The RoutledgeFalmer Guide t
Key Debates in Education

Education is never out of the news. It is not just an obsession with politicians and journalists but has become the main focus of ordinary people's lives. But there is no real debate about any of the issues reported in the media. Debating is out of fashion. No one raises the question of what has gone wrong when the entire political project of a society is seemingly reduced to 'education, education, education'.

The aim of this lively and challenging book is to provide the stimulus for further thinking about key educational issues by exposing and explaining the assumptions behind this obsession. Over 40 contributors – all experts in their fields – have written short, accessible, informed and lively articles for students, teachers and others involved in education. They address broad questions that are central to any understanding of what is really going on in the education system.

Topics covered include: the new relationship of the state to education; the changed nature of schools; whether teachers are afraid to teach; the problems with circle time, anti-bullying strategies, citizenship education, and multiple intelligences; the retreat from truth and the demise of theory in teacher training, and much more.

Everyone learning to teach in primary and secondary schools and further education colleges will find this book relevant to their programmes. In particular the book would be useful for students on Education Studies courses.

Dennis Hayes is the Head of the Centre for Studies in Education and Work at Canterbury Christ Church University College.

The RoutledgeFalmer Guide to Key Debates in Education

Edited by
Dennis Hayes

RoutledgeFalmer
Taylor & Francis Group

LONDON AND NEW YORK

First published 2004 by RoutledgeFalmer
2 Park Square, Milton Park, Abingdon,
Oxfordshire OX14 4RN

Simultaneously published in the USA and Canada
by RoutledgeFalmer
29 West 35th Street, New York, NY 10001

RoutledgeFalmer is an imprint of the Taylor and Francis Group

© 2004 Dennis Hayes for editorial material and selection,
individual chapters the contributors

Typeset in Sabon and Futura by
Florence Production Ltd, Stoodleigh, Devon
Printed and bound in Great Britain by
TJ International Ltd, Padstow, Cornwall

British Library Cataloguing in Publication Data
A catalogue record for this book is available from the
British Library

Library of Congress Cataloging in Publication Data
RoutledgeFalmer guide to key debates in education / edited
by Dennis Hayes.
   1. Education – Great Britain. I. Hayes, Dennis, 1950–
   LA632.R68 2004
   370′.941 – dc22   2004000259

ISBN 0–415–33243–5 (hbk)
ISBN 0–415–33244–3 (pbk)

CONTENTS

CONTRIBUTORS

Professor Richard Bailey (Canterbury Christ Church University College) is the author of numerous articles and conference presentations. His recent books include *Supporting Physical Development and Physical Education in the Early Years* (with Jonathan Doherty); *Teaching Physical Education 11–18* and *Education in the Open Society: Karl Popper and Schooling*.

Mike Blamires (Canterbury Christ Church University College) is a Principal Lecturer in Special Educational Needs. He runs the famous Xplanatory website and is the editor of *Enabling Technology for Inclusion*.

Professor Sonia Blandford (Canterbury Christ Church University College) is Dean of Education and is the author of several books and practical guides to school management including *Middle Management in Schools*. She writes a weekly column for the *Education Guardian*.

Jennie Bristow is commissioning editor for spiked-online.com and writes frequently on educational matters. Her most recent publication is *Maybe I Do: Marriage and Commitment in the Singleton Society*.

Jon Bryan (Newcastle College) is a National Executive Committee member of NATFHE. He is a sociologist who writes frequently on issues in post-compulsory education.

Professor Tyrrell Burgess (University of East London) is the Emeritus Professor in the Philosophy of Social Institutions. He has written extensively on education and public institutions and has acted as consultant to governments and such organisations as the World Bank and the United Nations Development Programme. He is the author of many books including *A Guide to English Schools*, *Education after School* and *The Devil's Dictionary of Education*.

Professor Tricia David (Canterbury Christ Church University College) has most recently published *Researching Early Childhood Education: European Perspectives*. She has also just published two further edited texts, both having been written by colleagues from Canterbury Christ Church University College: *Young Children Learning* and *Teaching Young Children*.

Professor Jon Davison (London Metropolitan University) is the author of many books on aspects of secondary initial teacher education and is one of the series editors of *Issues in Subject Teaching* for RoutledgeFalmer. He has recently been appointed Dean of Education at the Institute of Education, University of London.

Dr Shirley Dent is a former assistant editor of the *New Humanist*. She is a writer and is the co-author of *Radical Blake: Afterlife and Influence, 1827–2000*.

Dr Kathryn Ecclestone (University of Exeter) is a Senior Lecturer in Post-compulsory Education. Her most recent book, *Learning Autonomy in Post-16 Education*, is published by RoutledgeFalmer.

Professor Mary Evans (University of Kent) is Professor of Women's Studies. Her numerous publications include *A Good School, The Woman Question, An Introduction to Contemporary Feminist Thought* and (with D. Morgan) *The Battle for Britain*. Her most recent publication is *Missing Persons: The Impossibility of Auto/biography*, published by Routledge.

Claire Fox (Institute of Ideas) is the Director of the Institute of Ideas and a journalist. She has researched and written many articles and essays on issues around education, stress and bullying in the workplace. She lists being a regular on BBC Radio 4's discussion programme *The Moral Maze* among her many radio and TV credits.

Professor Frank Furedi (University of Kent) is a Professor of Sociology. His main intellectual interest is the institutionalisation of risk consciousness in western societies. He wrote *Culture of Fear*, which dealt with the ascendancy of risk aversion and the tendency for society to panic. More recently, his best-selling *Paranoid Parenting* examined the way in which risk aversion shapes contemporary parenting. His latest book, *Therapy Culture*, was published by Routledge in 2003.

Dr Ray Godfrey (Canterbury Christ Church University College) has written many articles on philosophy and mathematics. He has recently turned his attention to research problems and is one of the authors of *Early Childhood Educational Research*, published by RoutledgeFalmer.

Teresa Grainger (Canterbury Christ Church University College) is a Reader in Education, the former President of the United Kingdom Reading Association (UKRA) and the author of *Traditional Storytelling in the Primary Classroom*.

Professor Kathy Hall (Leeds Metropolitan University) is Professor of Childhood Education. Her colleagues in the research that provides the basis of her chapter are Shereen Benjamin (University of Birmingham), Kieron Sheehy, Janet Collins and Melanie Nind (Open University).

Richard Harris (London Metropolitan University) is Director of Primary Programmes. Among his publications are 'The law, rights and excluded children', in *Education, Exclusion and Citizenship*, and 'Black exclusions in a moral vacuum', in *Educating our Black Children*, both published by RoutledgeFalmer.

Dr Dennis Hayes (Canterbury Christ Church University College) is a philosopher by training. He has written widely on educational issues. He is the editor (with Robin Wynyard) of *The McDonaldization of Higher Education*. His most recent book is *Defending Higher Education: The Crisis of Confidence in the Academy*, published by RoutledgeFalmer.

Alan Hudson (University of Oxford) is the Director of Studies for Social and Political Science in the Department for Continuing Education. Among his recent publications are 'The trouble with planners', in *Audacity: Sustaining the Profession of Architecture*, and (with Dennis Hayes) *Basildon: The Mood of the Nation*.

Simon Hughes (Canterbury Christ Church University College) has written several books on religious education, including *KS4 RE Homework*. He runs the website RE-NET.

Simon Knight is a Project Manager, working with young people for community services near Glasgow, Scotland. He has a wealth of experience of working with children at risk and in trouble, including group, individual and family work, and school-based alternatives to exclusion. Simon is a founding member and now Director of Generation Youth Issues, the Scottish-based youth research charity. (www. GenerationYouthIssues.org.)

Dr Shirley Lawes (St Martin's College, Lancaster) is the Editor of the journal *Francophonie*. She has written many works on modern foreign language teaching and is one of the authors of *Understanding Teaching and Learning Modern Foreign Languages*, published by RoutledgeFalmer.

John Lea (Canterbury Christ Church University College) is the Programme Director for the Advanced Certificate in Education. He has just edited a book, *Working in Post-Compulsory Education*, and is researching political correctness in colleges in Britain and the United States.

Dr Laurie Lomas (Kings College, London) is a Senior Lecturer in the King's Institute for Learning and Teaching and has written many articles and papers on management and organisational change in education.

Toby Marshall (Havering College) teaches media studies and writes on topical issues in further education.

Lyn Martin (Torpoint Community School, Torpoint, Cornwall) is a teacher of citizenship.

Professor Gill Nicholls (Kings College, London) is Director of the King's Institute for Learning and Teaching and the author of several books, including *Professional Development in Higher Education*.

Professor Jon Nixon (University of Sheffield) is Professor of Educational Studies and Head of the School of Education. He has written widely on the changing nature of professional identity and currently edits the academic journal *Teaching in Higher Education*.

James Panton (University of Oxford) is a Lecturer in Politics at Lady Margaret Hall and Carlyle Scholar in the History of Ideas. He writes and broadcasts frequently on topics relating to higher education.

Professor Carl Parsons (Canterbury Christ Church University College) seeks to inform debate and policy options in the area of school exclusion, the recurring focus in his work. He has published many books on this topic, including the very well received *Education, Exclusion and Citizenship*, published by Routledge.

David Perks (Graveney School, Tooting, London), a science teacher since 1986, is currently Head of Physics in South London at Graveney School. As well as writing on education, he is the originator of the IOI Debating Matters sixth form debating competition.

Dr Gavin Poynter (University of East London) is the Head of the Department of Cultural Studies and is the author of *Restructuring in the Service Industries*. He is an authority on the economics of change, particularly as it has affected the service sector.

Dr Mike Radford (Canterbury Christ Church University College) is responsible for the Ed.D. Programme. He writes on philosophical issues related to aesthetics and spiritual education.

Dr Lynn Revell (Canterbury Christ Church University College) has researched new approaches to teaching children in Britain and the United States. She writes on issues related to religious belief and her forthcoming book is on the decline in churchgoing.

Dr Glenn Rikowski (University College Northampton) is a Senior Lecturer in Education Studies in the School of Education. He is the author of *The Battle in Seattle: Its Significance for Education* and co-editor (with Dave Hill, Peter McLaren and Mike Cole) of *Marxism Against Postmodernism in Educational Theory*.

Kevin Rooney (Queen's School, Bushey, Hertfordshire) is Head of Social Science. He has written several papers critical of the introduction of citizenship education into schools.

Jerome Satterthwaite (University of Plymouth) organises a very successful series of annual conferences around the theme of *Discourse, Power, and Resistance in Post-compulsory Education*, and is the editor of a book with the same title.

Professor Sir William Taylor CBE is a Visiting Professor at the University of Southampton and a consultant for a number of national and international higher education organisations. He was formerly Chair of the Council for the Accreditation of Teacher Education (1984–93), Vice Chancellor of Hull University (1985–91), Principal of the University of London (1983–5), and Director of the University of London Institute of Education (1973–83). He was made CBE in 1982 and knighted in 1990, and has been awarded honorary Doctorates by sixteen British universities.

Dr Linden West (Canterbury Christ Church University College) recently completed research into doctors and their learning and published it in his book, *Doctors on the Edge: General Practitioners, Health and Learning in the Inner-City*. His previous work includes *Beyond Fragments: Adults, Motivation and Higher Education, A Biographical Analysis*, published by Taylor & Francis.

Joanna Williams is a parent, a home tutor and a freelance journalist who writes frequently for many publications, including the *Times Educational Supplement*.

Dr Dominic Wood (Canterbury Christ Church University College) is a Senior Lecturer in the Department of Applied Social Sciences. He is a controversial and radical critic of environmentalism.

Professor James Woudhuysen (DeMontfort University) is Professor of Innovation and the author of many books, including *CULT IT*. He is also a regular contributor to *IT Week*.

Dr Robin Wynyard (Canterbury Christ Church University College) has been a visiting Professor in India, Pakistan and the United States. He writes on cultural transmission theory and its relationship to popular culture, and on the sociology of art and literature. He is one of the editors of *McDonaldization Revisited: Critical Essays on Consumer Culture* and (with Dennis Hayes) *The McDonaldization of Higher Education*.

PREFACE

Education in Britain is contested territory. Calls for the theory and practice of schooling to be 'taken out of politics', for restoration of the consensus about ends and means claimed to have existed in the early post-Second World War decades, are increasingly seen as unrealistic.

What happens in classrooms and campuses is now too important for the lives of individuals, for the management of the polity, for the health of the economy, for the stability of society, to be other than a central concern for governments, employers, workers, families – indeed, for everybody.

Labour set its top three priorities as 'education, education and education'. A Conservative claimed his party had similar priorities – although not necessarily in the same order. So there is no disagreement about whether education matters, but plenty about how best to put that commitment into practice.

Ours is a society of competing interests and diverse circumstances. We share a common commitment to the peaceful resolution of disputes and to the rule of law. We live in a democracy, in which governments have regularly to be elected. Inevitably, education is now increasingly an area of vigorous and sustained debate.

Two cheers, then, for debate. But there are also risks in considering educational issues in these terms. Perhaps calls for education to be de-politicised are a response to these risks. Debate is necessary. But debate is not enough.

Debate involves taking sides. It is not the job of the pros and the antis to do justice to the arguments of their opponents. Each must set out their own case convincingly enough to command a majority.

In the politics of democracy, debate is a means of reaching decisions. If these are to be successfully implemented and to achieve their objectives, the debate that leads up to them must be informed by close reasoning on the basis of carefully gathered and evaluated evidence, within traditions of public knowledge that embody appropriate and rigorous tests of truth.

Beginning teachers need to be aware of what is being debated, not in order to be recruited to a particular cause, but to be encouraged to think about the basis of particular convictions or beliefs – their own as well as other people's.

They need to acquire a career-long commitment to informed enquiry about themselves, their role in society, the subjects they teach, the children whom they strive to educate. Only by these means can their choices be well-founded, their actions constructive, their commonplace decisions well judged – and their own participation in debate made effective.

Faced with a need to speak or to act, and to do so quickly, none of us reaches for a historical, philosophical, sociological or psychological textbook or research report. Yet without some familiarity with and respect for what can be learned from such sources, and awareness of the assumptions and presuppositions reflected in our own beliefs and practices, we are poorly placed to learn from our experience and to develop the professionalism which enables us to speak, write and act appropriately – a point made strongly in one of the contributions that follow.

Without a shared language in which to describe what we see and hear, without a vocabulary of tested ideas and concepts that permit our experiences to be analysed and interpreted, the promise of 'reflective practice' – also subject to critical appraisal in this volume – cannot be fulfilled.

As teachers we have a particular responsibility to be well informed about the nature of the evidence on the why, the where, the when and the how of teaching and learning. We must recognise that decisions and choices we make – and those that, more than in the past, are made for us – reflect particular views of human nature, of human potential, of what constitutes the good life. We need to be able to see that claims that some practices are no more than 'common sense', that some courses of action are 'obvious', are often ways of covering up motives – our own and those of others – and of suppressing what needs to be a genuine, evidence-based debate.

The chapters that make up this book are rich in material for encouraging such debate. The authors take up positions on issues both broad and specialised – education and the state, citizenship, spirituality, the role of ICT and lifelong learning, multiple intelligences, reflective practice, bullying, circle time, school meals and much else. On each topic, there are questions to be asked, comments to be made, further evidence to be sought out. Everyone who reads the book will find some statements and assertions with which to agree, others to dispute. But they cannot fail to be stimulated by the range of opinion expressed and its relevance to many of the educational dilemmas of our times.

William Taylor

DEBATING EDUCATION
A beginner's guide

Dennis Hayes

Debating is out of fashion because of a widespread assumption that, if you challenge people's beliefs, opinions or arguments, this could damage their self-esteem, or worse. This assumption is having a detrimental effect on education at all levels. Increasingly, we are encouraged to see children and young people, and even adults, as emotionally *vulnerable*. Instead of emphasising their mental resilience, strength and their intellectual potential, it is their frailties, flaws and fears that naturally come to the fore. Evidence for this claim, if anyone doubts it, can be gathered by listening to discussions about children and young people in the lecture theatre, the classroom or in the school staff room.

Of course, young people are just as mentally strong, lively, intelligent and curious as ever. But these qualities are coming to be seen as undesirable or dangerous. The tendency for them to be seen as actual or potential victims in political pronouncements, in the media and in education policy and practice will inevitably affect their view of themselves. They may come to accept an emotionally vulnerable, impoverished and diminished view of their personal and of human potential.

The current focus on victimhood arose out of the collapse of the political contest between 'left' and 'right' that had been the feature of public debate for over 200 years. A popular way of looking at this is to say that the opposition between left and right has no meaning any more. It would be better to simply see the 'left' in the form of socialism or of any alternative driver for social change as simply *absent*. To fill this vacant societal space, social commentators, politicians and educationalists have, largely spontaneously, adopted the two central notions of victim culture: first, that ordinary people are emotionally vulnerable and, second, that their betters have something to offer, namely forms of therapeutic intervention.

It would clearly be a crude caricature to see the political world as no longer divided between 'left' and 'right' but between 'victims' and 'therapists', but this is an interpretation that is hinted at in several of the chapters in this book. What is not a caricature is the replacement of political debate about big issues with personality conflict. In parliament we have clashes of personality and disputes about personality and character. In the media we have more of the same. Even in education, where there might be more interest in debating 'the best that has been known and thought', discussion of issues relating to personality, character and psychology take priority.

Why debating matters

Debating matters because it is the precondition of the advancement of knowledge that is the spur to human progress. It is another way of expressing John Stuart Mill's belief that humanity is 'capable of being improved by free and equal discussion' (Mill 1859/1995: 69). Human beings, almost by nature, seek out challenges and question what appears to be 'true'. If we do not allow confrontation, criticism and contradiction we cannot begin to distinguish truth from falsehood and any restriction on these activities will stunt the human capacity for intellectual development. Mill puts this very well in *On Liberty*:

> the peculiar evil of silencing the expression of an opinion is that it is robbing the human race; posterity as well as the existing generation; those who dissent from the opinion, still more than those who hold it. If the opinion is right, they are deprived of the opportunity of exchanging error for truth; if wrong, they lose, what is almost as great a benefit, the clearer perception and livelier impression of truth produced by its collision with error.
>
> (Mill 1859/1995: 76)

Mill's rationale for freedom of speech, is now held to be old fashioned:

> the great weight of his position comes down on his assumption that human beings are progressive, capable of learning from experience. Does the experience of the Twentieth Century give the lie to this view? If so, the heart drops out of Mill's position.
>
> (Wolff 1996: 137)

But without debate we cannot even improve on society's failures, if that is what they are, and try to change society for the better.

It might be argued that we do not need to debate now because each and everyone of us has access, through the wonders of new technology, to a huge quantity of information unimaginable in Mill's day. However, even if we take the hype about living in an 'Information Age' seriously, we can see that we cannot even make sense of this information unless we are engaged in debate. Christopher Lasch, in a work published posthumously, put this argument very succinctly:

> What democracy requires is vigorous public debate, not information. Of course, it needs information too, but the kind of information it needs can be generated only by debate. We do not know what we need to know until we ask the right questions, and we can identify the right questions only by subjecting our own ideas about the world to the test of public controversy. Information, usually seen as the precondition of debate, is better understood as its by-product. When we get into arguments that focus and fully engage our attention, we become avid seekers of information. Otherwise we take in information passively – if we take it in at all.
>
> (Lasch 1996: 162–3)

Lasch also saw the need to engage in debate if society was to be truly democratic:

> If we insist on argument as the essence of education, we will defend democracy not as the most efficient but as the most educational form of government,

one that extends the circle of debate as widely as possible and thus forces all citizens to articulate their views, to put their views at risk, and to cultivate the virtues of eloquence, clarity of thought and expression, and sound judgment.

(Lasch 1996: 171)

The education provided in any society embodies that society's vision of its own future. If, as is the case today, the education on offer eschews debate and intellectual challenge then that society is going nowhere. It is no exaggeration to say that reintroducing a vigorous debate about education is the precondition for social change.

How to read this book

This book should simply be read from cover to cover. All the chapters are concise and accessible. They are not restricted to one area of education but seek to raise arguments across the field. This was quite deliberate. In part it was done to avoid a professional narrowness of focus, but also because what is happening in one area of education influences others. If in higher education, educationalists are putting the emotional before the intellectual, the message is carried to the next generation that education is a therapeutic activity. Reading the book from cover to cover will provide an introduction to a range of debates about education and, more importantly, a range of critical perspectives.

The contributors write from different standpoints but all of them are putting their views 'at risk' and rising to the challenge of initiating serious and public debate about education. For, in a sense, there are no 'key debates' about education any more. There is a climate and culture of compliance. The only issues that get raised concern the form of delivery of whatever the government and its quangos desire to see in education. There is much comment and groaning about the burden of inspections, testing, league tables and the underfunding of education. These complaints are well aired and, by and large, they are not to be found in this book. The 'key debates' the authors seek to raise are about the *content* of the education that is currently on offer to children, young people and adults. Traditionally a school, for example, was an institution that existed to provide an education based on subject knowledge. Beyond this essential role, schools performed a range of other peripheral tasks, such as socialising young children, imposing religion and morality upon them and preparing them for work. A clear distinction could be made between 'education' and 'schooling'. The once peripheral 'socialisation' functions now hold centre stage and we have *schooling* rather than education. This point is generalisable across the education system. Of course, there is still some education on offer, or our educational institutions would be empty shells. But the transmission of knowledge and culture is now secondary to other tasks, and what 'knowledge' needs to be 'delivered' is provided in an easily digestible, factory-like or 'McDonaldised' form. The inversion of the traditional relationship between education and the socialisation functions of educational institutions schooling is destroying education. However, the response of educationalists to the emptying of education of any meaningful content is *silence*.

It is tempting to suggest that argument and debate, although the essence of education, are lacking today because educationalists are too fearful about taking intellectual risks, putting their views forward and being challenged. Teachers often bemoan the imposition of a dominant 'discourse' about education by powerful players such as the Department for Education and Skills or the Teacher Training

Agency. However, when challenged to put forward alternatives they argue for a variation on what is already on offer. Except for the views expressed in this book there is no alternative to current policy. Any reader, whether a student, an educationalist or someone interested in education seeking challenges to orthodox views, some original perspectives and fresh arguments, will find them here. Students in particular will find useful arguments to use in lectures, seminars and essays.

The book is divided into seven parts, the content of which should be clear from their titles. A short summary of the issues raised might help the reader find their way through the book, but it is impossible with so many different and challenging contributions to comment on each one.

Part I, 'The state of education', discusses how the state, often not directly, but through a range of institutions, agencies and interventions, is transforming education. In a keynote piece, Frank Furedi argues that traditional relationships of trust in education are being formalised to the extent that schools engage in 'defensive teaching' with the possibility of litigation always in teachers' minds. Other contributors to this section look at how intervention is changing the way we work, offering people a diminished form of education, and how policy makers have abandoned the pursuit of knowledge and, as a result, have no coherent educational philosophy.

Part II, 'Policing the classroom', examines from a variety of perspectives how the lives of parents, teachers and pupils are subject to more and more intervention. Whether it is using parents as teachers and formalising a normal loving relationship, or restricting what pupils, read, think, feel and eat or how they play and build relationships, more and more aspects of education are being regulated. There are different perspectives on these issues. Taking one example, Teresa Grainger argues that we must not be obsessed with a notion of literature based on the book, as pupils today have 'multi-modal' literacies, whereas Shirley Dent argues for the power of literature to transform pupils' lives.

Part III, 'The search for lost values, communities and citizens', explores another series of interventions in the school curriculum that attempt to promote new and sometimes old values. These interventions are aimed at supporting troubled families, giving children 'rights', teaching them 'spiritual' values and encouraging them to be 'citizens' are often seen as positive and progressive but are shown to be deeply problematic and failing pupils. Citizenship education, for example, is seen by Simon Hughes as problematic because it rejects any consideration of how the best citizens are, like Socrates, often a threat to the status quo, whereas Kevin Rooney sees 'citizenship' as a political project entirely inappropriate as a 'subject' in school.

Part IV, 'Changing times? Changing education', looks at how ideas and rhetoric about a new fast-changing contemporary world have led to projects in social engineering that are transforming education into something very impoverished.

The importance of information and communication technology (ICT), new or 'multiple' intelligences and the 'greening' of education are critically examined. In a provocative chapter James Woudhuysen challenges the view that 'play' is an important part of education.

Part V, 'Lifelong learning – lifelong dependence', responds to the current concern with learning through life by showing how the education of adults and young people is no longer the transformative project that it once was. Through the interaction of an agenda aimed at meeting economic goals, with an attempt to cushion the impact of this through therapeutic intervention, the creative potential of the majority of people is wasted. Kathryn Ecclestone provides an overview. Linden West is sympathetic to this new philosophy and Glenn Rikowski examines why the creative potential of people will always be wasted unless the submission to economic necessity is challenged.

Part VI, 'The diminished academy', provides some of the most important arguments in the book, because what people experience in higher education determines their educational outlook for life. Each chapter shows that higher education is no longer offering the intellectual challenges that are needed to produce the brightest and best young graduates to take society forward.

Part VII, 'The study of education', presents arguments for a return to a study of education not based on philosophical fads or policy directives but on theory, the pursuit of reason, truth and real scholarship.

In the Postscript, Tyrrell Burgess provides a personal overview of what he considers are the real debates in education. Although his emphasis differs from that of several of the other contributors to this book, this difference is an important part of the search to identify what are the 'key debates' in education. He concludes with a hope and a truth: 'There is a lot to talk about'.

The contributors

The contributors to this book are from a variety of backgrounds: some are academics with an interest in education, others are teacher trainers, several are teachers and some are journalists and writers. It was particularly important to include a group of teachers who advance arguments that challenge orthodox ideas and theories about education and do not merely reflect 'practical' or 'practitioner' views. All the contributors wrote independently without knowledge of the contributions of others.

Many books on education are published and sold but how many are read? The success of this book will not be in the sales figures but in how many people take up the arguments presented here and develop or challenge them. The contributors all welcome robust discussion and criticism of their views. Given the many sacred cows they challenge they can be certain of that criticism.

References

Lasch, C. (1996) *The Revolt of the Elites and the Betrayal of Democracy*, New York and London: W.W. Norton & Co.
Mill, J.S. ([1859] 1995) *On Liberty*, Harmondsworth: Penguin Classics.
Wolff, J. (1996) *An Introduction to Political Philosophy*, Oxford: Oxford University Press.

PART I

THE STATE OF EDUCATION

THE STATE OF EDUCATION

CHAPTER 1

THE FORMALISATION OF RELATIONSHIPS IN EDUCATION

Frank Furedi

Back in 1999, when I was working on a sociological study of litigation, I was genuinely surprised to discover that litigation was fast becoming a serious problem in British education. Until very recently, parents did not sue their children's schools or local authorities. In previous times, teachers in schools or academics in universities faced complaints and grumbles but they did not have to worry about the threat of being forced into formal court proceedings. A closer inspection of this phenomenon shows that this development is the outcome of the formalisation of the relationship between parents and schools and between teachers and their employers.

The formalisation of relationships in education has been encouraged by the growing tendency towards extending the scope of bureaucratic intervention in the everyday life of schools and universities. Increasingly, every aspect of education is subjected to rule-making and regulated through inspection and auditing. As a result of a highly centralised system of education managed by an interventionist bureaucracy little is left to chance. It has been noted that even primary school teachers are allowed little initiative to exercise their professional judgment. The National Curriculum dominates the classroom and teachers' activity is regulated by the need to respond to the demands of standardised tests and inspections. In the university sector, a system of auditing has succeeded in influencing the minutiae of teaching and even of research.

The expansion of bureaucratic control is justified on the grounds that it ensures the maintenance of standards of education. It is argued that it helps hold teachers, lecturers and their institution to account. While the impact of the standardisation of teaching on the quality of education is debatable, its consequences on the relationship between the different parties – teachers, students, local authorities, parents – is strikingly clear. Bureaucratic intervention in education has led to the transformation of the basic relationships involving pupils, teachers, academics, students, parents and bureaucrats into carefully regulated transactions. Sadly, a focus on transactions distracts teachers from cultivating their relationship with students and parents. They are, above all, answerable to external agencies and not to those whom they teach. Whether they are successful or not depends not on what happens in the classroom but on their ability to meet the formal criteria established by inspectors and auditors. Such a development has had the effect of distancing people from one another. It has had the effect of transforming face-to-face relationships into transactions that are vetted according to a bureaucratic formula established outside the site of learning.

The formalisation of education has the negative effect of diminishing trust between people. Whether explicitly stated or not, it is a process that calls into question trust in the professional authority of the educator. Rules are enacted because it is believed that they are preferable to leaving matters to informal decision-making or the professional judgement of the teacher or the school. Through calling into question informal decision-making, the professional authority of the teacher is compromised. This process does not simply diminish the authority of the teachers. In recent years there has been a discernible trend towards the enactment of contracts between schools and parents. Such contracts are expressed in the language of a formal transaction. The school and the parent both undertake certain responsibilities stated in the agreement. Although such contracts are primarily symbolic in character, they contain an implicit statement about the status of the parent. It suggests that parents cannot be relied on to do the right thing for their child. They need to be reminded of their role and held to account by a contract. As in the case of the professional role of teachers, parental authority is called into question. Blaming parents for their child's truancy is already institutionalised. How long before parents are blamed for their children's examination performance?

Ironically, the very attempt to formalise human relations and to codify appropriate forms of behaviour actually feeds mistrust. Contracts and rules are made in circumstances where we don't trust people to do the right thing. Inevitably this alters the behaviour of the people who regard one another from the perspective of a transaction. Since a transaction and a contract implicitly assume a conflict of interest between the different parties, everyone concerned alters their behaviour. Differences become sharper and in an atmosphere of suspicion it becomes difficult to manage disputes informally. When confronted with an inspector, many teachers are encouraged to become more concerned with how they are seen to be doing their job rather than with what they actually do. In the university sector, lecturers lose the incentive to take a chance and become experimental. Once lecturing becomes an auditable object, it has little in common with the subtle, ambitious, critical and open-ended phenomenon that once went by the name of a good university education.

In universities, the formalisation of the student–teacher relationship into a transaction creates the potential for a permanent, silent conflict of interest between two parties who have every reason to act in a calculating way towards one another. Gone is the idea that a student is there to be inspired and challenged by his or her academic mentor. Lecturers who are concerned with avoiding hassle, complaints and litigation have little energy to provide a high standard of education. Worse still, the pressure of a contractual relationship forces teachers to adopt a formulaic style that treats everyone the same. The formalisation of the student–teacher relationship fosters a disregard for the individual. It limits the room available for flexible and spontaneous interaction. Why? Because the contract comes between teacher and student. Even with the best will, academics are likely to risk their position if they deviate from the contract in order to do what is right for the individual students.

In schools, the formalisation of relationships has led to the emergence of *defensive teaching*. Like defensive medicine, this form of teaching is influenced by concerns that have little to do with professional judgement. The encroachment of the process of formalisation of relationships on pedagogy is one of the least researched developments in education. Yet its impact is a formidable one. At present the impact of the formalisation of education in schools is most visible in relation to the rise in conflict between parents and teachers. Parents increasingly feel that they need to defend the interests of their child. They often act as the child's advocate and, as in any transactional relationship, assume that there is at least a potential conflict of interest with the school. In turn, teachers adopt a defensive posture and as a result sometimes become distracted from doing what is really in the best interest of their pupils. Research by Sarah Thomson of Keele University shows that the climate of litigation seriously compromises children's educational experience. She believes that 'because of the fear of litigation, teachers have become more guarded in their spontaneous responses to children and children's activities'. Certainly, many teachers have lost their enthusiasm for taking their pupils on school trips because of their concern with facing legal proceedings if something goes wrong. This reaction is an understandable response to recent developments. In 2000, a MORI survey found that 57 per cent of those questioned stated that they would seek compensation from their school if their child had suffered an avoidable injury.

Accidents involving pupils inside and outside schools are by no means the sole focus for the activities of lawyers specialising in promoting litigation in education. Some parents have hired lawyers to ensure that their children gain access to the school of their choice. There has been a spate of lawsuits on behalf of children who claim that the quality of their lives has been diminished by bullies. Parents who believe that their children's special needs have not been catered for have won major victories against their schools. Inevitably, some parents who feel that their children have underachieved are considering suing their schools or local authorities for failing to fulfil their duty to educate.

Supporters of the growth of litigation in education claim that this development indicates that parents have become more confident about exercising their rights. Opponents of this trend respond by emphasising the high financial cost of litigation. This emphasis on rights and finance overlooks what constitutes the most significant outcome – the destructive impact of classroom litigation on teacher–pupil relations and on the quality of education. Experience has shown that the rise of litigation leads to a further decline of trust. Invariably, institutions become more interested in preventing litigation than on doing what is in a child's best interest. The American experience is instructive in this respect. US schools do not initiate any activity before considering how to avoid a lawsuit. Some American schools have eliminated breaks in order to avoid any potential injuries that children may suffer as a result of running around. British schools are now travelling down the same road – some have banned skipping ropes from the playground. This climate of suspicion has also incited teachers to turn towards the courts. Encouraged by their unions, some are demanding compensation for malicious allegations made by children and for other adverse experiences encountered in the classroom.

Probably the most destructive consequence of the formalisation of education is that it transforms the relationship between teachers, heads, pupils and parents into one of potential conflict. Worse still, it fosters an environment in which growing ranges of educational experiences are subject to influences that have little to do with pedagogy. Defensive teaching is shaped by the activities of lawyers. And that cannot be good for our children's education.

Key readings

Furedi, F. (1999) *Courting Mistrust: The Hidden Growth of a Culture of Litigation in Britain*, London: Centre for Policy Studies.
Lowe, C. (2002) 'Legal Issues', *Times Educational Supplement*, 22 December 2002.
Thomson, S. (2002) 'Harmless Fun Can Kill Someone', *Entertainment Law* 1(1) (Spring): 95–103.

Focus question

Drawing on your own experience of education, can you find examples of relationships becoming more formal through fear of litigation?

CHAPTER 2

THE INTERVENTIONIST STATE AND THE STATE OF UK EDUCATION

Gavin Poynter

The 1997 White Paper, *Excellence in Schools*, declared that the newly elected Labour government's 'top priority' was raising standards. Since then reports into schools, further and higher education and 'lifelong' learning have reaffirmed the government's commitment to the modernisation of the whole education system (Dearing 1997; DfEE 1997a, 1997b, 1999a, 1999b). The government's purpose has also been clearly signalled – education is valued less for its intrinsic qualities of self-development and more for its contribution to creating a new kind of society. Britain's future prosperity rests with its capacity to develop and harness the skills required to be a significant player in the new knowledge-based international economy, following the path pioneered by the United States (DTI 1998; Reich 2002).

An unprecedented level of state intervention into all sectors of education has flowed from, and been legitimated by, this perspective whose underlying assumptions were broadly shared with those of earlier Conservative governments (Ainley 1999). The daily life of the student, teacher, lecturer and administrator has been reshaped by such measures as curriculum reform, the shifting of responsibility for fees to higher education students, the introduction of performance targets and league tables, changes to quality and audit systems and the introduction of targeted funds for teaching and learning, research and staff development and appraisal systems. The sector has, in turn, experienced significant financial and structural change that has brought it into a closer relation with the business world.

Has modernisation, or perhaps more accurately, 'marketisation' worked? On the surface, the answer must be in the affirmative. The market, and the mechanisms introduced by the state to regulate it, have been embedded with relatively little opposition (particularly in England). Students, parents and staff have absorbed the language, norms and values associated with the educational marketplace and the range of performance measures that delineate the successful from the failing. Students seek courses that offer 'employability'; parents move, if they can afford it, to the catchment areas of top-performing schools and staff create endless paper chases to conform with quality, audit and risk assessment requirements. If the success of state intervention is measured by the elevation of education towards the top of the domestic political agenda and a significant change in the behaviour of institutions and individuals in the sector, there is strong evidence to suggest that the policies of successive Conservative and Labour governments have, indeed, been successful.

All is not what it seems. It is argued below that the real success of government over recent years has been less to do with improving the performance of the education sector and more to do with enhancing the sector's role in reshaping the domestic social order. In this sense, 'Learning has become the basic principle for organising society' (Brown and Lauder 2001: 208). In developing this role, the cumulative impact of government reforms over the last two decades has been regressive rather than progressive. Rather than education becoming a centrepiece of what recent Labour governments have called a progressive economic policy, in practice it has become the centrepiece of a regressive and pervasive social policy, whose implementation has invariably led, according to its perceptive critics, to the creation of a 'Certified Society' regulated by a 'Workfare State' (Ainley 1999; Jessop 2000).

From welfare to workfare

In industrialised and modernising economies, the state has typically played a vital role in reconciling the relationship between civil society and the market or, more specifically, the social relations within a nation with the process of capital accumulation on which the dynamic of that society relies. In the nineteenth and twentieth centuries, as the demands of industrialisation required wider access to education, the state in countries like France and Germany established mass education systems that were centrally directed. By contrast, successive attempts in the first half of the twentieth century by the British state to develop a 'national, democratic and technically effective system' were a failure (McKibbin 1998: 269).

This failure was moderated in Britain at the end of the Second World War. The post-war welfare system arose from a series of social settlements through which the state responded to pressures for greater social and economic equality. The implementation of the 1944 Education Act helped safeguard social stability and provided limited opportunities for some working-class boys and girls to move up the rigid occupational structure of post-war Britain. The education system remained, however, a repository of social inequality with its main role being to educate the social elite, especially in the higher education sector, and accommodate the children of an expanding professional class (Perkin 1989). Private (public), grammar and secondary modern schools emerged as the repositories of compulsory secondary education, with secondary moderns being renamed comprehensives in the mid 1960s.

The creation of comprehensive schooling in 1964 initiated a decade of educational debate and reform involving the review of primary education (the Plowden Report 1967), the creation of new curricula in secondary schools, the introduction of new universities and the conversion of some technical colleges to university status (Robins Report 1963). The disruption of the prevailing social order, reflected in unprecedented levels of industrial and student unrest in the late 1960s and early 1970s, generated debates within the education sector that challenged the traditional 'elitism' of the British educational system but also, paradoxically, provided many of the arguments that could be used to recast the role of education as a regressive 'therapeutic' social policy in subsequent decades (Nolan 1998: 128–81; Hayes 2002: 143–59). Throughout the 'progressive' decade, successive governments found themselves encouraging and inviting local education authorities to create an educational system that diluted selection and offered greater opportunities for social mobility. Even during the Conservative administration of Edward Heath (1970–4), Margaret Thatcher, as Education Minister, 'designated more schools officially comprehensive than any other minister before or since' (Ainley 1999: 60).

These reforms took place during the last few years of the social compact that had given birth to the 'welfare' state. The reforms marked the end of the hegemony of the welfare state model rather than its consummation. In the 1970s educational reform occurred while successive governments sought to control and reduce public expenditure. As the UK economy weakened, particularly after the oil crisis of 1973,

an increasingly influential analysis from the media, business and academic worlds
was presented in terms of the unproductive public sector being a significant cause
of the decline of the British economy (Bacon and Eltis 1975). Put simply, in Britain's
de-industrialising economy, there were 'fewer and fewer real jobs and more and more
phoney ones' (Joseph 1975). The critique of the vast growth in public sector employment rested upon distinguishing between productive and unproductive labour, an
analytical distinction that has a long and much-debated pedigree dating back to the
foundations of modern political economy.

Much of the labour expended in all types of societies is useful or productive. Such
labour may be expended in the social reproduction of that society. An example today
might be voluntary work that helps society to look after, for example, the young or
elderly. What concerned the critics of the public sector in the 1970s was not this
productive labour in general but the proportion of productive labour that worked
directly for capital. In working for capital, labour creates the equivalent of its own
value – a wage. It also produces a new magnitude of value, a surplus value, which
eventually takes the form of profit for the entrepreneur. Labour is purchased by an
employer and put to work in production. The money capital, initially used to purchase
the labour, when brought together with constant capital (machinery and equipment),
becomes productive capital and in so doing creates the historically specific capitalist
labour process. In the course of this process, commodities of a higher value are
produced 'by the extraction of surplus labour from the workforce' (Savran and Tonak
1999: 124–8). The dynamic expansion or accumulation of capital rests upon the
successful extraction and expansion of surplus value from the productive labour that
is brought into its service. For the critics of the burgeoning welfare state in the 1970s,
an insufficient amount of labour was directed towards this purpose. The public sector
took the blame for Britain's economic decline; its reform became a pressing matter
for government, eventually giving rise to a new pattern of state intervention.

The new form of state intervention that became popularly known as 'Thatcherism'
in the 1980s had its origins in the policies of the Labour government (1974–9). The
'Great Debate on Education' initiated in 1976 sought to address the role of education in tackling the ills of the low skill, low productivity UK economy. Schools were
chastised for failing to prepare young people for work (HMSO 1977) and the
Manpower Services Commission (MSC), created in 1974, assumed an increasingly
important role in developing vocational training programmes and skills inventories
that provided the basis for the standards for National Vocational Qualifications
(NVQs) (Ainley 1999: 93). These inventories were subsequently translated into the
curriculum and the framework was created for an extensive reform of the education
provision for young people in secondary and further education – a trend that has
also taken hold of higher education over the last decade.

From these origins in the late 1970s, governments have engaged in successive
phases of 'modernisation' of state education. These have several common features.
First, the purpose of education has been redefined primarily in terms of its relevance
to the needs of the labour market and the changing occupational and skill requirements of enterprises. Second, the state has progressively reduced the role and
importance of democratically elected authorities in providing compulsory and post-
compulsory education (Jessop 2000). Third, the state has established audit and quality
regimes that are designed to determine relative market positions (often through the
publication of league tables) and regulate the relationship between educational institutions and their clients or customers, once known as students. Finally, this
appropriation of market mechanisms, conceived within a paradigm of consumption,

to regulate the education sector has enhanced the direct role of the state in the micro-management of schools, colleges and universities, while diluting its function as the guardian of the boundaries between the market and the state education sector.

This blurring of boundaries has accelerated since the return of the Labour government in 1997. Among the most visible examples include private companies taking over the running of schools; private training agencies securing contracts for the delivery of Learning and Skills Council (LSC)-supported training schemes and universities being required to engage in technology and knowledge transfer partnerships with private enterprise, securing private sector funding for 'close to market' research and consultancy. For critics these examples illustrate the acceleration of a trend towards the semi-privatisation of the state education sector. This trend was clearly evident in the free market individualist ethos that underpinned Thatcherism. Since 1997 successive Labour governments have attempted to reconcile this market ethic with the reconstruction of the concept of society through its social and educational policies (Driver and Martell 1999). The outcome is a heady and contradictory mix – the flowering of a 'shadow' market, arguably more pernicious in its operation than the real thing, and the consolidation of a highly bureaucratised, centrally directed system of education provision.

From government to governance: 'modernisation' and the rise of the 'shadow' market

The new state form of governance of a semi-privatised education system is designed, so the argument goes, to improve the system's responsiveness to the needs of a new knowledge-based economy. Who owns, manages and directly or indirectly finances the education sector is secondary. By improving education standards and regarding education and training as a lifelong pursuit, the state encourages and facilitates access and opportunity. The potential to enhance social mobility and individual opportunity rests with schools, colleges and universities moving closer to the market, emulating the behaviour of the capitalist enterprise. In turn, the establishment of a 'shadow' market induces among students the classic behaviour of the consumer. The ethos underpinning the welfare state model is turned upside down. Created as a vehicle for enhancing social mobility and providing free access to opportunity, the ethos underpinning the concept of public sector 'service' is now presented as the main obstacle to the attainment of these goals. The multi-dimensional character becomes the mono-dimensional consumer (Sennett 1998).

The emergence of a state education system in the post-1945 period in Britain, provided the opportunity for enterprises to be 'freed' from many of the basic tasks of maintaining and training their potential and current workforce. The expansion of the public sector rested upon the revenues secured by the state from business and private citizens. The various forms of partnership between the contemporary state and the private sector in funding hospitals, schools and universities is drawing back private enterprise into assuming a role in the reproduction of labour. This activity is leading some employees – trainers, academics, technicians and researchers – to expend a growing proportion of their work time directly in the service of private enterprise or engaged in 'income-generating' activities that reduce the dependence of their university or college on publicly funded grants.

This shift, however, is not necessarily illustrative of a move towards a new kind of dynamic 'knowledge-driven' economy. The marketisation of education policy and practice has generated for students a move towards a narrower form of instrumental learning and a confusion of skill with competency (Ainley 1999). Equally, there is little evidence that this approach has done much to enhance the UK's economic performance over recent years. Economic growth rates, as measured by the annual rise in Gross Domestic Product (GDP), have been consistently lower than during the days of the post-war boom (Poynter 2002). Indeed, the move of private enterprises towards investing in the state education system is, arguably, indicative of their own aversion to risk and their failure to generate innovative new businesses and industries themselves. The changing pattern of state intervention has been successful in modifying the behaviour of students and education workers with some even becoming 'productive labour'. The changing balance, however, between public and private, and productive and unproductive labour within the education sector, reflects less the emergence of an innovative new economy and more the loss of dynamism in contemporary society. Education has become the repository of the regressive social values and policies that are deployed to keep it glued together.

References

Ainley, P. (1999) *Learning Policy: Towards the Certified Society*, Basingstoke: Palgrave.

Bacon, R. and Eltis, W. (1975) *Britain's Economic Problem: Too Few Producers*, London: Macmillan.

Brown, P. and Lauder, H. (2001) *Capitalism and Social Progress*, Basingstoke: Palgrave.

Dearing, R. (1997) *Higher Education in the Learning Society: Summary Report of the National Committee of Enquiry into Higher Education*, London: HMSO.

Department of Trade and Industry (DTI) (1998) *Our Competitive Future: Building the Knowledge Driven Economy*, London: HMSO.

Department for Education and Employment (DfEE) (1997a) *Excellence in Schools*, London: DfEE.

Department for Education and Employment (DfEE) (1997b) *Excellence for All Children*, London: DfEE.

Department for Education and Employment (DfEE) (1999a) *Excellence in Cities*, London: DfEE.

Department for Education and Employment (DfEE) (1999b) *Learning to Succeed*, London: DfEE.

Driver, S. and Martell, L. (1999) 'New Labour: Culture and Economy', in L. Ray and A. Sayer (eds), *Culture and Economy After the Cultural Turn*, London: Sage, pp. 246–69.

Hayes, D. (2002) 'Taking the Hemlock? The New Sophistry of Teacher Training for Higher Education', in D. Hayes and R. Wynyard (eds), *The McDonaldisation of Higher Education*, Westport, CT: Greenwood, pp. 143–58.

HMSO (1977) *Education in Schools: A Consultative Document*, Cmnd. 6869, London: HMSO.

Jessop, B. (2000) 'The State and the Contradictions of the Knowledge-driven Economy', in J. Bryson, P. Daniels, N. Henry and J. Pollard (eds), *Knowledge, Space, Economy*, London: Routledge, pp. 157–75.

Joseph, K. (1975) *New Statesman*, 18 April, 1975, quoted in P. Bullock and D. Yaffe, 'Inflation, the Crisis and the Post-War Boom', *Revolutionary Communist*, No. 3/4, London: RCG Publications, p. 9.

McKibbin, R. (1998) *Classes and Cultures in England 1918–1951*, Oxford: Oxford University Press.

Nolan, J. (1998) *The Therapeutic State*, New York: New York University Press.

Perkin, H. (1989) *The Rise of Professional Society*, London: Routledge.

Poynter, G. (2002) 'Modules and Markets: Education and Work in the Information Age', in D. Hayes and R. Wynyard (eds), *The McDonaldization of Higher Education*, Westport, CT: Greenwood, pp. 57–70.

Reich, R. (2002) *The Future of Success*, London: Vintage.

Savran, S. and Ahmet Tonak, E. (1999) 'Productive and Unproductive Labour: An Attempt at Clarification and Classification', *Capital and Class* 68 (Summer): 113–52.

Sennett, R. (1998) *The Corrosion of Character*, New York: Norton.

Key readings

Ainley, P. (1999) *Learning Policy: Towards The Certified Society*, London: Macmillan.
Brown, P. and Lauder, H. (2001) *Capitalism and Social Progress*, Basingstoke: Palgrave (chapters 10 and 14).
Department of Trade and Industry (DTI) (1998) *Our Competitive Future: Building the Knowledge Driven Economy*, London: HMSO.

Focus question

To what extent has the 'modernisation' of education that commenced with the 'Great Debate' in 1975 contributed to the creation of a new knowledge-driven economy in the UK?

CHAPTER 3

EDUCATING THE PEOPLE

Alan Hudson

'A little learning is a dangerous thing' is a piece of folk wisdom that we are all familiar with.[1] We're inclined to believe it and assume that everyone else does too. But what can it possibly mean?

I suspect that the way it is read now is not that we should aspire to a great deal of learning – to break the pain barrier of learning. But that we shouldn't open the Pandora's box of knowledge to many people at all. After all what good would it do them, or it wouldn't do to give people ideas above their station! Much better, as the New Labour Department of Education does, to witter on about the pre-eminent educational values of vocational competence and individual self-esteem. It is the old reactionary trope that humankind cannot bear too much reality, but given a contemporary and more philistine spin.[2]

The value of education for the masses can only be seen as an accretion of social competence. In contrast, 'a little learning' might stimulate discussion about matters that have no immediate policy resolution in the world of 'joined up' government. 'A little learning' may reinvigorate the presumption that literacy is not about bumping up measured reading skills or voting on *The Big Read* but the capacity and willingness to take part in public discussion.

There is a perverse merit in the reactionary reading of the possibilities of education. The value, risk and potential of education is recognised. Education has to be denied to people, or in the modern case eviscerated as life skills, because the reactionary, for which read government 'policy wonk', fears and loathes nothing more than the people and democracy. The fear is that even a rudimentary education will imply criticism, contestation and an unwillingness to accept the natural order of things. Galileo mutters 'eppur si muove' after finessing the instruments of torture; people start reading the Bible in their own language and denying the divine right of kings and, Bob's your uncle, before you know it the whole social order comes crashing down. Far better to take the content out of education and to have some nice, measurable outcomes all conducted in an unchallenging and non-judgemental atmosphere.

It may seem perverse to say so but the official view of education owes more to the Church Fathers via Emile Durkheim than it does to a spirit of democratic enquiry. If you cannot get rid of education entirely then transform the content and claim that by giving it to a wider audience you are empowering them. At the same time you argue that anyone who opposes extending the shallow and fetid pool is anti-democratic and elitist.

The uncontested merit of widening participation, the government mantra of parental choice inside universal provision and the explosion of qualifications and preoccupation with student need are all but uncontested as evidence of government's commitment to the people. They all represent both the democratisation of our society and the exorcism of elitism, in the face of the cross of accreditation and the garlic of self-esteem. It is not so.

I believe that the present state of education is much closer to another familiar adage – 'ignorance is bliss'.[3] Contemporary education is not democratic, nor can it possibly liberate people. It is the opiate of the masses.

This is not to argue that higher levels of our present education system do not require some intelligence, nor that some individual economic and behavioural outcomes and outputs will accrue. Neither is it to suggest that individuals will not experience an intense desire to learn and understand. It is to argue that such results are either the spontaneous outcome of individual intellectual endeavour or that educational success owes far more to social position than it does to education itself.

It is wrong to view education in such a narrow and instrumental fashion, which incidentally does not work anyway. But this does make education such a resonant example of the pre-eminent ratio of modern political life: the more often the people are invoked the more they are disdained.

The people as consumer brand

In our times 'The People' has become a ubiquitous term of self-proclaimed legitimacy, in which self-interest masquerades as public duty. The common currency, in fact, denotes a peculiar set of social circumstances in which the historical threat of the people as a democratic agent has been marginalised. But at the same time the elites who were traditionally threatened by insurgency have survived, at the expense of their own project and inner convictions. Such a disoriented elite can only give itself coherence and attempt to reach a population it cannot inspire by invoking the people. It courts popularity by applying marketing to government, sorry governance, in order not to convince the citizen but to satisfy the consumer. When the citizen becomes a consumer it is the focus group rather than political debate that moves centre stage. When the people are not democratic insurgents but 'middle England' then the point of education is to deliver a product, not a gateway to civic life.

The last 50 years have seen the accelerating erosion of hierarchy and deference in many aspects of British life. This is good. But what this has meant is that we have achieved the semblance of democracy even when there is a widening gap in social and economic opportunity. This has led to a peculiar relationship between culture and politics. Culture has been levelled and carries the torch for the democratic component of our society and is ill equipped to do so, while to politics, the sphere of democratic engagement, sticks all the opprobrium and disenchantment that we feel when we are not being culturally diverted. We have substituted and mistaken the popularisation of cultural forms for political engagement. We accept the way things are as natural but laugh at them in our cultural practice.

Even in cultural terms this does not escape ambivalence and tension. The dominant cultural motif is to debunk the difficult and the critical as obscure and pompous. But there is a powerful theme of nostalgia in contemporary culture – the invention of a lost world of community, especially working class communities, which become a source of cultural identity. The nostalgia is cloying rather than bittersweet, because it allows for neither the harsh nature of those lost communities nor their search for educational and social betterment – a world captured in works as diverse as those of Richard Hoggart and Dennis Potter; works, both difficult and engaged, which now raise the voices of the debunkers higher than Simon Cowell's waistline.

Education, democracy and the citizen

In education the possibility of knowledge is questioned, examinations are seen as discriminatory and in turn discrimination is seen as judgemental and presumptuous. The content of education is diluted because subject discipline is presumed to be the mark of a hierarchical society and of no economic value.

Examinations are not elitist. The denial of social and economic possibilities to the majority is. This will be the fate of the majority of working-class children who will go to schools where traditional subjects are no longer taught. In the name of the people, economic efficiency and anti-elitism any real possibility of an engaged, participatory democracy will shrink and vanish.

Democracy in education is about giving the best content to an active citizen; the bastardised form of widening participation is about formal inclusion in passive mediocrity. The tools for understanding the world are replaced by worthless credits for the purpose of measuring targets and patronising twaddle about raising self-esteem.

Much of the discussion about education, whether it be about specialist schools, entry into Higher Education or continuing adult education, which is my particular concern, is presented as a battle between standards and widening participation. This is misplaced. The argument should rather be about the relationship between the people, or citizens and education. The question should be re-posed as to how the aspiration for the highest quality in education should be and can be constituted to encourage literacy or active participation in public affairs. At the heart of this conviction is an idea of literacy as public discourse associated with individuals such as Richard Hoggart and Dennis Potter. In this sense literacy presumes not merely reading skills, but a willingness and capacity to engage with public concerns and difficulties. In the public sphere cultural practice can in turn be understood, refined, explored and enhanced.

As current educational policy demonstrates, it is dangerous to have prescriptive models but it is legitimate to describe good practice. When we look to the past, we must guard against nostalgia, but to advocate the role of education in the spirit of democracy we have to make historical comparisons. The years following the Second World War were years in which the democratisation of our society, although it remained underdeveloped, was still associated with the capacity of individuals to act as citizens. And all the better, if they schooled themselves.

In 'The Great Tradition in University Adult Education', Harold Wiltshire argues for an emphasis on studies which can reasonably be expected to concern us as men and women, not as technicians or functionaries; nor even as examinees.[4] This means the pursuit of subjects as diverse as physics and music; history and languages.

The purpose of this education, and the nature of the curriculum, illuminates man as a social being rather than an economic asset or a self-actualiser. Learning for learning's sake is not, however, an end, although it is a pleasure. Learning is a means of understanding. The typical student, says Wiltshire, is not a specialist, whether scientist or solitary, but the reflective citizen. I would add that the reflective citizen will be a scientist, fire officer or shop worker, but is better at both because specialisation and training are predicated on education and not a substitute for it. Since the vocational aspect of education then becomes a derivative function of the whole process examinations cease to be accreditation hoops but a necessary component of intellectual discipline.

This conception of education combines a democratic notion about equality of educational opportunity with what Wiltshire was already acknowledging might be seen as unwarrantably optimistic assumptions about the educability of normal human beings.

It is the cynicism and condescension about the possibilities of people in the educational and wider social and political world that are driving education policy. This in turn makes education policy both a prime example of our degraded public life and a crucial battlefield for democrats.

There should be less concern for higher percentages of the population to achieve qualifications. It is dubious, already, whether this reflects any higher level of skill or achievement and it certainly does not enhance knowledge or critical enquiry. We should assert much more forcefully that self-improvement is not primarily or essentially economic or therapeutic but a fuller capacity to understand the world, articulate a view on it and participate in civic life.

Education is not the provision of a consumption good, the quality of which is to be measured against economic criteria, whether the benefit accrues to the individual, state or both. Education is not a mechanism to convince or reassure any individual that they and their experiences are of any intrinsic worth, but to encourage people to be discriminating about what is of worth and to give meaning to a wider set of relationships than their personal experiences. Education cannot and should not have a prescribed set of outcomes. Education cannot and should not reassure us that criticism is unjustified and negative.

The possible, or potential, merit in education is transformative. Learning – our own active engagement with learning – opens up a sense of dissatisfaction, not about our income or our identity but with our own knowledge of the world and perhaps even the way we choose to organise it.

The present state of education reflects the prevailing, New Labour, view of the people: it offers only the lowest common denominator of low expectations and disdain. We need to set against this an ambitious highest common factor achieved through rigour, conflict and argument.

Notes

1   A little learning is a dang'rous thing;
     Drink deep, or taste not the Pierian spring:
     There shallow draughts intoxicate the brain,
     And drinking largely sobers us again.

Pope, A. (2003) *An Essay on Criticism*, in Roger Lonsdale (ed.), *The New Book of Eighteenth Century Verse*, Oxford: Oxford University Press, p. 88.

2   Go, go, go, said the bird: human kind
     Cannot bear very much reality.

Eliot, T.S. (1969) 'Burnt Norton', in *Complete Poems and Plays*, London: Faber, p. 172.

3   No more; where ignorance is bliss,
     'Tis folly to be wise.

Gray, T. (2003) 'Ode on a Prospect of Eton College', in *The New Oxford Book of Eighteenth Century Verse*, Oxford: Oxford University Press, p. 352.

4   Wiltshire, H. (1956) 'The Great Tradition in University Adult Education', *Adult Education* XXIX, 2 (Autumn): 88–9.

Key readings

Brown, P. and Lauder, H. (2001) *Capitalism and Social Progress: The Future of Society in a Global Economy*, London: Palgrave.

Hoggart, R. (1958) *The Uses of Literacy*, Harmondsworth: Penguin.
Lester Smith, W.O. (1957) *Education*, Harmondsworth: Penguin.
Timmins, N. (1995) *The Five Giants: A Biography of the Welfare State*, London: Fontana.

Focus question

Is it possible to distinguish between elitism, social hierarchies and the pursuit of excellence in formulating education policy?

CHAPTER 4

THE PHILOSOPHY GAP

Claire Fox

Does anyone know what New Labour's educational philosophy is? Having been a teacher and having written on education I still can't fathom it out. Before someone from the DfES drowns me in sound-bites and jargon, yes I know all about diversity, aptitude and choice. There's certainly plenty of choice: take your pick from specialist schools, city academies, training schools, CTCs, beacon schools and now a cadre of advanced schools. And then there were Estelle Morris's schools that she 'wouldn't touch with a bargepole', and Alistair Campbell's 'Bog Standard Comprehensives'.

It's ironic that, when New Labour was in opposition and throughout their first term, the mantra was 'standards not structures'. Now all there seem to be are 'structures'. Everyone gets hot under the collar about types of schools and yet the philosophy behind the government's approach to education is anybody's guess. Every month, new ideas are floated – more exams, fewer exams, vocational GCSEs, fewer AS levels – adding up to a bewildering array of disjointed ideas conspicuous by their lack of educational vision.

In the past, whether in 1870, 1902 or 1944, Education Acts were accompanied by raging debates about epistemology, the relationship between schooling and society, technology and progress, the meaning of curricula, vocational versus academic, etc. The structures of schooling were only a reflection of a philosophy, not the end point. For example, when the comprehensive system was launched 40 years ago, the type of school was just an expression of a bigger idea. Love it or loathe it, comprehensivisation marked a complete shift in philosophy around the clarion cry 'opportunity for all' and represented an ideological assault on the iniquity of selection. Post-war pioneers of state education had a clear intellectual project and rejected the previous era's instrumentalism that treated schooling as a vehicle for skilling the workforce. Their philosophy was explicitly academic and egalitarian; it promised to open up the wonders of knowledge and the life of the mind to all. The transmission of the best that has ever been known or thought would no longer be the preserve of a narrow social elite.

That was then, but what of now? Of course we must be wary of an easy slippage into nostalgia. But noting the passing of an education system, which aimed at a knowledge-based philosophy, is no lament for a golden era. Allowing everyone access to knowledge for its own sake was indeed an ideal that was rarely realised. But at least it was an ideal valued by significant sections of society and certainly by those who ran state education. Now they have abandoned it.

Today, the idea of knowledge as an end is derided as elitist, irrelevant and old-fashioned. Charles Clarke, the Secretary of State for education no less, gave a speech at University College Worcester dismissing university scholarship as a medieval prejudice and the ideal of knowledge for its own sake as 'a bit dodgy' (Smithers and

Woodward 2003). This approach best epitomises an increasingly philistine ethos that haunts education policy.

Clarke is simply echoing a new breed of state education bureaucrat who seems to regard knowledge per se – knowledge with a capital K – at best with ambivalence, but more often with hostility and contempt. For example, despite the rhetoric of a commitment to the K word in today's knowledge economy, the discussion about ICT in education shows the confusion at the heart of the debate. When Michelle Selinger wrote in a much-cited New Labour think-tank pamphlet: 'It is no longer unusual for students to know more than their teacher about a particular topic because they have used e-mail and the web to delve deeply into something that engages their interest' (2001: 12), she gave succour to the new orthodoxy that pupils can know as much as their teacher because they can use a search engine. Such an approach has had serious consequences for how we view knowledge, and indeed how we view teaching.

Transferring knowledge is confused with simply passing on information (think A–Zs, telephone directories, even dates and names of kings and queens). By suggesting ICT transforms teachers from knowledge providers to information facilitators, teaching is reduced to the merely technical. After all a machine can spew out facts, opinions, statistics and even ready-made lessons. But expert teachers have spent years immersed in the knowledge associated with their specialist subject, have thought about that poem, that period in history, that chemistry experiment, from every angle and have practised sharing insights and truths with children of various abilities.

Increasingly then, our definition of knowledge in an educational setting is emptied of all intellectual content. But another contemporary trend is just as worrying – knowledge is also treated in a narrow instrumental fashion. Government ministers queue up to proclaim that the government values university research *not* as the expansion of human knowledge, but for its contribution to UK plc. Charles Clarke's predecessor, Estelle Morris, told academics to quit their ivory towers and forge links with business and communities to make knowledge count.

The most vivid example of these market-orientated demands was the major review of universities commissioned by the New Labour government when they first came to power. Sir Ron Dearing's review demanded that all undergraduate courses proved their employability quota and flagged up a new role for universities to produce more 'work ready graduates'. Thus knowledge was promoted not as a glorious end in itself, but as no more than a means to an end, i.e. getting a (better) job. Dearing suggested year-long work experience placements even on non-vocational courses such as classics. He noted employers' criticism that academics should spend less time researching and writing books, and more time teaching their students the core skills that are fundamental to the modern age (Dearing 1997). Dearing's recommendations have now become so internalised that it no longer seems surprising that the government regularly argues for the expansion of university education using the language of the workplace and the economy rather than as an intrinsic good.

Since Dearing, instrumentalism has gone far beyond the crude demands of the market. Once schools and colleges are loosened from their knowledge-based moorings new instrumental demands can be placed on the sector. Increasingly these have little educational content at all. Whatever the social problem, from obesity to teenage pregnancies, government calls on schooling to solve the problem. There is rarely a government social initiative that doesn't have an 'educational' angle: youth unemployment – get them back to college; over-40's unemployment – get them into lifelong learning; young single mothers – enrol them on college courses; poverty trap – the answer lies in getting more qualifications; community fragmentation – use education to improve self-esteem. The ever-expanding remit of PSHE testifies to schools becoming substitute arenas for government intervention into matters that were erstwhile the responsibility of parents and the private sphere.

Examples are endless. Politicians, obsessed with youth apathy and having failed to inspire young voters, turn to schools and charge them with the non-educational task of re-engaging pupils with politics. Hence we have compulsory citizenship classes, even though this topic does not pass the test of any academic, or indeed vocational, criteria. This is a subject with no intellectual core, no syllabus and driven not by educational demands but rather by the motive of socialising children.

If not acting as a surrogate election agent, education is being turned into a branch of social services. The new green paper *Every Child Matters* (DfES 2003) demands that schools take a lead in the child abuse jamboree and head teachers are told that one way of assessing their educational performance is by reaching targets in child protection. The DfES is to be the lead agency in bringing all children's agencies together, from social services to the police, and Ofsted will oversee an integrated inspection framework to assess the joint agency working. In the same month Children, Young People and Families Minister, Margaret Hodge, unveiled 61 extended schools in which the health and social care of the local community, and family and adult support will be the key focus.

When education is treated as a panacea for social ills, it is little wonder that teachers are demoralised. More broadly, teachers are being encouraged to forget that they are in the knowledge business. Instead they are expected to act as social includers, a new branch of social work. Consequently, many have lost their nerve in the battle for ideas. Scared of failing people, and being held responsible for social exclusion, teachers constantly cave in to their new role. Teachers are now not focused on subject knowledge because the subject has been sidelined in favour of social policy and state education has been politicised for non-educational instrumental ends. Is it any wonder then that the General Teaching Council has just revealed that a mere 24 per cent who enter the teaching profession do so because of a love of their subject? And only 14 per cent of teachers are motivated to stay because of the subject.

The sickly annual 'Teacher Oscars' ceremony, initiated as a carrot for a worn-down profession, illustrates the point. Teachers are rarely rewarded for the depth of their subject knowledge, their scholarship or their ability to stretch pupils with intellectual rigour and pedagogy. Instead there is a concentration on those who leave nobody out, who care most, and who make their pupils feel good about themselves. This is a hollow task. Rewarding pupils for being themselves rather than for what they achieve is not education – but it is the task of the socially inclusive teacher.

Indeed, if there is one idea that has usurped 'knowledge as an end' it is that of the social inclusion agenda. Being inclusive is now packaged as an educational end. No one is to be excluded; participation is all. But substituting Knowledge for its own sake with Participation for its own sake begs the question, participation in what? Inevitably, if the principal goal of education is to 'include' people, the content of that education and the standards it sets cannot fail to suffer. The passion of government officials and teachers is not reserved for the quality of ideas assimilated in schools, but for how many pupils are socially included by gaining the latest spurious qualification. When the former education secretary, David Blunkett, stated boldly, that 'instead of patronising the children of families in challenging circumstances we will target support to help them learn and remove, one-by-one, the barriers that prevent them from achieving their potential' (Blunkett 1999), he was not talking, as radicals did in the past, about removing the social barriers denying people access to knowledge and ideas. He was talking about removing the educational 'barriers', which make judgements about ability and attainment.

The issue of qualifications is instructive. In socially inclusive Britain everybody must 'ave 'em. Rather than this leading to a debate about how best to teach the depth and rigour that this might require, New Labour simply changes the qualification regime to make sure everybody is included. First, they created GNVQs that you couldn't fail, and which were given to all the pupils who were 'excluded' from passing GCSEs and A levels (because they were not educated well enough to pass). But even that was considered too exclusionary – so now we have glorified work experience dressed up as academic qualifications. (GNVQ-style qualifications in topics such as travel and tourism and beauty and hairdressing have been rebranded as (vocational) GCSEs). The meritocratic impulse behind the objective assessment of knowledge is being replaced with government favours and patronage. New guidelines from the Qualifications and Curriculum Authority (September 2003) have suggested that GCSEs should abolish the F grade (i.e. Fail) and replace it with N for Nearly (Harrison 2003). The new positive marking schemes are justified as important for pupils' self-esteem, to ensure no exam-taker feels excluded. An emphasis on inclusivity is reducing education to feel-good 'therapy'.

Getting people to participate in education has now become a bureaucratic target. The content of what is being participated in is increasingly marginalised and side-lined. Look at the fate of music colleges. The government are concerned that too few students from poor areas are studying classical music. Conservatoires have been told to widen participation and give 10 per cent of their places to students from disadvantaged backgrounds or face heavy financial penalties. But if it is true that too few of the intake in music colleges are from state schools, one has to ask why they are not able to fulfil the necessary entrance requirements of a grade 8 in Instrumentation, a grade C in Maths A level and an audition. Perhaps the problem lies in the fact that the level of instrumental teaching in state schools has been in decline since the 1990s. But what solution did the Higher Education Funding Council come up with to tackle this problem? It has suggested that music colleges are in danger of being elitist and exclusionary by concentrating on classical music; instead they should widen the curriculum to include pop and rock. So there we have it! The original aim of encouraging wider participation in classical music has been drowned by the demand for participation per se and the knowledge available at conservatoires is sidelined.

There has been a similar end result in initiatives to get more young people to take science at school. The common perception is that the individual subjects of physics, chemistry and biology have put pupils off because they are too difficult and abstract. Instead, there has been the growth of modular (combined) science GCSEs, packaged around themes, which claims to make science 'relevant to concrete reality' so that it will allegedly connect with young people's concerns, such as global warming and environmentalism. But while this strategy has seen more pupils participating, it's not in science per se. After all, science is based on abstract ideas for a very good reason – it has to be to deal with the counterintuitive behaviour of the natural world. One can only conclude that inclusion as an end is leading to contempt for knowledge, whether in classical music or scientific theory, and is producing a 'content-lite' curriculum.

These examples are an interesting insight into the educational philosophy and ethos of today's education mandarins. This new anti-elitist elite has an incredibly conservative imagination. The only way they can imagine including more and more people into intellectual life – whether into classical music or physics, academic GCSEs or university level education – is by transforming intellectual life itself and emptying it of its contents to make it more hospitable to the majority. What they never emphasise is transforming pupils or students by means of education and making young minds more hospitable to knowledge.

In conclusion, today's educational policy pundits have avoided developing a clear educational philosophy. But the vacuum is filled with some dangerous implicit ideas which use the egalitarian language of access and inclusion, but which redefine education as a thin gruel with low expectations. The majority of pupils are not expected to be able to engage with the best, the abstract and the most difficult. An educational project, which disavows knowledge, never imagines that pupils might aspire to the life of the mind. Today's social engineering lacks educational ambition for today's youth, and is leading to the abandonment of education's most ambitious project – a commitment to the transformative potential of knowledge and ideas.

References

Blunkett, D. (1999) The Secretary of State, address at the President's Reception at the CBI, Centre Point, London, 19 July.

Dearing, R. (1997) *Higher Education in the Learning Society*, National Committee of Inquiry into Higher Education, London: HMSO.

DfES (2003) *Every Child Matters*, Nottingham: DfES Publications.

Harrison, D. (2003) 'It's Official: You Can No Longer Fail Your Exams', *The Daily Telegraph*, 21 September.

Selinger, M. (2001) 'Can ICT Improve the Recruitment, Retention and Morale of Teachers?', in M. Selinger and C. Yapp (2001) *ICTeachers*, London: IPPR, pp. 8–17.

Smithers, R. and Woodward, W. (2003) 'Clarke Dismisses Medieval Historians', *The Guardian*, 9 May.

Key readings

Bentley, T. (1998) *Learning Beyond the Classroom: Education for a Changing World*, London: Routledge.

Phillips, M. (1996) *All Must Have Prizes*, London: Little, Brown & Company.

Smithers, A. (2001) 'Education Policy', in A. Seldon (ed.), *The Blair Effect*, London: Little, Brown & Company, pp. 405–26.

Focus question

Is it a step forward to be more concerned with issues such as social inclusion rather than the advancement of subject knowledge?

PART II

POLICING THE CLASSROOM

CHAPTER 5

RE-ENCHANTING EARLY CHILDHOOD?

Tricia David

According to current reports (Stone 2003), many women in their twenties and thirties are deciding to give up work when their children are born – and here we are talking about women who have a university education behind them and promising careers, potentially, ahead. Best-selling books, like Allison Pearson's *I Don't Know How She Does It* (2002) and Danielle Crittenden's *Amanda Bright@ Home* (2003) are said to be exemplars of this fashion for 'yummy mummies'. They may even be role models.

Despite the government's policies to encourage women to return to or remain in the workforce and their increased funding to enable the development of provision for young children's Education and Care, the enticements to give up and stay at home for a few years can be very strong. To begin with there is the fact that one is quite likely to have 'fallen in love' with one's new offspring, and to want them to have an enchanting early childhood. Once life becomes pressured by too much work and chores at home, the idea of enchantment can be forgotten or lost.

Second, there is still some moral pressure in English society which can lead to feelings of guilt about handing this precious new being over to someone else, often someone hitherto unknown to the parents. For many, particularly those whose work options are relatively uninspiring, policies like the New Deal and inducements to employers to take account of work–life balance issues for their employees (of both sexes) may not add up to sufficiently rewarding incentives to stimulate further developments in women's employment patterns. (By the Spring of 1999 just over half of women in the UK with a child aged under five were in employment.)

When all this is combined with the often insurmountable challenges one faces in order to combine motherhood with work, as detailed by research (Brannen *et al.* 1997; Skinner 2002), it is hardly surprising that, viewed from a mother's perspective, too little has been done to support them.

Of course, it must be acknowledged that the current government has done far more than any before to ameliorate the situation. If one examines the history of provision for the youngest children in England, especially in comparison with most of our European partner countries (Moss 1990; David 1993, 1998; OECD 2001), the English Early Childhood Education and Care (ECEC) situation has been bedevilled by attitudes to the family and laissez-faire government policies (Gauthier 1996), which have at times spelt out the edict that it was not the responsibility of government to provide services so that women with small children could go out to work, but that if they wished or were forced to do so, then the responsibility was their own.

Integrated ECEC: examples from abroad

In other countries, more comprehensive and integrated services, providing meaningful (to the child) care and education (i.e. planned opportunities for learning, not formal lessons), have developed as a result of recognition that both strands are important – essential in fact.

For example, in France the *école maternelle* system started over 100 years ago, with an educative intention, aiming to instil in the very young a love of learning and the beginnings of an understanding of their future as French citizens. In Sweden, a 1960s' shortage of workers meant that their government created a climate in which childcare was central and children seen as a collective responsibility. Both have now developed further, so that in France schools can accommodate to help parents cover their work hours and in Sweden the educational aspects of their services are more consciously elaborated.

The current situation in England is one in which the growth of the ECEC sector, in terms of numbers of places, is positively encouraged by the government, especially by the Treasury. This appears to emphasise the care aspect. However, at the same time there are other government-initiated developments concerning the need for improvements in the quality of provision, such as a new training pack for those who work with children aged from birth to three (Abbott *et al.* 2002) and the Secretary of State Charles Clarke's pledge for more resources (Tweed 2003).

UK history

The UK's Early Childhood Education and Care history is more chequered and perhaps more difficult to develop as a result. Apart from the innovations of a few pioneers, such as Robert Owen and the McMillan sisters, whose work was subsequently emulated in industrial areas of the country where women's labour in light industries resulted in unsupervised young children being seen as a problem, nursery provision in the UK was not a priority. Almost a century ago, women school inspectors presented a report advising the government to develop nurseries. During the years of the two World Wars, some attention was paid to the needs of women working for the war effort, and after the Second World War, the 1944 Education Act actually laid a duty on local authorities to open nursery schools and classes for children aged between three and five. Most ignored this requirement and no action was taken. Local authority day nurseries tended to be reserved for those young children whose families were experiencing extreme difficulties and there were very few private nurseries. Childminding was relatively unregulated.

In the 1960s, the playgroup movement began, involving mainly mothers who sought out-of-home, group experiences for their children, in the absence of any meaningful government strategy. Again, this type of group experience was generally for three- to five-year-olds, and it developed rapidly, in church halls and other available spaces rather than in purpose-built settings, especially in those areas of the country where there was no maintained nursery provision.

What all this has meant is that many working parents have to depend on informal care by relatives, nannies or au pairs, who may be the best solution for some, while others would prefer a properly regulated system with trained educarers.

The lingering effect of maternal deprivation theory

Perhaps as a result of the ways in which John Bowlby's work on maternal deprivation (Bowlby 1953) was used, debate about Early Childhood Education and Care has been infused with the idea that individual women have the major responsibility for their own children, and that women's and children's rights are bound to be incompatible. This is despite the fact that, historically, women have always worked, often outside the home, and children have been raised by people other than their own mothers. Decisions about child-rearing, like those about the nature of Early Education and Care, are made within the context of particular times and places, as the roles of mothers, fathers, children and other family members shift in relation to social, cultural and economic factors (David *et al.* 2001). The problem in the UK has often been the confounding of the issue of care, so that a parent may work, and education (i.e. early learning opportunities), to benefit the child. The fact that Early Education and Care go hand-in-hand is paramount, since young children are learning all the time.

Yet there is at present funding only for part-time places for children aged three and four. In other words a substantial burden still falls upon parents if they seek employment. Further, if mothers choose to, or must, work as soon as their maternity leave ends, there is still a shortage of places for babies and toddlers.

Additionally, some provision, especially that in maintained schools, continues to be limited to traditional school hours. The growth in breakfast and after-school clubs is very welcome, but there are still too many cases of children needing to be 'bussed' to a different setting. This is more likely to happen when the children are in the earliest years, rather than when they can fully understand what is happening to them and why. For too long it has been considered 'normal' for children younger than five to move from one setting to another, not only year on year, but sometimes within a single day. Were schooling for 11–16-year-olds to be made on this pattern, there would no doubt be uproar. Then there is the question whether the quality of Early Childhood Education and Care provision can be sufficiently high to be equivalent to that a 'good parent' would offer ... but what is meant by quality? Can one define meaningful criteria for such a value-laden concept? What does research tell us about what very young children need?

What babies and young children 'need'

It is important to acknowledge that the concept of a 'need' is culturally defined (Woodhead 1990) – apart from needs such as food, shelter, etc. – so that research is often premised on assumptions about the kind of society in which children are being raised to participate. Knowing what children are like, what they can do and how they make sense of their worlds at this age is essential if we are to promote beneficial provision, whether that is at home or in another setting. We know that babies can form attachments with several significant people in their lives, both adults and children, not simply with their mothers. We also know that:

- All areas of learning and development are intricately intertwined, young children develop and learn holistically and their emotional and social development seems to form the bedrock of other areas.

- Babies seem to come into the world primed for attachment to warm, familiar carers, who will usually be mothers, fathers, grandparents, older brothers and sisters and key adults in ECEC (Early Childhood Education and Care) settings.
- These attachments form the basis for subsequent relationships, and for a person's sense of self/self-assurance – those children who have had experience of warm attachments and positive responses become socially adept, self assured, independent, interdependent and higher achievers in their later ECEC and school settings.
- Parents who express negative narratives concerning their own early relationships with their parents need support to overcome perpetuating such patterns and to form joyful, mutually loving relationships with their babies and small children.
- Babies are born with the ability to perceive differences in languages and they can recognise the sounds used in the languages spoken in their homes.
- Between 12 and 36 months of age, young children grasp what is and is not culturally acceptable behaviour and speech and this is the result of being involved in interactions during the first year of life, where one is treated as if one is a person who understands and can respond.
- Babies seem to be tuned to learn from, with and about first the people and the cultural environment around them, followed by the material environment – they come into the world primed to be curious, competent learners.
- Play, in which the baby or child takes the lead and makes choices, is a process which fosters cognitive development.
- Language and thought are developmentally linked – each depends on and also promotes the development of the other.
- Children 'make sense' of and 'transform' knowledge, experiences and events through imaginative and creative activity.
- Children's developing memories and use of narrative help them make sense of their lives.
- They want to share and express their ideas playfully through the 'hundred languages of children' (for example, dancing, singing, talking, 'storying', music-making, painting, making patterns, building, model-making, 'animating' puppets and other toys, dressing up, gardening, looking after animals, drawing and mark-making – to list but a few possibilities).
- Once again, the research points to the centrality of positive relationships with parents and other key people in young children's lives.

Research also directs us to suggest that parents and practitioners need to be able to:

- Understand attachment and the importance of a child being special to at least one significant person in order to promote resilience.
- Be informed about young children's development.
- Provide opportunities to explore and play in a safe and secure environment – children's mobility and movement are important for their development.
- Know about brain development and the importance of 'nourishment' (a good diet – in both the form of food and of physical and psychological stimulation).
- See that intimate behaviours such as *bugging and nudging*, *pet names* and *idiosyncratic behaviour* are important and that children's development sometimes seems difficult because they are trying to become independent people with a sense of self.

- Have reasonable rules which fit with children's rhythms and give a pattern to life.
- Know that parents, as well as children, need support.

(David *et al.* 2003)

Meanwhile, research also suggests that policy makers need to help communities and the public understand the importance of positive interactions and experiences in the first three years for all areas of development, including brain development, and for enjoyment in the here and now. Further, it is time they acknowledged that practitioners need help in accessing education and training, as well as appropriate pay and conditions of work, to enable them to fulfil their important role.

Re-enchanting early childhood

Researchers such as Belsky (2001) continue to argue that we should be wary of encouraging mothers to hurry back to work in their child's first year, despite indications for effects due to variations in the quality of provision and the number of hours worked. What certainly seems to be crucial to future well-being for the individual child is the influence of close relationships. The prognosis is good if they have loving, responsive, sensitive key persons around them. These should be people who not only ensure all their health needs are met. They should also be able to recognise young children's fascination with and curiosity about what is going on in their world, to cater for their drive to explore and problem-solve through active learning, and to provide opportunities to play, make friends and share experiences. At this age, children also seem to need time to be deeply focused alone but near others. In other words, babies and young children grow and learn best when they share their life experiences through playful exchanges with people who love them (Gopnik *et al.* 1999).

It is in this understanding of young children's ways of learning and appreciation of their amazing abilities that we can perhaps begin to grasp what is needed if we are to bring women's and young children's lives into a positive and synergistic whole. It will require a new kind of 're-enchantment' of early childhood.

That re-enchantment will depend upon how, as a society, we set about ensuring the fulfilment of these apparently obvious and simple conclusions about young children and how we support their mothers as both parents and workers.

References

Abbott, L., Langston, A., Ackers, J., Baron, I., Bradbury, C., Holmes, R. and Johnson, M. (2002) *Birth to Three Matters: A Framework to Support Children in Their Earliest Years*, London: DfES.

Belsky, J. (2001) 'Emanuel Miller Lecture: Developmental Risks (Still) Associated with Early Child Care', *Journal of Child Psychology and Psychiatry* 42(7): 845–59.

Bowlby, J. (1953) *Child Care and the Growth of Love*, Harmondsworth: Penguin.

Brannen, J., Moss, P., Owen, C. and Wale, C. (1997) *Mothers, Fathers and Employment*, London: DfEE.

Crittenden, D. (2003) *Amanda Bright@ Home*, New York: Warner Books.

David, T. (ed.) (1993) *Educational Provision for our Youngest Children: European Perspectives*, London: PCP.

David, T. (ed.) (1998) *Researching Early Childhood Education: European Perspectives*, London: PCP.

David, T., Goouch, K. and Jago, M. (2001) 'Cultural Constructions of Childhood and Early Literacy', *Reading* 35(2): 47–52.

David, T., Goouch, K., Powell, S. and Abbott, L. (2003) *Birth to Three Matters: A Review of the Literature*, London: DfES.

Gauthier, A.H. (1996) *The State and the Family*, Oxford: Clarendon Press.

Gopnik, A., Melzoff, A. and Kuhl, P. (1999) *How Babies Think*, London: Weidenfeld & Nicolson.

Moss, P. (1990) 'Work, Family and the Care of Children: Equality and Responsibility', *Children and Society* 4(2): 145–66.

OECD (2001) *Starting Strong*, Paris: OECD.

Pearson, A. (2002) *I Don't Know How She Does It*, London: Chatto & Windus.

Skinner, C. (2002) *Running Round in Circles: Coordinating Childcare, Education and Work*, London: Policy Press.

Stone, K. (2003) 'From Yummy Mummy to Walled-up Wife', *The Sunday Times, News Review* 5 (October): 5.

Tweed, J. (2003) 'Clarke's Pledge to Early Years', *Nursery World*, 103(3887): 4–5.

Woodhead, M. (1990) 'Psychology and the Cultural Construction of Children's Needs', in A. James and A. Prout (eds), *Constructing and Reconstructing Childhood*, London: Falmer Press, pp. 60–77.

Key readings

Crittenden, D. (2003) *Amanda Bright@ Home,* New York: Warner Books.

David, T. (ed.) (1993) *Educational Provision for Our Youngest Children: European Perspectives*, London: PCP.

Gauthier, A.H. (1996) *The State and the Family*, Oxford: Clarendon Press.

Focus question

Why does the state not put sufficient resources and money into supporting young children and their mums?

CHAPTER 6

AFRAID TO TEACH?

Joanna Williams

Our increasingly risk-aware society has witnessed an explosion in panics concerning children. Parents worry that children are at risk of abduction by paedophiles or abuse by relatives. If they remain at home, children could be prey to 'groomers' in Internet chat rooms or at risk of obesity from a couch-potato lifestyle. The food children eat could cause cancer or the vaccinations designed to protect them could trigger autism. Teachers are not immune to these panics and we need to question the extent to which concerns over child-rearing can be allowed to influence classroom practice.

Changing roles

Recent years have witnessed substantial change in the relationship between teachers and parents and the role each is expected to fulfil. Parents are now more involved than ever before in the education of their children. Sheila Wolfendale and Keith Topping, two of the leading proponents of incorporating parents into the world of professional educators, point out that 'Education legislation in the UK from the early 1980's onwards almost without exception has contained provision for the extension of parents' rights in education' (1996: 2). Alongside legislation there are formal classes in parenting skills, a plethora of advice manuals suggesting how to be a better parent and informal discussions in the media – 'Mums Make a Difference' (headline from *The Independent*, 3 April 2003). Frank Furedi argues that 'Parental responsibility for child development has been expanded so that mothers and fathers are expected to play a direct role in their children's education' (2001: 73).

At the same time, the role of the teacher has also been expanded. Teachers can no longer concern themselves solely with teaching subject knowledge. Teachers are expected to take on a broader role involving care of the social, moral and physical welfare of the children in their care. This takes place formally through the teaching of citizenship and personal and social education classes and informally through a continual awareness of child protection issues. The duty teachers have to care for the children in their charge has gone beyond *in loco parentis*, 'since this fails to acknowledge the full range of teachers' responsibilities' (*Education Law Monitor* 2002). In order to fulfil this broader role, teachers had to forge links with parents: 'Partnerships with parents were seen as a considerable help in providing holistic support to the "whole child"' (Pollard and Triggs 2000).

Lack of trust

Furedi argues that 'The erosion of the line of demarcation between parent and teacher opens the way to conflict and mutual recrimination' (2001: 77). The resulting relationship between teachers and parents can be characterised by a lack of trust. Teachers no longer trust parents to adequately protect and care for their children or to prepare them for starting school. Teachers expend considerable time and energy compensating for the perceived defects of parents. As one headline in *The Independent* puts it: 'Schools Must Teach Parents How to Talk to Children' (3 April 2003). Numerous family literacy schemes have developed, such as Hackney PACT (Parents and Children and Teachers) and CAPER (Children and Parents Enjoying Reading) (detailed in Wolfendale and Topping 1996), all of which require substantial teacher input.

Parents, meanwhile, have little faith in teachers to do the best for their children academically or to protect them emotionally or physically. Teachers are aware of and react to the concerns of parents. We need to examine how classroom practice is influenced by this lack of trust.

Academic attainment

Parents no longer trust teachers to ensure their child achieves his or her academic potential and instead consider 'The behaviour and performance of school children ... to be a direct reflection of the quality and support they receive from their fathers and mothers' (Furedi 2001: 73). Recent years have seen an explosion in the number of educational games, learn-at-home computer programmes and National Curriculum self-test books. This is certainly an industry that is booming. Alongside this is an increase in the demand for home tuition, '65% of the pupils at one primary school had private tuition'. Tutors are perceived to be 'making up for the deficiencies of both the private and state education sectors' (Brian 2002: 16). However, parents cannot sit back and relax once the tutor is employed and are warned to be on their guard: 'alarmingly, anyone can set themselves up as a private tutor, or even as a tutoring agency, with no licensing or registration' (Brian 2002: 18).

Schools have not attacked the notion of parents as substitute teachers, or, to any notable degree, questioned the need for extra tuition on top of the school day. Instead, schools have been eager to exploit the enthusiasms of parents as extra teachers. The educational charity Campaign for Learning suggests that, 'Children whose parents are involved in their schooling do up to 25% better than pupils with families who are not involved' (*The Independent*, 8 October 2003). Many schools run programmes to involve parents, although, 'Interestingly, few schools feel the need to evaluate ... the worth of their programmes' (Hancock and Gale 1996). Involving parents has come to be seen as a positive in itself, although few studies report children making significant academic progress as a result of increased parental involvement: 'the evidence was anecdotal since no school undertook the kind of evaluation which would withstand rigorous examination' (Branston 1996). Parental involvement is sought largely through the sphere of homework. Parents may be asked to formally sign a home–school agreement declaring their part in the responsibility for their child's academic attainment. In some schools, homework is set with the prime aim of using children to involve their parents. 'Schools have devised homework tasks which require discussion with a parent about the chosen book' (Hancock and Gale 1996).

By incorporating parents as fellow educators, teachers run the risk of undermining their own professionalism. In the current climate of parental anxiety about children's attainment, incorporating parents serves only to further reinforce the notion that education cannot be trusted to teachers alone. A vigorous defence of teacher professionalism and the specialist skills of teaching would help alleviate parental concerns.

Teaching requires specialist subject knowledge that teachers should have acquired through studying at a higher level and completing teacher training. To deny pupils access to specialist teachers has much more damaging consequences for their academic attainment than their parents not listening to them read. Likewise, if teachers could hand responsibility for the social and moral welfare of pupils back to parents, more time would be freed up for teachers to engage with their subject specialisms.

Physical protection

The blurring of the boundaries between the role of teachers and parents can be dated back as far as the Plowden Report (CACE 1967) but it only took on momentum when it met with the climate of panic and anxiety around children that built up in the 1990s. If parents are no longer to trust teachers with their child's academic attainment then they no longer feel confident entrusting schools with their child's physical protection. Parents lack trust in teachers to defend children from risk of injury, accident or abduction. Concerns over children's safety become most apparent when teachers seek to take children away from school on day trips, evening theatre visits and residential stays. Several high-profile cases have aroused parental fears. The death of 13-year-old Caroline Dickinson in a French youth hostel in 1996 caused alarm over the organisation of residential stays out of all proportion to the reality of the risks faced. The drowning of Gemma Carter while on a school trip to France in June 1999 caused similar panic.

Despite the high-profile nature of such tragedies, they remain, fortunately, incredibly rare occurrences. Gemma's mother, Sharon Carter said, 'I always wonder if more had been done would Gemma still be here today?' (*TES*, 16 May 2003). This is a perfectly understandable reaction from a grieving mother. However, educational professionals should be in a position to take a step back from the situation and make an accurate assessment of the dangers faced on school outings in relation to both the risks faced by children in their everyday lives and the benefits gained by children participating in such trips. For example, foreign exchanges provide many children with a fantastic opportunity to learn a language, immerse themselves in another culture and gain independence. However, concerns over children staying alone with a strange family have led to many schools arranging for children to stay with a family in pairs (*TES Scotland*, 25 July 2003), surely diluting the educational experience. As this shows, schools take on board the concerns of parents and alter their practice accordingly.

Judges in the case of *Woodbridge School v. Chittock* noted that schools have, 'a duty to ensure that in the changed environment of a school trip pupils are placed at no greater risk than they would be when at school on a normal day' (*Education Law Monitor* 2002). This is a nearly impossible demand. The DfEE publication, *Health and Safety of Pupils on Educational Visits* (1998) offers 68 A4 pages of guidelines that must be followed before, during and after school trips take place, including 15 pages of forms to be completed. Five-page consent forms sent home to parents for a day trip can surely only serve to reinforce the notion that children are at risk. While there is little other than (considerable) anecdotal evidence to suggest that the number of school trips has been reduced, what has happened is an increase in the monitoring of pupils on such trips. One alarmingly extreme suggestion is that children are electronically monitored while off school premises: 'Radar wrist and ankle tags are being developed to help teachers keep track of pupils' (*TES*, 12 September 2003). As a result of teachers acquiescing to parental panics children miss out on learning opportunities and experiences from which to gain independence.

Emotional support

Parental fears are also raised over entrusting teachers with their children's emotional well-being. This first became apparent over the issue of bullying – covered in detail elsewhere in this volume. What is significant is that concerns over bullying originated in schools. It was when the parents of quite happy children heard about anti-bullying initiatives that the panic spread. The message was sent home that schools could be emotionally stressful places for youngsters. The extent to which this belief has taken hold was made apparent in the summer of 2003 when we witnessed 'building anger over the national tests for seven, 11 and 14-year-olds' (*TES*, 16 May 2003). Parents reported horror stories of children so stressed they couldn't eat or sleep. Teachers, parents and the teaching unions joined forces to campaign against the SAT (Standard Assessment Test) exams.

Testing children came to be equated with emotional abuse, a term most often used by education professionals 'to convey the warning that even insensitive remarks and criticisms by parents can unwittingly cause damage to their child' (Furedi 2001: 31). School tests serve a purpose in assessing what children have learnt and what still needs to be taught. It could be argued that by dealing with exams at school children learn how to cope with challenges in later life. Yet, as Furedi continues, 'what underpins definitions of emotional abuse is the belief that since children are extremely fragile, they are easily traumatized and vulnerable to a wide variety of risks'. Because teachers have already accepted the import of this definition they are in no position to mount any defence of testing. Once again children are denied an experience that could help them grow in emotional maturity and independence.

Lowering expectations

The demise of the traditional roles of teacher and parent has served to eradicate the trust that was once the underpinning of the relationship. This makes both parties more susceptible to the numerous panics surrounding children. Teachers can no longer respond critically and confidently to parental anxieties and so end up altering the experience of schooling in a highly reactionary way. Where schools once strived to push children to their limits academically, physically and emotionally to encourage them to grow up, learn and mature; they now seek to cushion children and protect them from risk. A safe school becomes a place without risk or challenge, a place where children cannot be allowed to stretch themselves for fear of failing or exposing the weaknesses of others – in effect a place where little learning can take place.

References

Branston, P. (1996) 'Children and Parents Enjoying Reading: Promoting Parent Support in Reading', in S. Wolfendale and K. Topping (eds), *Family Involvement in Literacy*, London: Cassell Education, pp. 18–33.
Brian, K. (2002) 'Slaves to Studying', *Parentwise* 1: 16–18.
CACE (1967) *Children and Their Primary Schools* (The Plowden Report), London: HMSO.
DfEE (1998) *Health and Safety of Pupils on Educational Visits*, London: HMSO.
Education Law Monitor (2002) 'Negligence: School Trips, and the Teachers' Duty of Care', June: 8–12.
Furedi, F. (2001) *Paranoid Parenting*, London: Penguin.
Hancock, R. and Gale, S. (1996) 'Hackney PACT: Reflecting on the Experience of Promoting Home Reading Programmes', in S. Wolfendale and K. Topping (eds), *Family Involvement in Literacy*, London: Cassell Education, pp. 7–18.

Pollard, A. and Triggs, P. (2000) 'Childhood and Education', in A. Pollard, *Readings for Reflective Teaching*, London: Continuum, pp. 51–7.
Wolfendale, S. and Topping, K. (1996) *Family Involvement in Literacy*, London: Cassell Education.

Key readings

DfEE (1988) *Health and Safety of Pupils on Educational Visits*, London: HMSO.
Education Law Monitor (2002) 'Negligence: School Trips, and the Teachers' Duty of Care', June: 8–12.
Furedi, F. (2001) *Paranoid Parenting*, London: Penguin.
Wolfendale, S. and Topping, K. (1996) *Family Involvement in Literacy*, London: Cassell Education.

Focus question

To what extent should the concerns of parents influence classroom practice?

CHAPTER 7

LITERACY

Singular or plural? For today or tomorrow?

Teresa Grainger

Over the last decade, new technologies have markedly transformed the landscape of literacy and reshaped the frames of reference for meaning making and communication. Today's children, born into this changing world, spend their early years in an environment fundamentally different from that experienced by their parents. Popular cultural and media texts are part and parcel of their everyday lives and frequently constitute their first curriculum, as well as contribute to the formation of their cultural identity. Yet when these children make the transition to school, their emergent techno-literacy practices are neither officially recognised nor built upon in the early childhood curriculum. In the UK, later curricular guidelines also retain a limited 'autonomous' model of literacy, 'a single thing with a big L and a single Y' (Street 1993: 81). The consequences are multiple:

> The disjunction between the multimodal world of communication which is available to school children in the wider community and the constipated, book bound modes of the standard curriculum has resulted in the increasing alienation of pupils from the schooling on offer.
>
> (Millard 2003: 4)

Such alienation, Millard argues, increases with age and as gendered preferences in literacy widen. This chapter, in contrast to current curricular conceptions, argues for the plurality of literacy practices and highlights the growing disparity between home and school literacy. It examines the increasing chasm between teachers' and pupils' textual knowledge and experience and explores the professional challenges ahead if the curriculum is to be transformed in response to the multimodal competencies of today's young people.

Multiple literacies

The common sense view that literacy is an unvarying competence or skill, which can be taught and tested, may have political appeal, but fails to recognise that it is shaped by culture and by the pattern of its use. Research studies have shown that the language and culture of home and community structure and influence ways of making meaning and communicating. Such ethnographic work has challenged the assumption that literacy is a static set of skills, acquired through individual learning, and has encouraged a pluralist view, which recognises multiple literacies and accepts that their acquisition is the result of social involvement. We need to re-conceptualise the traditional conception of literacy and, as Barton (1994) suggests, focus instead on literacy practices – sets of social practices associated with written language in a culture.

In a recent longitudinal study, Gregory and Williams (2000) reveal the literacy practices of past and present generations of families living in two square miles of London: Spitalfields and the City of London. They document, for example, the Bangladeshi children's remarkable ability to use strategies learned in their Bengali and Arabic classes in their mainstream English school in Spitalfields, and also show that, for the monolingual children in the City of London, a clear distinction exists between the 'emergent tradition' of literature associated with popular culture, which the children selected and enjoyed at home, and the 'residual tradition' of literature sanctioned at school (Luke 1992). Local or vernacular literacies, which have their roots in everyday life, often remain unrecognised and sidelined, while dominant literacies, those that originate in the powerful institutions of society, are both promoted and reified. This is problematic, since, as research has shown, when mismatches occur in the way literacy is defined at home and school, the chances for school success are severely compromised (e.g. Au 1993; Cairney and Ruge 1996; Gee, 1999; Luke and Carrington 2002). In school, teachers need to acknowledge difference and build on the contrasting literacy practices of the children they teach, acknowledging that the current 'net generation' is differently literate.

The multimodal textual experience of today's children

Young children at home routinely engage with a myriad of new texts and forms. They play with computer games, text message on cellphones, go online and access the internet, email friends, enter chat rooms, watch television and films and engage with image-based comics, magazines and newspapers with interest and enthusiasm. Such texts, whether online or offline, are often multimodal, combining words and pictures, photographs, sounds, symbols, moving images, graphics, diagrams, gestures and/or facial expressions. The varied nature of these texts has altered the ways in which young readers expect to read and to construct meaning:

> Not only are there now many more kinds of text to refer to than in the past, as children make meaning of new experiences, events and practices, they also think differently from adults' developed frames of reference. ... Adults may struggle with the conceptual differences of the 'textnological' revolution, but children are already there, reading and producing texts in many dimensions and investing them with meaning drawn from their own wide repertoire of cultural experience.
>
> (Bearne 2003a: 135)

Digital technologies have transformed traditional text genres and have created new modes of textual practice in which the importance of visual, aural and physical ways of making meaning are evident – in this way children's orientation to online information, knowledge, learning and communication is formed.

This textual complexity represents a real challenge to teachers who may find it hard to keep up with their pupils' repertoires. As Luke warns, the partitioning of the curriculum into subjects which are divided in time and space means that the classroom often works to 'discourage children from blending, mixing and matching knowledge drawn from diverse textual sources' (2003: 398). Children represent their thinking by drawing on their text experience, and boys in particular 'seem to draw more heavily on their visual and multi-media experience than girls, who tend to use written text as models' (Bearne 2003b: 27). Yet the curriculum assessment arrangements fail to acknowledge their multimodal literate practices. This may reduce the interplay between dominant and vernacular literacies, and in turn may limit teachers' awareness of children's verbal–visual semiotic practices.

Teachers' and pupils' literacy: a widening divide

Even though children are fast becoming multimodally literate, many of their teachers remain bound by the conventions of print. Today's professionals are constrained, at least in part, by the narrow skills-based definition of literacy found in the National Literacy Strategy in England. Such conceptions of school literacy perceive it as relatively fixed and not continually changing and give clear precedence to written texts over spoken ones, as well as profiling the delivery of skills-focused objectives at the expense of the interactive development of a living twenty-first-century literacy curriculum. Despite an apparent rise in the use of new media in classroom contexts, the gap between children's everyday literacy practices and those of their teachers is increasing. Too often, technology such as video is used merely to offer another version of a set book and opportunities for production or transduction are lost. Additionally, the widespread misuse of television and video in school (to substitute teaching, to fill time and so on), discourages more rigorous and creative use of new media, and this situation may be exacerbated by the limited inclusion of work on techno-literacy practices in initial teacher education courses. In documenting school practice in Queensland, Luke and Carrington (2002) describe how the impact of cultural differences, new economies and technology was perceived by teachers there as a sign of student 'deficit'. They reveal that the teachers, for all their assiduous intentions, were frankly unaware of the children's living literacy practices and felt unsure of the literacy demands of the new century. As a result they were offering a skills-based programme, which was not only irrelevant in approach but was virtually pre-digital and anti popular culture.

New technologies which are unfamiliar to adults can create feelings of loss of control and this may well undermine the confidence of teachers whose pupils are technologically far more advanced. The generation divide may never have been so marked, and has resulted in 'an irrational loyalty to reading and writing' (Flood *et al.* 1997: xvi) on the part of the profession and the reaffirmation of the printed word as the exclusive form of representation and communication in the classroom. Each older generation appears to perceive that the culture of younger people is both less complex and less demanding (Marsh 2002), but such perceptions towards children's current cultural interests are partly founded on prejudice and not on a considered review of research evidence. Negative views about the role of media and popular culture, which are often associated with traditional conceptions of childhood, are in evidence both inside and outside the profession. Furthermore, anxiety over children's loss of innocence and their perceived vulnerability to the seductive powers of the media are widespread, fostered by the increasing uncertainty of postmodern society.

However, new technologies and media texts are not only embedded with young children's lives, but also serve significant purposes. They encourage children's active viewing and the production of their own hybrid texts built upon a range of media resources. Tyner (1998), too, has challenged the notion that exposure to the media is disadvantageous and offers an alternative asset model. He argues that mass media and popular culture can work as a benefit to literacy instead of as a social deficit (Tyner 1998: 7), offering new opportunities for creative engagement and transformation.

Literacy: the challenge ahead

In accepting the existence of multiple literacies, the role of the visual and multimodal nature of texts and the need to effect a transformation from a linear print- and page-based culture to a screen-based hyperlinked mode of communication, the profession needs to consider three issues, namely: rethinking the landscape of literacy, revisiting pedagogical practice and developing a broader understanding of critical literacy – a literacy for tomorrow.

In relation to rethinking literacy, the place of techno-literacy practices in young people's lives and the concept of multi-literacies need to be widely accepted and endorsed in revised national curricula as well as in assessment arrangements. Teachers will need to keep abreast of how new media actually work, to recognise their potential and to build upon and extend their pupils' capacity to innovate and transform existing resources. In particular, the cognitive and affective strategies that children need to cope in this multi-textual universe must be identified and acknowledged. As online and offline worlds reshape one another, literacy represents 'a set of travelling practices' (Clifford 1992) within and between them, which will continue to be used in many different context-dependent and value-laden contexts. Teachers need to be alert to new literacy practices as they evolve. Increased professional awareness of household access will also be essential, and an openness to listen to and learn from contemporary family literacy practices, values and attitudes. Over time this may necessitate a radical redesign of relationships between home, school and community.

In order to make schooling relevant and meaningful, teachers need to combine both old and new literacies and also extend their pedagogic practices in the light of the different access to knowledge offered by new technologies. The new modes of communication and representation offer new opportunities for reading and writing and richer intertextual links, and will focus the profession's attention on the significant role of oral language. As Luke observes:

> When learning is no longer geographically tied to a desk, the school library, the book or the teacher who demands 'all eyes up front', then old style transmission and surveillance pedagogy becomes less stable and less defensible.
>
> (2003: 398)

Traditionally framed pedagogies, reinforced by the recent priority given to whole-class teaching, will need to give way to alternative practices, and an emphasis on both the production and consumption of texts, which encompasses inquiry-based learning in a community of learners. Such collaborative and constructivist approaches place learning and knowledge at the centre of pedagogy. In working towards a literacy of fusion, Millard (2003) describes a transformative pedagogy which is open to the children's own resources for learning, but requires teachers to develop a richer understanding of what particular modes of communication best suit the task in hand. Effective fusion, she suggests, should enable children to transform their knowledge and give them agency in a wider world, as well as develop their critical awareness of their own and others' meanings.

Literacy is 'not just a skill or knowledge, but an emerging act of consciousness and resistance' (Giroux 1993: 367), which should develop children's ability to read both the words on the page and the world behind the text. If we are not to alienate the children of today, then developing a critical literacy for tomorrow, both in curriculum design and practice, is a pressing professional need.

References

Au, K. (1993) *Literacy Instruction in Multicultural Settings*, Fort Worth: Harcourt Brace Jovanovich.

Barton, D. (1994) *Literacy: An Introduction to the Ecology of Written Language*, Oxford: Blackwell.

Bearne, E. (2003a) 'Rethinking Literacy: Communication, Representation and Text', *Reading Literacy And Language* 37: 3.

Bearne, E. (2003b) 'Every Picture Tells a Story', *Times Educational Supplement*, Opinion, 3, October: 27.

Cairney, T. and Ruge, J. (1996) 'Examining the Impact of Cultural Mismatches between Home and School: Coping with Diversity in Classrooms'. Paper presented to the American Association for Educational Research Conference, New York, 8–12 April.

Clifford, J. (1992) 'Traveling Cultures', in L. Grossberg, C. Nelson and P.A. Treichler (eds), *Cultural Studies*, London: Routledge, pp. 96–116.

Flood, J., Heath, S.B. and Lapp, D. (1997) *Handbook of Research on Teaching Literacy Through the Communicative and Visual Arts*, New York: Macmillan.

Gee, J.P. (1999) 'The New Literacy Studies: From "Socially Situated" to "the Work of the Social"', in D. Barton, M. Hamilton and R. Ivanic (eds), *Situated Literacies: Reading and Writing in Context*, London: Routledge.

Giroux, H. (1993) 'Literacy and the Politics of Difference', in C. Lankshear and P. Mclaren (eds), *Critical Literacy: Politics, Praxis and the Postmodern*, Albany, NY: State University of New York Press, pp. 367–7.

Gregory, E. and Williams, M. (2000) *City Literacies: Learning to Read Across Generations and Cultures*, London: Routledge.

Luke, A. (1992) 'The Social Instruction of Literacy in the Primary School', in L. Unsworth (ed.), *Literacy, Learning and Teaching: Language as a Social Practice in the Classroom*, Melbourne: Macmillan.

Luke, A. and Carrington, V. (2002) 'Globalisation, Literacy Curriculum Practice', in R. Fisher, M. Lewis and G. Brooks, *Raising Standards in Literacy*, London: Routledge.

Luke, C. (2003) 'Pedagogy, Connectivity, Multimodality and Interdisciplinarity', *Reading Research Quarterly* 38(3): 397–403.

Marsh, J. (2002) 'Popular Culture, Computer Games and the Primary Curriculum', in M. Monteith (ed.), *Teaching Primary Literacy Through ICT*, Buckinghamshire: Open University Press, pp. 127–43.

Millard, E. (2003) 'Towards a Literacy of Fusion: New Times, New Teaching and Learning?', *Reading Literacy and Language* 37(2): 3–8.

Street, B. (1993) *Cross-cultural Approaches to Literacy*, Cambridge: Cambridge University Press.

Tyner, K. (1998) *Literacy in a Digital World: Teaching and Learning in the Age of Information*, Mahwah, NJ: Erlbaum.

Key readings

Gregory, E. and Williams, A. (2000) *City Literacies: Learning to Read Across Generations and Cultures*, London: Routledge.

Kress, G. (2003) *Literacy in the New Media Age*, London: Routledge.

Marsh, J. and Millard, E. (2001) *Literacy and Popular Culture*, London: Paul Chapman.

Focus question

What arguments do you think make a good case for multiple literacies?

CHAPTER 8

'LITERACY' AND THE 'LITERARY'

Shirley Dent

'Literacy' is not simply about being able to read or write proficiently, although it of course requires those skills. Robert Pattison lays the gauntlet down in the opening to *On Literacy*: 'We are inadequately literate in part because we have inadequate ideas about literacy' (1982: v). He then leads us to a brave new world of 'new literacy', where The Who's lyrics can apparently stand their ground with Milton's blank verse and the new poet is 'the literate man of rock culture' (1982: 205). I agree with Pattison that the reason we are inadequately literate is that we have inadequate ideas, but I would modify the statement: 'We are inadequately literate because we have inadequate ideas about the literary'. Whereas Pattison applauds a Caliban's progress of a popular literacy, where the freshness and immediacy of vernacular English replaces the literary tradition, I am dismayed at the gradual erosion of the literary in literacy.

The ability to read or write is about functional literacy, or the ability to cope with the everyday requirements of reading and writing in a developed society. It is a skill that you have or don't have. Although the teaching of that skill may involve complex techniques (phonics, etc.) and theories of teaching basic literacy may be disputed, the teaching of functional literacy demands a pragmatic approach. At the end of the day it is the teaching of a defined skill. Literacy that looks towards the literary, however, can never be only about teaching a skill. Whereas functional literacy is about a defined objective (i.e being able to read and write), the literary is an open-ended aim, a continuous engagement and grappling with the critical tradition of literature.

Functional literacy calls for a skill set to be taught and learnt. Only the most arcane or deranged educationalist is going to quibble about the need to teach children to read and write effectively. But my concern here is not with that very important but also very basic functional acquirement of literacy. It is with literacy's connection with the literary, or the historical meaning of 'literate' as described in the American Heritage Dictionary: 'For most of its long history in English, *literate*, has meant only "familiar with literature", or generally, "well-educated or learned"'. How we judge the status of what literature is, how we transmit knowledge of good literature and how we equip students with the critical faculties to make judgements about the quality of a text before them are all important parts of teaching literacy. And this is where the real problem with the National Literacy Strategy (DfES 1998) lies, and not with the Framework stifling creativity, being prescriptive, expecting the earth tomorrow, being about political targets or any of the other reasons teachers may criticise it for.

The problem is that the Framework gives no sense of the literary, of what distinguishes literature that enlightens and challenges from literature that is merely entertaining or informative. The Framework constantly bucks the need to critically engage with, and articulately defend, great literature. If we look at the Framework for Teaching English to KS3 Year 9, we will see that this lack of confidence manifests itself not so much in relation to pupils' potential ability to appreciate great literature. Disconcertingly, the Framework's lack of certainty about the literary is apparent in its lack of faith in teachers' authority to convey what makes one text superior to another one.

What the National Literacy Strategy *says* it is about seems to encapsulate both the utilitarian objectives of mere literacy and the imaginative aims of the literary:

> The notion of literacy embedded in the objectives is much more than simply the acquisition of 'basic skills' that is sometimes implied by the word: it encompasses the ability to recognise, understand and manipulate the conventions of language, and develop pupils' ability to use language imaginatively and flexibly. ... By the end of Year 9 we expect each pupil to be a 'shrewd, fluent and independent reader' with, among other skills, the ability to be 'reflective, critical and discriminating in response to a wide range of printed and visual texts'.
>
> (DfES 1998)

There seems little to take issue with in what the National Literacy Strategy hopes to achieve for pupils and the type of reader the strategy wants to produce. But the lack of literary ambition and literary insight in the strategy reveals itself in the inclusion of visual texts and virtual texts. Their mandatory inclusion shows that the National Literacy Strategy is either philistine where literature is concerned or prepared to take short-cuts in what the curriculum offers. The strategy happily promotes new media but makes no mention of quality of content, and innovation in technology seems to be interchangeable with literary value.

There are no short-cuts to grappling with difficult and unfamiliar texts: the graduate student who wrote an essay on Jane Austen's *Mansfield Park* full of references to that wised-up flirt Fanny Price, Austen's prig *par excellence*, having seen Patricia Rozema's sexed-up big screen version and having neglected to read the actual book, deserves their apocryphal life as an idiot. But we also need to ask what sort of education system produces an English literature undergraduate who thinks that seeing the film of a great novel is the same as *reading* a great novel. If this is a growing trend, and we are on the way to the world of Raymond Bradbury's *Fahrenheit 451*, where literature is literally reduced to ashes and the visual reigns supreme, then we need to seriously challenge that system rather than shrugging our shoulders and forgetting about literature.

Almost against expectations, the Framework for Teaching English at KS3 emphasises critical evaluation. In its student objectives for text level reading at KS3 the Framework asks that students are able to, among other things, 'evaluate their own critical writing about texts', 'comment on interpretations of the same text or idea in different media, using terms appropriate for critical analysis' and 'review and develop their own reading skills, experiences and preferences, noting strengths and areas for development'. Analysis is another buzz word, particularly in relation to understanding the historical and cultural contexts of literature: for example one explicit objective is to 'analyse ways in which different cultural contexts and traditions have influenced language and style, e.g. *black British poetry, Irish short stories*'.

What is missing in all of this is a sense of authority in making judgements about literature, particularly in judging what good literature is and inspiring a desire to read great literature. The fetishisation of diversity over quality is indicative of this lack of confidence in what can and should be classified as literary, rather than merely written, material. The result is a bunching together of writers by extraneous and personal factors, such as race, nationality or 'personal history', rather than by what really differentiates them: there is as much difference between Buchi Emecheta and Wole Soyinka as there is between Edna O'Brien and James Joyce, and the poems of Benjamin Zephaniah and Derek Walcott have little in common if we discount the fact that they could both be squeezed on to a list of 'black British poetry' to be dutifully studied. I would argue that Soyinka, Joyce and Walcott are literary writers – that their writing exhibits the values of literary tradition and innovation. How do I know? As T.S. Eliot puts it, we know because we look at the poetry not the poet, and poetry and literature do not come into being out of nowhere or exist on their own individual terms. A poem or a play cannot be syphoned off to explain social ills or provide political comment. It first and foremost exists as part of its own living, critical tradition. Eliot argues, 'I have tried to point out the importance of the relation of the poem to other poems by other authors, and suggested the conception of poetry as a living whole of all the poetry that has ever been written' (1932: 17). For Eliot, the great poet – the literary writer – brings a particular consciousness to their writing – a constant engagement with, and innovation on, literary history:

> What is to be insisted upon is that the poet must develop or procure the consciousness of the past and he should continue to develop this consciousness throughout his career. What happens is the continual surrender of himself as he is at the moment to something which is more valuable. The progress of an artist is a continual self-sacrifice, a continual extinction of personality.
>
> (1932: 17)

To suggest that what makes Zephaniah and Walcott equal as writers is the fact that they are black, and neglecting to interrogate the literary value of their poems, is racism masquerading as liberalism.

No one springs fully formed from the womb armed, Athena-like, with literary knowledge, able to appreciate Hamlet's soliloquy or understand *Ulysses* unaided. Literary aims, like literacy skills, need to be taught with authority. Without the authority to judge literature as good or bad, how do we expect students to engage with 'critical analysis' and what are we expecting such analysis to produce? Even more seriously, without somebody who is an authority on the living tradition of literature and literary criticism, who can criticise and correct pupils' unformed and ill-formed judgements, and what is the purpose and outcome of asking students to 'evaluate their own critical writing about texts'?

The lack of critical authority is also present in the National Curriculum's prescribed reading for KS3 and 4, which is as follows:

- two Shakespeare plays;
- drama by major playwrights;
- two pre-1914 fiction texts;
- two post-1914 fiction texts;
- four pre-1914 poets;
- four post-1914 poets;
- recent and contemporary works;
- writers from different cultures and traditions;

- literary non-fiction;
- information and reference texts;
- media and moving image texts.

It is at this point that the concept of literacy as something beyond the merely functional begins to slip-slide away in the bullet points of the National Curriculum. Where differentiation is needed, for example between pupils of differing abilities for whom a different curriculum may be called for, very little is offered. Instead, we have a nod to diversity of all sorts, including multiculturalism and multimedia. In this sense diversity seems to have become a tick-box-twitch for a strategy with no confidence in literacy as a skill that leads to literary understanding, that goes beyond the nuts and bolts of being able to read and write. This is not to say that an appreciation of the literary is a static state that teachers must strive to achieve in every pupil. On the contrary, being literate is something you *begin*, something you embark on and engage in. To be literate is a process that is determined by engagement and aspiration. The difference between being illiterate and beginning to be literate is highlighted in Maya Angelou's truism, 'always be intolerant of ignorance but understanding of illiteracy' (1984: 97). Historically, to be illiterate meant you were potentially excluded from certain sorts of knowledge, and you usually would have little choice in the state of your illiteracy: education was beyond the reach of most workers.

But many people did not accept this enforced state of ignorance. They aspired to be educated and to learn and know about a literary tradition from which they had been excluded: in short they aspired to the literary and to be considered literate. And these aspirations resulted in institutions such as the Mechanics Institute and the Working Men's College. These aspirants concerned themselves with intellectual improvement and looked to authoritative judgement from the likes of E.M. Forster and John Ruskin. Autodidacts, such as the pit-poet Joseph Skipsey, would simply not have understood the concept of self-evaluation or multiple literacies. His role models were Shakespeare, Heine and Blake. Although he occasionally used North-umbrian dialect in his poetry or metaphors of the pit to great effect to explain poetry (for example when he describes Swinburne's interpretation of Blake as illuminating the dark pit of our understanding like a Davy lamp), he aspired to write like a meta-physical poet rather than to indulge his personal history. Such people were not, as Richard Hoggart terms it, 'the victims of what we might call the "stay as sweet as you are" society' (2001).

In the great print revolution of the eighteenth and early nineteenth centuries, the birth of the common reader did not mean the death of great literature or a shift of literacy away from the literary (Altick 1957; Raven *et al.* 1994). William Cobbett expresses the excitement of engaging critically with the world and ideas, when he recalls his experience of reading Jonathan Swift's *A Tale of a Tub* as a 14-year-old: 'The book [...] was so different ... it delighted me beyond description; and it produced what I have always considered a sort of birth of intellect' (quoted in Porter 2000: 74–5). The Enlightenment viewed reading as an intellectual quest, a challenge and something to actively engage with and which actively engaged in the world. Aspiration was a delight rather than a burden and critical judgement was not seen as an imposition but as a necessary part of becoming literate. Pupils actively wanted to enter a tradition, take possession of it and even change it. It would be wrong to suggest that very much has changed in human aspirations: individuals do still strive to change their situations, and to progress beyond what is expected. A recent study by researchers from the Policy Studies Institute shows that although 7 out of 10 Bangladeshi children live in poverty compared to 3 out of 10 of white children,

79 per cent of children from Bangladeshi families remained at school beyond leaving age in 2001, compared with only 69 per cent of their white counterparts. Despite the odds, these children have educational aspirations and act upon them (Marsh and Perry 2003).

So what is the teacher to do who wishes to help those aspirations along, to inspire, to challenge and to open up the world of literature without limit to their pupils? Trust your authority, trust great literature (whatever your subject is) and trust your pupils. This anecdote told by the author Philip Pullman during the Roald Dahl lecture at the Edinburgh International Book Festival in 2002 is both inspiring and instructive. He described a moment that, as a schoolboy, inspired him with an enduring love of literature. When Pullman was seven years old, a teacher read Coleridge's *Ancient Mariner* to his class. The teacher simply read the poem without attempting to explain it. The class was absolutely silent during the reading and the sense of awe imparted obviously remained with, and inspired, at least one of those children to explore the challenging, often difficult, world of literature and the literary.

References

Altick, R.D. (1957) *The English Common Reader: A Social History of the Mass Reading Public 1800–1900*, Chicago, IL: University of Chicago Press.

Angelou, M. (1984) *I Know Why the Caged Bird Sings*, London: Virago.

DfES (1998) *National Literacy Strategy's Framework for Teaching English for Key Stage 3 in Year 9*, available at http://www.standards.dfes.gov.uk/literacy/teaching_resources/nls_framework/.

Eliot, T.S. (1932) *Selected Prose*, London: Faber & Faber.

Hoggart, R. (2001) 'Adult Education: The Legacy and Future', a lecture to celebrate the Fiftieth Anniversary of the University of Glasgow's Department of Adult and Continuing Education, 18 October, available at http://www.gla.ac.uk/adulteducation/latestnews/RichardHoggart.html.

Marsh, A. and Perry, J. (2003) 'Ethnic Minority Families – Poverty and Disadvantage', in C. Kober (ed.), *Black and Ethnic Minority Children and Poverty*, London: End Child Poverty.

Pattison, R. (1982) *On Literacy: The Politics of the Word from Homer to the Age of Rock*, Oxford: Oxford University Press.

Porter, P. (2000) *Enlightenment: Britain and the Creation of the Modern World*, Harmondsworth: Penguin.

Raven, J., Small, H. and Tadmore, N. (eds) (1994) *The Practice and Representation of Reading in England*, Cambridge: Cambridge University Press.

Key texts

Cox, B. (ed.) (1998) *Literacy is Not Enough*, Manchester: Book Trust and MUP.

Hoggart, R. (1958) *The Uses of Literacy*, Harmondsworth: Penguin.

Ozik, C. (1997) 'The Question of Our Speech: The Return to Aural Culture', in K. Washburn, and J. Thornton (eds), *Dumbing Down: Essays on the Stripmining of American Culture*, New York: Norton.

Focus question

How can pupils and students be encouraged to read, read and read more?

CHAPTER 9

SCHOOLING YEAR 6
Inclusion or SATuration?

Kathy Hall[1]

Concern is mounting for the plight of children and young people condemned in our schools to a dreary diet of tests, tests and more tests. League tables and performance management have meant increasing pressure for pupils and teachers throughout the system, but most intensely at the 'pressure points' in Years 2, 6, 9 and 11, where pupil performance in national tests is made the subject of public scrutiny. The current system of assessment is nothing short of a regime of surveillance, and the recent A-level fiasco shows just what a political issue assessment really is. Our in-depth analysis of Year 6 classrooms in two inner-city schools reveals the power of these externally imposed and monitored regimes of assessment/surveillance in shaping children's experiences of schooling (Benjamin *et al.* 2003; Hall *et al.*, in press; Nind *et al.* in press). Assessment, which in Year 6 is usually reduced to testing, defines the school day, the curriculum and the teacher's responsibilities; it also defines what can count as success, and who (whether pupil, teacher or parent) can be seen to be succeeding.

SATs, and the prospect of SATs, in effect produce a hierarchy of what can be seen as pupil worthiness: we have called this a SATurated hierarchy. What emerges from our data is how pupils' worth is considered in relation to how well they comply with the demands of the testing regime. The ideal and most worthy pupil is someone who prioritises SATs success and who self-polices to this end, who does the allotted homework, who is seen to possess the necessary ability, who will achieve at least level 4 in all subjects, who is willing to be 'boosted' to achieve even higher levels and who is mature and popular. This ideal pupil participates in class by giving appropriate answers that model the type needed to do well in SATs papers, absorbs what the teacher offers and completes work without support in the time allowed.

However, there are differences between the ideal girl and the ideal boy pupil. The ideal girl pupil is not seen to need to suppress other priorities to the same degree as her boy counterpart, since she commits to the SATs agenda, producing 'immaculate' work: her desire to please by doing well predisposes her to hard work and makes other, non-scholastic pursuits undesirable to her. The ideal boy pupil, on the other hand, is assumed to be inherently able rather than inherently hard-working, and he can therefore accommodate the demands of SATs alongside 'having a life'. But he has to suppress, albeit temporarily, these other priorities since the demands of SATs (it is assumed) do not really suit him as much as they suit his girl peers. It follows, then, that choosing to be SATurated is seen as authentic for girls but inauthentic for boys.

Not far down the hierarchy of worthiness, we suggest, is the determined worker, who, although not seen to possess as much inherent ability as the ideal (especially the ideal boy) pupil, can compensate to some extent by diligence. Despite such hard work, the determined worker – who is most likely to be a girl – does not attain the stellar SATs levels of the ideal pupil, though she shares the ideal pupil's desire for SATurated success and can usually achieve the crucial level 4 benchmark. At a similar point in the hierarchy, and often more interesting to the teacher, is the pupil (usually a boy) who has competing interests outside of the classroom, quite often football, which interfere with his desire for SATs success. He is seen as having raw potential and as needing to be pushed in order to score at the 'expected level'.

Moving down the hierarchy is the accepting and acceptable pupil – acceptable in so far as s/he feigns interest in classwork, suppresses her/his own desires sufficiently to appear compliant with SATurated demands and, in sum, who presents as quietly accepting of the regime. We came across many instances where these children, by being quiet, could opt out and not complete work: so long as s/he appears to be on task, the accepting and acceptable pupil can avoid being challenged or supported to participate.

Towards the bottom of the hierarchy is the SATs resister. The SATs resister might, in some cases, have a disruptive effect on the classroom, but s/he is just as likely to resist quietly, through, for example, refusing to work, attending almost exclusively to other priorities and absenting her/himself from school. The SATs resister refuses to accept a SATurated identity, casting doubt on other children's (and often the teacher's) SATs project by her/his refusal to be made desirous of SATs success, and casting doubt on the project of continuous improvement by not seeming to care about setting or meeting targets.

The SATuration of the curriculum has further implications. The practice of setting for the SATs curriculum areas of English, Maths and Science exerts a powerful pressure on teaching and learning. Our data show that this manifests itself in minimal differentiation by task or lesson pacing, and it can often be driven by the need to fit children into the organisational requirements of the school instead of children's learning requirements. All too often it can seem that, in Year 6, setting exists to make it easier for the teacher to teach to the tests – and teaching becomes not just a process of coaching, but of *pushing*. Teachers find themselves talking about 'level 4 children', 'potential level 4s' and so on, leading to a very restricted version of individual differences in learning proficiency. Once set, the curriculum narrows to prioritise those particular areas. Learning in and through the arts, for example, becomes marginalised since those areas are 'outside' SATs. When the heat is on, these outsider subjects can be seen as expendable, and do not need to be part of the children's daily or weekly experience. In Year 6, we are increasingly seeing the length and content of the school day determined by SATs.

It would be unreasonable and unfair to blame schools and teachers who are working under pressure and publicly accountable for pupil performance. The point about SATs is that they are part of an apparatus designed to police the English schooling system, and to win – by coercion and co-optation – the consent of teachers and pupils. Teacher, as well as pupil, identities have been SATurated. The pressure experienced by teachers is surely unprecedented. What our research begins to make visible is the way in which different policy imperatives can contradict each other: the rhetoric of inclusion, with its emphasis on celebrating difference and maximising diversity, and the rhetoric of 'standards', defined and demonstrated through a highly particular version of curricular success, are irreconcilable. The demands of the standards agenda, reflected in the overwhelming emphasis on SATs, legitimate exclusion rather than promote inclusion, and the Audit Commission's latest report on the subject will be no surprise to teachers. Year 6 is well and truly SATurated with conflicting priorities, to the detriment of children's education, and at the expense of the teachers who are struggling with impossible and inhumane demands.

Note

1   This is a research-based chapter and the full list of authors is: Kathy Hall, Shereen Benjamin, Janet Collins, Melanie Nind and Kieron Sheehy.

References

Benjamin, S., Nind, M., Hall, K., Collins, J. and Sheehy, K. (2003) 'Moments of Inclusion and Exclusion: Pupils Negotiating Classroom Contexts', *British Journal of Sociology of Education* 24(5): 547–58.
Hall, K., Collins, J., Nind, M., Sheehy, K. and Benjamin, S. (in press) 'SATurated Models of Pupildom: Assessment and Inclusion/Exclusion', *BJES*.
Hall, K., Collins, J., Nind, M., Sheehy, K. and Benjamin, S. (in press) 'Methodological Challenges in Researching Inclusive School Cultures', *Educational Review*.

Key readings

Benjamin, S. (2002) *The Micropolitics of Inclusive Education*, Buckingham: Open University Press.
Corbett, J. (1999) 'Inclusive Education and School Culture', *International Journal of Inclusive Education* 3(1): 53–61.
Gerwitz, S. (2000) 'Bringing the Politics Back In: A Critical Analysis of Quality Discourses in Education', *British Journal of Educational Studies* 48(4): 352–70.
Nind, M., Sheehy, K. and Simmons, K. (eds) (2003) *Inclusive Education: Learners and Learning Contexts*, London: David Fulton.

Focus question

How can teachers challenge a situation in which inclusion is undermined by other valued aims of schooling?

CHAPTER 10

CIRCLE TIME

Lynn Revell

Schools everywhere have been experimenting with an activity called circle time. Circle time involves sitting children or adults in a circle and discussing and sharing issues, themes or ideas. The teacher or a designated adult plays a facilitative role and encourages participants to realise that they can resolve the problem or deal with the issue themselves (Mosley 1996).

Circle time has become so popular that it is now routinely recommended in government inspections and policy reports (DfES 2002). The government not only recommends the use of circle time in schools but where Ofsted inspectors have observed the practice in schools they have praised its effectiveness (Dawson and McNess 1998)

Circle time is unusual in that it is championed by government inspectors, head teachers and teachers alike (White 1990) and educationalists in more specialist areas such as inclusion (Barrow *et al.* 2002) and bullying (Sullivan 2000; Rigby 2002; Suckling 2002), anti-racism, pupils with emotional difficulties (Long and Fogell 2003) and citizenship all recommend circle time as a way of enabling children to talk and discuss issues.

Supporters of circle time believe it is an effective way of prompting children to discuss their feelings and engage in discussions of sensitive or controversial issues. As a result, many teachers and educationalists believe that circle time can enable children to take responsibility for their emotions and thereby address a multitude of behavioural and social problems. The most comprehensive research into the effectiveness and use of circle time in primary schools confirms the reasons for its popularity: 97 per cent of the school teachers interviewed thought that circle time improved their children's behaviour and over half thought it improved the child's ability to communicate (Dawson and McNess 1998).

However, the assumptions behind circle time are not neutral, nor are its underlying principles open-ended and nor are all emotional expressions or views expressed by participants permitted. An examination of some of the principles behind circle time suggest that it compels children to behave in certain ways and more seriously that it legitimises various emotional and behavioural responses while undermining others. The implications for the role of the teacher are even more dramatic. By encouraging the teacher to play the role of circle time facilitator the teacher is expected to act as therapist and counsellor as well as educator.

The overriding assumption behind circle time is that it raises the self-esteem of participants and that this in itself is a positive development (Dawson and McNess 1998). In *Turn Your School Around*, Jenny Mosley argues that the use of circle time throughout the school should lead to a whole school policy on self-esteem and that those principles are all included in the standards outlined in the National Curriculum.

There is, however, little research on the effect of circle time or evidence of any relationship between circle time and self-esteem. The research by McNess and Dawson concentrates on teachers' perceptions of the effects of circle time and does not acknowledge that links between self-esteem and behaviour is contested (Dawson and McNess 1998: 2). Mosley's work also contains the assumption that self-esteem is crucial to the development of the child – an assumption that is common to many educational and child development theories (Kraemer 2000).

Proponents of the importance of self-esteem stress that how we feel about ourselves influences other aspects of our lives. In his history of the term, Steven Ward notes that high levels of self-esteem have been attributed to good academic performance, happy marriages and well-adjusted children (Ward 1996). Similarly, Dukes and Lorch argue that where there is low self-esteem there is not only poor academic performance but a diminished purpose in life which can lead to delinquency (Dukes and Lorch 1989).

The presumption, however, that high self-esteem results in good behaviour or better academic achievement is contested. In a study conducted by the University of Michigan, psychologist Harold Stevenson showed that, while American students ranked above all others in their levels of self-esteem, this was not matched by their actual ability. A comparison of maths and science achievement by schoolchildren in 20 countries showed Americans ranked near the bottom, below those with lower self-esteem (Nolan 1998).

Other research showed that, when a standard maths test was given to 13-year-olds in six different countries there was no relationship between self-esteem and their results. Korean children scored the highest and Americans scored the lowest. All children were asked to respond to the statement, 'I am good at mathematics'. Only 23 per cent of Korean children answered yes to this statement (the lowest percentage of the six countries) and 63 per cent of Americans answered yes, the highest of all the countries (Nolan 1998: 170).

Not only is the relationship between self-esteem and achievement questionable but even the most passionate supporters of self-esteem recognise that, even where there is a correlation, it is unclear which is the causal factor (Covington 1989; McKay 1992). High self-esteem may be the product of academic and social success. That high self-esteem can produce, in itself, success is unproven and indeed is not even a reliable indicator of cognitive development.

The subsequent assumption, that circle time improves self-esteem, is also unproven. Teachers who are already committed to circle time report positive results, but, as yet, there has been no independent assessment of the effect of circle time on children's own self-esteem, their behaviour or their academic results.

Circle time itself is also underpinned by questionable assumptions, particularly because they disguise and confuse the teacher/pupil relationship. The first is that circle time is a non-coercive activity; second, that children have no right to keep their feelings private; and third, that teachers are merely facilitators, allowing the children to develop their own ideas.

The first assumption is that children are free to participate in circle time. In most models of circle time, children are given the opportunity not to speak or to participate. However, most circle time manuals recommend that children are asked to explain why they do not wish to contribute. This means that young children are expected to challenge a practice their teacher has introduced and in which their peers are participating. Peer and teacher pressure are compounded by the fact that involvement in circle time is invariably accompanied by a system of formal and informal rewards, such as praise from the teacher, the giving of golden time, smiley faces and other perks of the classroom. Publicly divulging one's emotions and feelings is acceptable and rewarded. The pressure for even the most reluctant of children to participate would be enormous. Far from being a voluntary activity circle time is a coercive psychological tool, even though it is presented as being voluntary. This confusion between its presentation and the reality can only confuse children about what it means to say that something is voluntary, and undermines their understanding of what freedom to choose may mean, and their sense of their own decision-making ability.

The second assumption is related to the issue of the privacy of the child. The focus on raising self-esteem criminalises all personalities, emotions and responses that are not positive, upbeat and warm or deemed to fit in with a raised self-esteem. This ignores the fact that all children have personalities and moods that are diverse and individual. Early years practitioners have noted that even very young children can form different types of relationships based on different feelings and criteria and that the management of their emotional responses is a part of the maturing process (Hurst 1997). The policing of negative feelings assumes that only positive feelings and emotions are acceptable or normal.

The third assumption raised by the common use of circle time in schools is the way it transforms the role of the teacher. We have already seen how the very use of the circle time in the first place is biased towards raising self-esteem, which in itself will mitigate the apparent neutrality of the teacher. However, there is a wider point at stake here. Circle time is frequently described by its supporters as a form of therapy or psychological intervention (Barrow *et al.* 2002). Is it the place of teachers to indulge in therapy in the classroom? Proponents of circle time believe that not only it is the place of teachers to do this but that it is now the purpose of education as a whole to perform this role (Mosley 1996: 4). In championing the psychological responsibilities of teachers, advocates of circle time are reinforcing a growing trend in education to transform the teacher from educator to amateur therapist and councillor.

This transformation can be traced back to the introduction of self-esteem in education. In America and Britain the principles behind circle time are based on the psychological theories of Abraham Maslow (Dawson and McNess 1998). In *Towards a Psychology of Being*, Maslow argued that individuals should work towards becoming a self-actualised person – an individual who was able to utilise their inner psychological strengths to deal with problems.

In *Freedom to Learn* Carl Rogers developed this idea in an educational context. He dismisses the view that education should be about the outpouring of facts and challenges the view that teachers should be concerned with what they teach their pupils. Instead he urges teachers to identify with the 'feeling qualities of life' (Rogers and Freiberg 1994: 37) and to question whether as teachers they are justified in believing that they know more than the young (Rogers and Freiberg 1994: 152).

In her critique of the growth of self-esteem as a current within educational thinking, Maureen Stout (2000) traces the development of these ideas in the work of Harvard psychologist Jerome Brunner and more recently in the work of Howard Gardner. The common theme uniting their work is not only that emotions and feelings are key in the way people learn but that the role of the teacher is not to teach but to facilitate the young as they construct their personal identities. In *Culture and Education* Brunner not only champions 'emotions and feelings' over the myth of objectivity (1996: 12) but argues that children learn more effectively when education is seen as a process of discovery rather than instruction by the teacher. Similarly, Gardner also argues for the teacher as facilitator. The teacher's role in the classroom geared towards multiple intelligences is transformed into one of identifying pupils' individual intelligences and catering to their specific needs (Fogarty and Bellanca 1999).

Ironically, through their participation in strategies like circle time, teachers are not helping children to develop emotionally or academically. Through policing children's emotions and encouraging them to take responsibility for difficult issues teachers are abdicating their own responsibilities as educators. Teachers do know more than children and for them to pretend that they do not is not only disingenuous but a denial of the fundamental tenet of the teacher/pupil relationship – for the one to teach and the other to learn.

Circle time proposes that it teaches children responsibility, whereas in fact it shows them a teacher refusing to take responsibility for their own moral views and pretending that these views are arrived at through consensus.

Whether any form of therapy or counselling is neutral or even appropriate in schools is a separate question, but the use of therapy with children through circle time forces them to participate in strategies that are intrusive and which they are powerless to oppose. It allows teachers to act as judge and jury in relation to the way children feel about themselves and their emotions and teaches them that only some emotions are good while others are bad. Teachers should not have the right to do this with the children in their care, especially when their understanding of psychology is so limited and unprofessional.

Teachers need to use their professional understanding of teaching to reach their aims. If they want to improve their pupils' listening or communication skills or improve their pupils' behaviour, they need to do so as teachers, which they are trained for, and not as psychologists, which they are not.

References

Barrow, G., Bradshaw, E. and Newton, T. (2002) *Improving Behaviour and Raising Self-esteem in the Classroom*, London: David Fulton Publishers.
Brunner, J. (1996) *The Culture of Education*, London: Harvard University Press.
Covington, M. (1989) 'Self-esteem and Failure in School: Analysis and Policy Implications', in A. Mecca, N. Smelser and J. Vasconcellos (eds), *Social Importance of Self-esteem*, London: University of California Press.
Dawson, N. and McNess, E. (1998) *A Report on the Use of Circle Time in Wiltshire Primary Schools*, Bristol: University of Bristol, Graduate School of Education.
DfES (2002) *Intervening Early*, Nottingham: DfES Publications.
Dukes, R. and Lorch B. (1989) 'Concept of Self, Mediating Factors and Adolescent Deviance', *Sociological Spectrum* 9: 301–19.
Fogarty, R. and Bellanca, J. (eds) (1999) *Multiple Intelligences: A Collection*, Palatine, IL: IRI/Skylight Publishing.
Holden, C. (2003) 'Citizenship in the Primary School: Going Beyond Circle Time', *Pastoral Care in Education* 21(3): 24–9.
Hurst, V. (1997) *Planning for Early Learning*, London: Paul Chapman Publishing.
Kraemer, S. (2000) 'Promoting Resilience', *International Journal of Child and Family Welfare* 4: 273–87.
Long, R. and Fogell, J. (2003) *Supporting Pupils with Emotional Difficulties*, London: David Fulton Publishers.
McKay, M. (1992) *Self-Esteem*, Oakland, CA: New Harbinger Publications.
Mosley, J. (1996) *Turn Your School Around*, Wisbech: LDA.
Mosley, J. (2002) *Quality Circle Time in the Primary Classroom*, Wisbech: LDA.
Nolan, J.L. (1998) *The Therapeutic State: Justifying Government at Century's End*, London: New York University Press.
Rigby, K. (2002) *Stop the Bullying: A Handbook for Schools*, London: Jessica Kingsley.
Rogers, C. and Freiberg, H.J. (1994) *Freedom to Learn*, Oxford: Maxwell Macmillan International.

Stout, M. (2000) *The Feel-good Curriculum*, Cambridge, MA: Perseus Publishing.
Suckling, A. (2002) *Bullying: A Whole School Approach*, London: Jessica Kingsley.
Sullivan, K. (2000) *The Anti-bullying Handbook*, Auckland: Oxford University Press.
Ward, S. (1996) 'Filling the World With Self-Esteem: A Social History of Truth Making',
    Canadian Journal of Sociology 21(1): 1–23.
White, M. (1990) Circle Time, *Cambridge Journal of Education* 20(1): 53–6.

Key readings

Mosley, J. (2002) *Quality Circle Time in the Primary Classroom*, Wisbech: LDA.
Stout, M. (2002) *The Feel-good Curriculum*, Cambridge, MA: Perseus Publishing.

Focus question

Why do you think the government is so keen to promote circle time in schools?

CHAPTER 11

ANTI-BULLYING STRATEGIES IN THE UK

Simon Knight

Since the early 1990s bullying has become the panic to eclipse all panics. In fact it could be said that bullying has now ceased to be a panic as such, as concern about it is now incessant. The profile given to bullying and more particularly the obligatory anti-bullying policies generated are damaging to children and should be scrapped.

Modern concern about the impact of bullying in school seems to be built on two assumptions: first, that there is a high incidence of bullying that is either new or previously unrecognised; second, that the impact of bullying on children is more serious than it has been believed to be up to now.

The old adage about sticks and stones has truly had its day:

> The word 'tease' is derived either from an old English word meaning 'to pull apart', or from a Norwegian word meaning 'to tear to bits'. To tease also means to 'torment or irritate'. Teasing can be cruel and destructive and it should not be dismissed automatically as trivial and unworthy of attention.
>
> (Elliott and Kilpatrick 1994: 23)

Andrew Mellor, the Scottish based anti-bullying guru, even believes that, 'deliberately leaving an individual out of a social gathering or ignoring them' (1997: 2) can be serious. Children say that they do not like being called names or being sent to Coventry. However, when these common unpleasant aspects of growing up are caught in the 'bullying dragnet', many peer interactions are included that would never have been considered bullying in the past. This has the effect of inflating the incidence of bullying and presenting it as more widespread than it actually is.

If we then conflate, as is the trend (see Duin 1997: 8), these exaggerated figures with the rare and tragic cases that make headlines, a scenario of highly risky school life is presented to all concerned. This generates unnecessary worry and fear. It is dishonest of the anti-bullying industry to present bullying as widespread and the norm. Worse still, it is damaging to children to make them feel that they will be bullied and as a result possibly even commit suicide.

Some children tragically do harm themselves after being systematically persecuted by their peers. Professionals should intervene in these cases, to stop victimisation and support the sufferer. But, as teachers and youth workers, adults modelling tomorrow's adults, we should also know when not to interfere. We should offer all children some perspective on experiences that they encounter. Pandering to their emotional, partial and consequently disproportionate reactions confirms them as justified and leaves children feeling damaged and vulnerable. We should stress that life does and should contain risks. Children might not like this approach, but the current climate encourages them to see a crisis at every turn. By discovering the 'horror' of bullying, adults are telling children to interpret as life shattering, something that in the past they may well have felt differently about.

A risky world is not one that is acceptable in today's safety-obsessed times though. Trusting teachers today to be the professionals they have been trained to be – adults acting on their own judgement rather than policies and procedure – has become an anathema. Consequently, in our risk-averse world, anti-bullying policies attempt to make school a completely 'safe' environment.

In his book, *The Bullying Problem: How to Deal with Difficult Children*, Alan Train, when discussing preventive strategies, states that, 'In essence, there should be no free time in school, whether in class or out of it' (1995: 173). Increased supervision of children is a common theme to most anti-bullying strategies and policies. Constant supervision is the key problem that arises for children from the barrage of anti-bullying initiatives.

Increased supervision takes numerous forms and ranges from reducing the number and length of breaks or playtimes and eliminating blind spots in the playground, to placing a constant staff presence in all areas of the school. Believe it or not, playtime supervisors are a relatively new phenomenon and teachers used to only have their morning cup of coffee disturbed to administer a sticking plaster – how did we all survive in days gone by?

Children need time and space away from adults for emotional development to take place. Developing independence is an essential component of growing up. Exploring, experimenting, taking decisions and making mistakes, not just physically but also in the realm of peer relations, all contribute to developing maturity. Peer relations act as a practice arena for children, where they can rehearse interpersonal relations prior to taking full adult responsibility.

James Youniss pulls apart and examines this social arena very well in his book, *Parents and Peers in Social Development*:

> Peer relations are the source from which critical characteristics of the mature personality come. These include a sense of equality, interpersonal sensitivity, the need for intimacy, and mutual understanding.
>
> (1980: 29)

Youniss isn't one-sided in this, in fact he stresses that, without adult input, 'there is no possibility for learning culturally established patterns of co-operation and mutual concern' (1980: xvii). What he does say is that certain learning opportunities *only occur* in peer relations and cannot happen anywhere else.

Children need 'private space'. The idea that unsupervised playtime and playgrounds are dangerous and problematic needs to be challenged. Research carried out by the Institute of Education has shown that for children school break time is a 'significant and generally enjoyable time [and that] the great majority of pupils throughout their school careers expressed a positive view of break time' (Blatchford 1999: 110). A young American girl quoted on the International Play Association website makes the same point but in a more straightforward fashion: 'When we don't have recess, I feel like screaming. When we do have recess, I do scream!'

The school playground is a place where many experimental social interactions are tried out. Life in the playground can help in the development of many social skills that are essential in later life. Even when in conflict, a normal experience for children and particularly so between close friends, important strategies for the management of difficulties are acquired. If denied the opportunity to experience real mistakes, with real consequences, children miss out on the important role of error in learning. Margaret Donaldson, the Edinburgh-based child psychologist, in her book, *Children's Minds* (1987), points out the fundamental urge of children to be independent, to manage by themselves. Not allowing children the freedom to make mistakes deprives them of the freedom to flourish. Adults need to pause, stand back and ask whether intervention, even helpful intervention, is necessarily a good thing.

When their peer relations are controlled by adults they cease to be peer relations. Children are prevented from acting as social agents themselves. Anti-bullying programmes are a great example of adult-led intervention.

Youniss quotes Piaget and Sullivan at length to illustrate the difference between adult/child (supervised) and child/child (unsupervised) relationships:

> In all spheres, two types of relations must be distinguished: constraint and co-operation. The first implies an element of unilateral respect, of authority and prestige; the second is simply the intercourse between individuals on an equal footing.
>
> (Piaget cited in Youniss 1980: 14)

> If you will look closely at one of your children when he finally finds a chum ... you will discover something very different in the relationship, namely, that your child begins to develop a real sensitivity of what matters to another person ... not ... 'what should I do to get what I want' but instead 'what should I do to contribute to the happiness or to support the prestige and feelings of worthwhileness of my chum'.
>
> (Sullivan cited in Youniss 1980: 14)

Anti-bullying programmes remove the experience of unfettered conflict and kindness. Children may well act towards one another in a more civilised fashion but 'acting' is precisely what they are doing. If children only give through a sense of duty, then they are not really giving. There can be no mutuality while an adult is standing on guard. The paradox of promoting constant supervision of children as a way of preventing bullying, at the same time as promoting the active citizenship agenda, is obviously too complex for some in the new education elite to grasp.

While it is not very productive to counter panics by merely replacing one worry with another, there are some real and potentially problematic consequences for society if we deny children the space and time they require.

The skills, competency and independence that currently define adulthood will become meaningless if children never practise them. If everyday life for them is constantly controlled and regulated, children will grow up expecting regulation and so depend on third parties to resolve their difficulties. The concept of independence will lose its reality.

Without independence there is no responsibility. Looking to blame others for our own misfortunes is an already well-established fact of modern-day society (Furedi 1999: 36). Sometimes the pressure that peers bring to bear on each other has a positive socialising effect. The collective voice of a child's classmates can bring about positive change that can banish childish or antisocial behaviour. Children need to be left alone to learn important lessons. Being encouraged to blame others when our own behaviour is the problem diminishes our own sense of self. Developing an identity that incorporates incompetence and victimhood will present considerable difficulties through adolescence and into adulthood.

Challenging the false perception that children are more vulnerable today requires that we become much more critical when risks facing children are inflated – either by other adults or by children. We should stress that risks are beneficial to children:

> Risks must be taken because the greatest hazard in life is to risk nothing, the person who risks nothing does nothing, has nothing, is nothing. They may avoid suffering and sorrow, but they cannot learn, feel, change, grow, love or live. Chained by their certainties they are slaves, they have forfeited their freedom. Only a person who risks is free.
>
> (Unknown author, cited by Barnes 1997: 42)

We must have the courage of our convictions when faced by children who feel that what they are experiencing is the end of the world. Teenage years are tumultuous and emotionally upsetting, but that is what they need to be. If we, in our various roles, neglect our duty to act as leaders, then we will be guilty of creating a generation of 'Lost Boys' who never grow up and consider themselves as 'damaged goods'.

References

Barnes, P. (1997) *Theory into Practice*, Glasgow: University of Strathclyde.
Blatchford, P. (1999) 'The State of Play in Schools', in M. Woodhead, D. Faulkner and K. Littleton (eds) (1998) *Making Sense of Social Development*, London: Routledge.
Donaldson, M. (1987) *Children's Minds*, London: Fontana Press.
Duin, N. (1997) *Bullying: A Survival Guide*, London: BBC.
Elliott, M. and Kilpatrick, J. (1994) *How To Stop Bullying: A Kidscape Training Guide*, London: Kidscape.
Furedi, F. (1999) *Courting Mistrust: The Hidden Growth of a Culture of Litigation in Britain*, London: Centre for Policy Studies.
Mellor, A. (1997) *Bullying at School: Advice for Families*, Edinburgh: SCRE.
Train, A. (1995) *The Bullying Problem: How to Deal with Difficult Children*, London: Souvenir Press.
Youniss, J. (1980) *Parents and Peers in Social Development*, Chicago, IL: University of Chicago Press.

Key readings

Bristow, J. (2001) 'Peer Groups Bad – Friends Good?', 24 April 2001, available at http://www.spiked-online.com/Articles/00000000558D.htm.
Donaldson, M. (1987) *Children's Minds*, London: Fontana Press.
Elliott, M. and Kilpatrick, J. (1994) *How To Stop Bullying: A Kidscape Training Guide*, London: Kidscape.

Focus question

Some educationalists believe that we should create 'rubber walls' to produce a safe environment in which children can take risks. What does it mean to take a risk?

CHAPTER 12

MENU CHANGE IN EDUCATION?

Robin Wynyard

I said in 1998:

> As a child I was forced to eat awful school meals and made to sit at the dinner table, all afternoon if necessary, until they were eaten. This did not stop me from inventing devious strategies, like throwing soggy cabbage under the table, so implicating as many unsuspecting scholars as possible.
>
> (Wynyard 1998: 166)

Looking back, perhaps they weren't quite so bad as I thought they were!

Also, in retrospect, I find that my attitude towards children and the food that they eat has not changed one jot – in short, I believe that children should eat what they want to! However, my view differs from that of successive governments who seemed determined to interfere with the diet of school children. Such interference has differed from what I term 'weak interference' to 'strong interference'. Both of these forms have a connection to a perceived governmental ideology. 'Weak' in ideological terms means that by and large the population can see the wisdom of the interference and thus they support any direct governmental intervention. 'Strong', alternatively, means that the population at large does not necessarily see the wisdom behind the ideology and are very sceptical concerning any direct government interference. Historically the ideology has passed from 'weak' to 'strong'.

For my parents and myself school dinners were as much an important part of life as free milk, the school doctor, school dentist and nit nurse. I might not have liked them, but unquestionably they were there! Today, unlike then, not only are they not always there, they are also part of a growing educational debate, with statements appearing daily in our newspapers:

> Glasgow City Council is the first authority in Britain to make a free breakfast available to every primary school pupil in a £1m healthy eating campaign, which offers toast and juice or milk with other options of yoghurt, cheese, or fresh fruit. Almost 15,000 pupils a day use the service.
>
> (*The Herald*, 22 August 2003)

In the 1950s parents and children took school dinners for granted as part of the newly formed Welfare State, where the aim was to *look after us from the cradle to the grave.*

But, in fact, the debate over school meals had rumbled on long before 1948. Reporting on the poor physical shape of recruits for the Boer War, the Inspector of General Recruiting spoke of the 'gradual deterioration of the physique of the working classes for whom the bulk of the recruits must be drawn' (Report of the

Inter-departmental Committee on Physical Deterioration 1904, vol. 1: 96). As a result, in 1906 the school medical service was established and part of its brief was the school feeding of children in elementary schools.

After the two World Wars, school dinners were seen by the state as essential for welfare because rotten teeth, rickets and malnutrition were prevalent among the nation's youth. To the politicians the connection between decent food and long-term health was crystal clear and if people didn't have enough of it then it was the job of the state to provide it. Allied to the rise in compulsory education, the argument ran that simply sitting down with other children to a meal was an important part of the wider socialisation programme.

The debate over school meals hasn't gone away – only the arguments used have changed! In the 1960s a relationship was seen between the lack of school meal provision and rising juvenile delinquency. With lack of lunchtime supervision in the schools all kinds of antisocial mischief would result.

In the 1970s the concern was economics not health or delinquency:

> Even if school meals are provided, the charge made for the meals influences whether they are taken, and the higher the charge the more children will choose not to accept them and go home instead and the less the mothers will work on the average.
>
> (Wynn 1972: 259)

So it seems we can expect interference in the dietary habits of schoolchildren, whenever the government of the day sees potential societal breakdown. Thus, with school meal provision we are never far away from ideology, but as life gets more complicated the reasoning behind it becomes far more diverse.

In 1948, the one simple implication was that the welfare of the individual was good for the nation as a whole. This struck a chord with the population, who saw justification in state interference. But, as the nation got wealthier and fatter, school dinners went downhill fast.

School meals were increasingly the most expendable bit of education and one of the softest targets of the educational system. As part of a constant cost-cutting exercise local councils, under the 1980 Education Act, are only obliged to provide school meals for those entitled not to pay for them. Finally, councils still providing a school meals service were required to make a profit by the 1988 Local Government Act. In the 1990s the argument seemed to be that, as parents are much wealthier, they and not the state are financially better able to feed their children.

With the new millennium this ideology is shifting dramatically as there is a fear that increased wealth has somehow gone to our heads. Suddenly we are prey to the machinations of the advertising budgets of huge corporations. Sir Liam Donaldson, the Labour government's Chief Medical Officer, has warned manufacturers that they must stop promoting unhealthy foods to children or risk curbs on their advertising. Julian Peto, an adviser to the government, told a House of Commons Select Committee in August 2003 that teachers should include a child's body mass index in their annual reports to parents. His concern was that our children are becoming obese and obesity is a killer which parents might not notice – the assumption being that teachers are best placed objectively to advise on a child's weight.

Obesity *is* on the increase in the UK, as it is in the United States and Germany. Along with the UK, these form three of the four richest *and* fattest nations in the world. There *is* an argument here: that in order for a nation to get rich, the people comprising it have to get fat! This harks back to 1948 when we were neither fat nor wealthy. Professor Alberti (BBC Radio 4, 25 August 2003), in explaining the exponential worldwide rise of Type 2 diabetes, saw obesity as a contributory factor. In this he bemoaned the passing of school meals. We know that a fifth of the population is overweight, costing the NHS an estimated £500m a year and the economy another £2 billion in fat-related illness. Such figures are awesome, but they do not explain the greater than average rise of diabetes in countries like India and Pakistan, where obesity is *not* the problem. In asking governments to actively intervene in what we eat, he was only referring to the wealthiest and not the poorest nations!

My argument remains clear that at the national level there is a correlation between fatness and wealth, the inevitability being that body growth goes with economic growth. This argument runs counter to the medical ideology that would like to see health warnings on unhealthy foods in much the same way we already have them on packets of cigarettes. But, if we are to see fat as an issue, there are many other factors than food to consider. These include the lack of compulsory games in school and the fact that playing fields have been sold off by cash-strapped schools. Media exaggeration also fuels a paranoid society where a 'safe indoor mentality' is the norm. This latter has led to the fact that children don't walk to school any more.

In the UK, the obesity argument is confused! So, too, is the argument about how much schoolchildren eat, or *what* they eat.

Schoolchildren can either spend the money their parents give them on junk food, or they can take in a prepared lunchbox to eat during the meal break. The latter is *supposedly* the healthier option. There is a third possibility: a reformulated school meal service based on nutritious meals concocted by famous chefs. The trouble is that children don't want asparagus and fresh vegetables; they want chips and beans! In any case a look at the figures spent on school meals is illuminating. For England and Wales, expenditure on school meals in 1996/7 was around £386m, or 2.1 per cent of total education spending, or £7.45 per head of population. School meals don't seem feasible, unless the budget for them is upped considerably. This means the money has to come from somewhere else, like fewer teachers or fewer schoolbooks.

From America the writing has been on the wall about *what* children eat: 'The American School Food Service Association estimates that about 30 percent of public high schools in the United States offer branded fast food' (Schlosser 2001: 56). The American sociologist George Ritzer wrote: 'However, many have had to alter school cafeteria menus and procedures to make fast food readily available. Apples, yoghurt, and milk may go straight into the trash can, but hamburgers, fries, and shakes are devoured' (Ritzer 2000: 9).

The difference between America and Britain concerning children's food is striking. At the end of the day Americans know they are fat but they choose to ignore it! If there is any tinkering with the food supply it is not done at a governmental level. For the American corporations supplying the bulk of the nation's food, the demand to change dietary practice only becomes a factor when company profits get eroded. McDonald's and Kraft's decision to cut the fat in products comes after fears that they might be sued for millions of dollars for turning American kids into 'fatties'. On the other hand my experience of Americans will not see them demanding smaller portions for their money!

Of course, obesity is not a good thing, but the arguments concerning it are not as clear as the government would like to make out. In America people are deemed to be able to spend their money on whatever they want even if this harms them physically. I don't argue that this is good or bad, simply that if you want laissez-faire economics then governments cannot prescribe what people eat.

In the UK anomalies abound, making government attempts at interference in children's food appear strange. Although, in theory, the government might sympathise with the views of scientists over what children are eating, for financial reasons they *do* seem to want to turn a blind eye to the manufacturers of *less desirable food* intruding into schools. Increasingly like the United States, cash-strapped schools in the UK can benefit from the workings of the free market. Adverts in schools for McDonald's products bring cash for much-needed school equipment. Cadbury has launched a marketing scheme, endorsed by a government minister, which involves collecting tokens from chocolate bars in exchange for school sports equipment.

Some points should be borne in mind when considering whether a government interferes in a child's diet. Without a doubt modern governments want the vast improvements in rising life expectancy and health, but can't accept that this goes along with increasing waist size. To look at this another way, I am sure that if you said to those in power in a country like Bangladesh, 'we can make your population both fatter and richer', they would jump at the chance!

In the UK it is to patronise children to see them as innocent dupes forced into eating McDonald's burgers simply by watching genial Ronald McDonald on the television.

Society is far more complicated with more pressure and anxiety, but can we go too far with the assumptions behind this statement? Some writers talk of a 'paranoid society', where family eating becomes a zero sum game: 'Mothers and fathers trying to cut down on their calorie intake now need to diet in secret in case their darling receives the wrong signals about eating' (Furedi 2001: 46). So the parents get thin while their children get fat! Considering it is adults the government wants illness-free in order to work and bolster GNP, might this not be a fair trade? At the end of the day it is up to the parents, not government, to stop children stuffing themselves with chocolate and burgers. As Furedi puts it, 'Isn't it time we were honest with ourselves and admitted that our weaknesses are just that – bad habits we can overcome, if we really want to. ... If we eat too many burgers, then we are to blame, not McDonald's or Wimpy' (*Daily Express*, 15 July 2003).

In any case the perceived danger of the food in children's school lunchboxes might be misplaced. The lunchboxes themselves might be the problem. 'Children have been asked not to bring lunchboxes (to a particular school) because they pose a health and safety risk to teachers ... modern lunchboxes ... were very bulky and teachers could trip over them' (*Sunday Times*, This Life, 13 July 2003).

As we live in a much healthier, wealthier and more interesting society than ever before, why should we want to turn the clock back to the hunger and poverty of my youth? So, unless it can be clearly explained why outside influence should intrude into what our children eat, then, for the time being, parents and children themselves should take responsibility.

As a child it never crossed my mind that I didn't eat liver, greens, marrow, turnips, baked potatoes and a myriad of other food stuffs. The fact that I eat all of these things with relish now seems to be the point. It also applies to my children when they were young and the fact that in adulthood they also eat them now. I daresay that it will also apply to their children and so on.

We all remember that as children we were fussy about certain foods, but the truth is that as adults we become more catholic in our tastes, trying a much wider variety of food. I don't have any argument with the fact that children should be allowed to eat what they want when they are young, because like most parents I know that offspring will work it out for themselves in due course.

References

Furedi, F. (2001) *Paranoid Parenting*, London: Allen Lane/Penguin.
Ritzer, G. (2000) *The McDonaldization of Society*, Thousand Oaks, CA: Pine Forge Press.
Schlosser, E. (2001) *Fast Food Nation*, London: Allen Lane/Penguin.
Wynn, M. (1972) *Family Policy*, London: Penguin Books.
Wynyard, R. (1998) 'The Bunless Burger', in M. Alfino, J.S. Caputo and R. Wynyard (eds), *McDonaldization Revisited: Critical Essays on Consumer Culture*, Westport, CT, and London: Praeger.

Key readings

Critser, G. (2003) *Fat Land: How Americans Became the Fattest People in the World*, London: Allen Lane/Penguin.
Furedi, F. (2001) *Paranoid Parenting*, London: Allen Lane/Penguin.
Ritzer, G. (2000) *The McDonaldization of Society*, Thousand Oaks, CA: Pine Forge Press.
Schlosser, E. (2001) *Fast Food Nation*, London: Allen Lane/Penguin.

Focus question

'Children should be allowed to eat what they like'. What are the educational arguments for and against this statement?

PART III

THE SEARCH FOR LOST VALUES, COMMUNITIES AND CITIZENS

CHAPTER 13

JUST BEING THERE FOR US

Carl Parsons

Early intervention work, preventative interventions and restorative and corrective practices for 'at-risk' and disaffected young people abound. Training in doing it, manuals to support practice, websites for ongoing support point to increasingly 'professionalised' strategies. North America has been prolific in developing and branding specialist, 'manualised' services. Along with this have gone powerful dissemination, merchandising and 'product testing'. To prevent education failure and the development of antisocial behaviour we have Headstart, High/Scope Perry Pre-school, DISTAR and Cognitive Enrichment Advantage, Webster-Stratton parenting programmes and Fast Track to name just a few. For addressing delinquency, there is an equally wide range of structured, restorative arrangements. In the UK, we demand *evidence-based practices* and that doesn't mean a bunch of committed practitioners and clients saying 'it works'. We want randomised longitudinal controlled trials. These impress us most of all. The High/Scope Perry Pre-school project reporting 20 years on that one dollar invested saves seven dollars and six cents is the star in that respect.

These approaches have a growing appeal in the UK and numerous government-funded projects, including Excellence in Cities, Sure Start, Children's Fund, On Track and Connexions, incorporate elements from the professionalised and mechanised American scene. However, they confront professional cultures that are more holistic and less specialised. Inter-agency, multi-professional, joined-up services are currently favoured, yet some evidence suggests workers with a key link role and limited training can have as much success by 'just being there for us'. Additionally, there is considerable effort invested in 'regenerating communities'; part of this is to train local activists to engage with the community in addressing its problems. Thus, befriending, mentoring, family visiting and volunteer family support are gaining ground as approaches that place *less* reliance on trained professionals to *deliver* services *to* a passive, troubled individual, family or community.

The discussion extends to a weighing of the special expertise external professionals bring to a 'problem' individual or family against notions of professional despotism, self-righteousness, personal advancement and 'client' disempowerment.

Hyper-specialisation

There are practical, moral, financial and sociological reasons for questioning the ever-greater specialisation and professionalisation of services to address disadvantage, delinquency and disengagement. The social inclusion agenda in the UK has a strong moral and rhetorical appeal despite, and perhaps because of, a conceptual vagueness. Increasing specialisation of the services is designed to 'target' children, families and schools, and most often designed to 'fix' the child. Yet there are more generalised community-based and interpersonally simple ways of approaching the problem. It questions notions of targeting and dosage and whether one needs to examine the child, school and family within a community context which itself lies within broader political and historical forces.

Gans (1995) has described the perverse tendency for professionals and professional groups to benefit greatly from the disadvantage of others and apply their professional and therapeutic skills to addressing this disadvantage – though it is deeply embedded and their efforts are likely to yield little.

We specialise, as professionals, in order to:

- provide a bounded, targeted rationale;
- prevent being drawn into diverse multiple problems;
- maintain and enhance status;
- acquire greater specialisation in socially valued work and esoteric mysticism;
- insulate from responsibility and community.

Hyper-specialised responses and 'just being there for us'

Brief therapy, Webster Stratton, parenting courses, etc. are highly structured inputs which have been widely tested and greatly refined in order to appeal to the client group. They also serve as great 'protectors' for the professionals who 'deliver' the package. They are seldom authentic interactions. They are abstracted from the inter-action networks and communities from which people come and they are not sustained.

Lloyd *et al.* (2001) report from the clients' side. Investigating inter-agency working in preventing school exclusion they visited many families and interviewed in order to determine what made a difference in maintaining young people in school. While single disciplinary teams may have some limitations, the multi-disciplinary team is much recommended to address the multiple problems that many children and families manifest, yet there is the suggestion that 'there is very little evidence regarding the efficacy of multi-disciplinary teams working in educational settings' (Wilson and Pirrie 2000: 4).

Lloyd and her colleagues question whether the professional role matters, particularly as the nature of their expertise and the organisation they belong to is often unknown by the client. Asked if the professional who had visited had come from Youth Justice, social work, the health authority, a local community group or somewhere else, they often did not know. The answer was not uncommonly 'There was this woman' (Lloyd *et al.* 2001: 181).

Interviewees talk also about good personal relationships with some 'helpers'. These individuals did not see the helper in a professional role but rather as someone who 'my dad used to talk to him all the time at the football'. Or 'my mum and my social workers are good friends' (Lloyd *et al.* 2001: 182).

Arguably, it is not the professional role nor the particular skills acquired in training but a manner, relationship, authenticity and trust. In much discussion there is the temptation to concentrate on measures to be taken by providers – the supply side – without taking account taken of the experiences, needs and hopes of the young people themselves.

At 'the hard end', professionals can be working with a client group that finds it difficult to turn up, keep appointments or carry through any decisions made; yet charities and projects working with these young clearly make an impact on their lives because of sustained interest and commitment to the young people.

The state of youth

In the UK, we do not treat our young people well. Some countries appear to be better at cherishing their young than others. The Innocenti Report Card begins by saying,

> The persistence of child poverty in rich countries undermines both equality of opportunity and commonality of values. It therefore confronts the industrialised world with a test of its ideals and of its capacity to resolve many of its most intractable social problems
>
> (UNICEF 2000)

The report sets out the facts about how poorly the UK supports young children and the gross variation in the proportion that are below the 'relative' poverty line. The '5 per cent club' consists of the Nordic countries, Luxembourg and Belgium. France has a proportion of 7.9 per cent, Germany 10.7 per cent, while the UK stands at a disturbing 19.8 per cent. It could be that only those at the lower end of the percentage scale are approaching meeting Article 27 of the UN Convention on the Rights of the Child, providing 'a standard of living adequate for physical, mental, spiritual, moral and social development'.

Convincing research links inequality and ill health, psychosocial welfare and even homicides (Benzeval *et al.* 1995). People who live in disadvantaged circumstances have more illness, greater distress, more disability and shorter lives than those who are more affluent. The inequalities which lie behind the unequal distribution of health hazards are much the same as those implicated in the poor participation and attainment in education. We cannot solve the education problems within that sphere alone.

In terms of criminal justice systems countries also vary widely and political decisions have defined the nature of the discourses about whether actions of young people are to be seen as punishable or remediable. In England and Wales 5,300 under 18-year-olds are detained in prison, as against 16 in Denmark, 134 in Finland, 850 in Spain, 25 in Portugal and 8 in Sweden. The United States and Canada boast numbers and rates of juvenile incarceration that should be an embarrassment.

Different proportions of pupils are in special schools in different countries: in the UK it is under 2 per cent, Flanders has 3.6 per cent of its pupils in special schools, the Netherlands 4.4 per cent, Scotland 1.2 per cent, Ireland 1 per cent and Spain 0.5 per cent.

The differences in allocation, treatment, status and life chances are conditioned by the socio-cultural environment and specific decisions made. The striking finding from looking back over different countries over a fairly extended period of time is that prosperity as much as morality leads us to care for the young and the vulnerable. This suggests a fairly shaky moral foundation.

Utopias, third ways and dreams

Youth's continued marginalisation and the compromised and partial entry to citizenship status are sources of concern. It is the social exclusion, with associated possibilities of crime, lack of participation, unemployment or unemployability and long-term dependency which the state apparatuses need to address. There continue to be groups that are predictably marginalised in contexts of competition and uncertainty.

The disadvantaged are exposed to alienation at multiple levels: being unproductive (unemployed or unemployable) members of a society with a strong work ethic (economic exclusion); being incapable of satisfying wants in a growing hedonistic ethos, being on social security or the dole in a materialist, consumerist society (social exclusion); and finally being clients of an institution, persons incapable of handling their own problems (political exclusion). The cumulative effect of all these is a sense of loss of dignity. The institutionalisation of strategies to mitigate poverty coupled with the breakdown of community solidarity develops a more acute form in the loss of 'social, economic, psychological and emotional well-being' which is reflected in various forms, such as the lack of coping or problem-solving mechanisms, lack of meaningful activity, extinction of structures of intra-group and inter-group solidarity, loss of dignity and low self-image.

Solutions?

In a study of what makes a difference in helping difficult young people stay in education, a medium-term follow-up report by Parsons *et al.* (2001) found that, in the examination of a whole range of factors associated with interventions and prevention, no particular strategy or professional skill stood out as making a distinctive difference. In looking at successful cases of children who had been excluded at primary school level but were succeeding later at secondary school level, the things which made a difference were not unlike earlier mentions of 'some woman came round':

1   Presence of a concerned adult in professional contact – these could be tutors or school year heads, staff in a Pupil Referral Unit, key workers in a children's home or special support staff from projects of various descriptions. It was somebody who really concerned themselves with the individual's welfare and believed they 'could make it'.
2   Flexibility of approach and provision. There is not one approach and you know it will work. Layers of provision are necessary. There must always be another option.
3   Recognition of individual strengths and abilities. Empowerment means allowing young people to make choices and build on their strengths. Professionals must acknowledge, value and provide opportunities for young people to build on their strengths.
4   The individuals themselves – in some cases people in contact with the young people wanted to emphasise the way they felt the individual should take credit for their own achievements, despite the fact that in such cases they had a great deal of support from particular individuals and/or agencies. In these cases, personal ambition, maturation and taking responsibility for one's own life, as well as not blaming others, was a key thing.
5   Change of school or education provision.

(Parsons *et al.* 2001: 52)

Solutions to problems of disaffection in young people are likely to be found in the management of moderately trained, well-supervised 'generic' workers. These will have good interpersonal skills and will be well cared for (burn-out is too frequent). We do not need the concentration of highly specialised and expensive professionals. There is the constant need to remind ourselves, and others, that we, as a society, make many of the problems with young people that we then proceed to address.

References

Benzeval, M., Judge, K. and Whitehead, M. (1995) *Tackling Inequalities in Health: An Agenda for Action*, London: Kings Fund.

Gans, H.J. (1995) *The War Against the Poor: The Underclass and Antipoverty Policy*, New York: Basic Books.

Lloyd, G., Kendrick, A. and Stead, J. (2001) 'Some Woman Came Round': Interagency Work in Preventing School Exclusion', in S. Riddell and L. Tett (eds) *Education, Social Justice and Interagency Working: Joined-up or Fractured Policy?*, London: Routledge.

Parsons, C., Hayden, C., Godfrey, R., Howlett, K. and Martin, T. (2001) *Outcomes in Secondary Education for Children Excluded from Primary School*, Research Report RR271, London: Department for Education and Employment.

UNICEF (2000) *Child Poverty in Rich Nations*, Florence: United Nations Children's Fund.

Wilson, V. and Pirrie, A. (2002) *Multi-disciplinary Teamworking: Indicators of Good Practice*, Edinburgh: Scottish Council for Research in Education.

Key readings

Hopkins, E. (1995) *Working-class Self Help in Nineteenth Century England*, London: St Martin's Press.

Parsons, C. (1999) *Education, Exclusion and Citizenship*, London: Routledge.

Riddell, S. and Tett, L. (2001) *Education, Social Justice and Interagency Working: Joined-up or Fractured Policy?*, London: Routledge.

Focus question

Why is it that we feel that some external person is now necessary to help the disadvantaged? What happened to the working-class tradition of self-help?

CHAPTER 14

ASSERTING CHILDREN'S RIGHTS

Richard Harris

Steven, a Children's Rights Advisor in the Office of the London Commissioner for Children's Rights, states that:

> The Office works to uphold the Articles in the United Nations Convention on the Rights of the Child. Three of these are:
>
> > Article 12: The right for young people to have their opinions listened to.
> > Article 16: All young people have a right to a private and family life.
> > Article 2: Children must not be discriminated against.
>
> (sortit.org.uk)

One might wonder why there is such interest in children's rights if this is all they amount to. And what do these rights mean, for example a 'right to ... family life'? Does it mean that a parents' divorce, which ends a child's family life, is no longer the parents' choice? No – see the Matrimonial Causes Act 1973 s.1 (2) (e), as amended. Perhaps this right refers to children having the right to a standard of living fit for family life? Certainly not! The Department of Work and Pensions (2002) document *Households Below Average Incomes 1994/95–2001/02* shows that, in the last year surveyed, around 14 million people were living below half average income after housing costs. This is three times the number of people in this position in 1979. Perhaps the establishment of a Children's Rights Commissioner for England will end the child poverty hidden in that figure? There is a Children's Commissioner for Wales. He has not ended child poverty. His role broadly consists in asking children 'what *you* think is most important' (childcom.org.uk).

What are children's rights?

Some of the UN Convention's rights define harms from which children should be protected. Article 19 declares, 'The State has an obligation to protect children from all forms of maltreatment perpetrated by parents or others responsible for their care'. The Article uses the language of rights to state what are, in reality, prohibitions upon the behaviour of others – behaviour controlled by the criminal law. Asserting these prohibitions as rights is just a convoluted way of mirroring a set of protections that all people are in fact granted.

In England, fathers used to have rights over their children. This meant in effect that children were a kind of property (Montgomery 1988). John Eekelaar interestingly suggests that children were rather 'agents for the devolution of property within the family' (1986: 163). Parental rights have now withered, replaced by the gentler notion of responsibilities (Law Commission 1988: para. 2.4). In a seminal study of

the origin of children's rights, Eekelaar suggests they have three spheres of operation. Rights cover a child's 'basic interest', essentially covered by child protection
legislation; a 'developmental interest' in having his or her capacities promoted to best
advantage; and an 'autonomy interest', i.e. the child's wish to take action free of
adult control. Not only can the autonomy interest clash with adult wishes, it can
also clash with a child's basic and developmental interests. It is as a device to resolve
these clashes that the concept of children's rights meets an essential test.

Eekelaar, a supporter of children's rights, says that identifying them is essentially
an empirical matter. The Children's Commissioner for Wales is doing exactly this.
Eekelaar argues that rights are important as they put children in the position of
subject rather than object. This position stems from an appreciation of the fundamental weakness of the English law approach to disputes involving children. This
requires the court to seek the welfare of the child (Children Act 1989 s. 1 (1)). The
problem is that claims made about where that welfare interest lies are made by adults
and are inseparable from their own claims with respect to the child. The 'welfare of
the child', in the absence of a measure of welfare, can be little more than the reifying
garb in which adults suggest what is best in accord with their own values and interests. The problem with Eekelaar's position is that it sticks with the English legal
fantasy that everyone who has a voice before the civil court is equal in reality, rather
than equal in legal fiction (Fitzpatrick 1992). In family law, decisions can turn on
which party commands the resources (the actual possession of a child being a resource
in this context, as having the child can trigger property transfers for the purpose of
supporting the child).

In the notorious case of *Nottinghamshire CC v. P*, the eldest of three sisters
claimed that her father had sexually abused her and that he was abusing her younger
sisters, aged 16 and 13. The local authority decided, apparently for financial reasons,
not to take action (Cretney 2003). Sir Stephen Brown, in the Court of Appeal, said
'as appears from this case, if a local authority doggedly resists taking the steps which
are appropriate to the case of children at risk ... the court is powerless' ([1993]
3 WLR 637 at 642). These children had a right to protection, firmly entrenched
in child protection law. The problem was that what happened to them depended
on the decisions of a politically controlled body, the Nottinghamshire County Council.
They controlled the resources these girls needed to get free from the household
of their abuser. Had they been independently rich, this case would not have been
before the civil courts. It was before the courts because the assertion of rights was
really an attempt to get someone with money and staff, Nottinghamshire County
Council, to take action to give these children a new home. The rock upon which
the ship of rights constantly wrecks is that hard place, politics. The civil law court,
a forum for adjudicating disputes between individuals, cannot deliver when faced
with a conflict between an individual and part of the state that has some form of
democratic or participatory governance. When rights are most needed, they most fail
to deliver their promises. The former poor law provenance of all this comes strongly
through the decisions of the courts when dealing with those now called the socially
excluded. In *Re W* [1971] AC 682, a mother of two toddlers became pregnant. She
believed she could not cope with another child in her small one-room accommoda-
tion. She offered her baby for adoption. The baby was placed with potential adopters.
Soon after, she was rehoused and wanted the baby back. She refused to consent to
the child's adoption. The House of Lords, considering the final appeal, held the determining issue to be whether or not the mother was reasonable in refusing consent to
the adoption. This is the test laid down in statute. But when would a mother be
unreasonable? In reality, the question the judges answered was who could give this

child a better life – the mother who lived on benefits or the prospective adopters, a comfortable middle-class family? It is simply the old story of the middle classes buying (they could afford the litigation) the children of the poor. If the mother had been given a small fraction of the eventual costs of the litigation at the time of the baby's birth, she would never have been separated from her baby. In this case, the language of rights was not used by the court to resolve the claims of child, mother or prospective adopters. The court stuck to the question, was the mother being reasonable to refuse to consent to her child's adoption? What difference to the deliberative process would that one word 'rights' have made? (Contrast this case with *Winnipeg Child and Family Services v. K.L.W.* [2000] SCC 48, in the Supreme Court of Canada, in which the *Canadian Charter of Rights and Freedoms* was held to be compatible with a child protection agency, without any judicial authorisation, snatching a newborn child from the maternity ward. A framework of rights does not prevent cases such as *Re W* as there is always a clash of rights – here the child's and the mother's – and so the court is still in the business of performing a balancing exercise conducted in accord with other principles. This is exactly what happened in *Winnipeg*.)

In the era before rights were asserted, the poor and the orphaned were treated rather differently. Jean Heywood reports that:

> in pre-Reformation England, the [poor] ... child had a place in a feudal and employed community. ... His safeguard ... lay in the communal nature of the society. ... In the fact that life was centred round the community rather than the family there lay the possibility of opportunity and protection for the unwanted child.
>
> (1978: 7–8)

The parental right of custody emerged in upper-class litigation in the nineteenth century, as a device to keep the realm of the family private (Hoggett *et al.* 1996: 573). Right is the concept of property as developed in the capitalist era, the right to personal possession and the right to exclude all others. It is the central legal tool that created the middle-class nuclear family. And the modern assertion of children's rights mirrors this Victorian parental claim. Both are claims to privacy and autonomy – a rejection of others' attempts to tell one what to do. The Victorian father who asserted his rights had to have money behind him. The rights of the child is an attempt to command others, primarily public bodies, to use their money in the child's interest.

In contrast, Onora O'Neill (1996) asks us to consider the foundations of rights thinking. She argues that ethical reasoning is an attempt to answer the question 'who counts?' Rights are essentially judicalised statements of 'I want'. Eekelaar's autonomous interest claim obviously is 'I want', dressed in lawyer's garb. Empirical surveys to establish the 'I want(s)' then breach an essential aim of moral discourse, the supervening of culturally specific views which limit the scope of justice. She argues that institutions, such as the institution of rights, are only just if they can take the claims of 'distant strangers' seriously (O'Neill 2000). Will the rights determined by the Welsh Commissioner do this? She suggests that the language of rights is overblown. It attempts to conjure into being ill-defined obligations, such as the obligation to help children or to be considerate towards them. These obligations are unlike the rights we know from property, the original setting of such talk. A rights possessor can abandon property (I have a right to my car – property in it – but if you want my car I can give it to you gratis). Children's rights are not seen as belonging to children in this way. That is one thing that is so odd with them. They are not capable of being waived by individual children as it is said this would harm the interests of all children. Not many think a 14-year-old girl should be allowed to legally consent to sex with an older man, even though she might consent in reality; or to starve herself to death as an anorexic. The paternalism of this thinking is obvious. A response to this might be to claim that rights do have teeth in identifiable relationships and it is precisely within those relationships that children need to be empowered. Here we see a mystification with words. Children will only be free of powerful adults if they are wealthy enough to avoid them. But that wealth will only get children what they want through buying the services of poorer and economically dependent adults.

Children's rights and human rights

Since the Human Rights Act 1998 became law, many rights, which overlap with those in the UN Convention on the Rights of the Child, are part of English law. These rights are imposed by the state and, as discussed above, the rights holder cannot surrender them. In contrast, property rights and rights which emerge through private contracts can be surrendered by the rights holder. The right itself is property (you can sell it, for example.) Human rights are not like this, but are akin to torts – those obligations imposed by the law on us all, independent of our will. A well-known example is the tort of defamation. Yet, even here, someone who has been defamed does not have to sue. (But, except in an abstract sense, do you have that right if you cannot afford to sue? As one judge memorably put it, you have the right to sue just as you have the right to dine at the Ritz Hotel.) The only part of the concept of right that connects with the realm of children's rights is the concept of obligation. O'Neill sees this clearly (O'Neill 2000), arguing that the only real questions in the field of rights talk are: what duties exist?, who has them?, and what are the boundaries of these duties? Duties bring us back to society and to asking the timeless question, what does society have to do to bring up its children well? Giving children rights, private claims against particular adults whom they might be able to force to act in their interest, is in my submission an odd way to care for children. It is abandoning them. It is to tell children the lie that they live in a world that cherishes their freedoms. If there are problems it is because of uncaring or neglectful adults or inertia (the McPherson view of the world).

The purpose of children's rights in the home is to allow children independence from parental authority and control – to assure autonomy; in effect, to end parental authority. The parents within a family are in a community of mutual support. If one parent fails to fulfil the obligations of parenthood or their relationship, the other parent can end the relationship. That is the reality of adult life. Rights do not, by their nature, entail obligations. Where rights arise from an agreement, they will only be granted as part of a package of benefits to the parties. Children's autonomy rights in the home highlight parents' obligations. That is, not that the maturing child develops an adult relationship with their parents, but that the child can continue to assert the demands of a child without the obligations that are naturally part of an adult relationship. To put this differently, children's autonomy rights in the home turn the parents from being the central human community in the child's life into a resource – a property. It is only with your own property that you have rights without duties. We are offered, not freedom, but total alienation. For an interesting observation on the law after *Gillick*, see Seymour (1992).

Other areas in which children's rights would be effective – at school and in relation to the social services – are areas central to public policy and political debate. Rights ignore the community and its democratic institutions as vehicles to resolve disputes and foster children's well-being. One can understand why, given the weakness of these institutions in caring for children. This weakness demands a political and community response. Creating rights, which is a private law tactic, further undermines the tenuous democracy we have. The concept of rights clashes with society's right to fashion its own rules. That's what rights are for. Above all, rights conveniently ignore the real evil that bedevils children's lives – *want*. Beveridge knew *want* was the key enemy. *Want* walks tall again while rights lobbyists run between its legs.

As Hon. Justice Michael Kirby of the Supreme Court of Australia said:

> It is important to be aware of the growing influence of . . . the international law of human rights, upon the decisions of courts everywhere in the world. Lawyers of the next generation will perceive a local legal problem through different spectacles. They will see local law and local solutions in a context of global law and global solutions. As the cases on parental-child relocation illustrate, this is something that is already happening in the field of family and children's law. We should alert our minds to a legal revolution that is underway.
>
> (2002)

References

Cretney, S., Masson, J. and Bailey-Harris, R. (2003) *Principles of Family Law*, London: Sweet & Maxwell.

Department for Work and Pensions (2002) *Households Below Average Incomes*, available at http://www.dwp.gov.uk/asd/hbai/hbai2002/contents.asp.

Eekelaar, J. (1986) 'The Emergence of Children's Rights', *Oxford Journal of Legal Studies* 6: 161–82.

Fitzpatrick, P. (1992) *The Mythology of Modern Law*, London: Routledge.

Heywood, J. (1978) *Children in Care*, London: Routledge & Kegan Paul.

Hoggett, B., Pearl, D., Cooke, E. and Bates, P. (1996) *The Family, Law and Society*, London: Butterworth.

Kirby, M. (2002) *Children and Family Law: Paramount Interests and Human Rights*, available at http://www.hcourt.gov.au/speeches/kirbyj/kirbyj_children_and_family_law_oct_2002.htm#_ftnref26.

Law Commission (1988) No. 172: *Guardianship and Custody*, London: HMSO.

Montgomery, J. (1988) 'Children as Property?', *Modern Law Review* 51: 323.

O'Neill, O. (1996) *Towards Justice and Virtue: A Constructive Account of Practical Reasoning*, Cambridge: CUP.

O'Neill, O. (2000) *Bounds of Justice*, Cambridge: CUP.

Seymour, J. (1992) 'An "Uncontrollable Child": A Case Study in Children's and Parents' Rights', in P. Alston, S. Parker and J. Seymour, *Children, Rights and the Law*, Oxford: Clarendon Press.

www.sortit.org.uk/your_voice.htm.

www.childcom.org.uk/english/index/html.

Key readings

Eekelaar, J. (1986) 'The Emergence of Children's Rights', *Oxford Journal of Legal Studies* 6: 161–82.

Harris, J. (1982) 'The Political Status of Children', in K. Graham (ed.), *Contemporary Political Philosophy*, Cambridge: Cambridge University Press.

Heartfield, J. (1993) 'Children's Rights WRONG', *Living Marxism*, October: 12–14.

www.childcom.org.uk/.

www.sortit.org.uk/your_voice.htm.

Focus question

How far does conferring rights on children diminish adults' rights?

CHAPTER 15

EDUCATION, CULTURE AND SOCIAL CLASS

Jon Davison

On examining official government documents it is difficult not to be struck by elitist attitudes to the working class displayed by educational policy makers throughout the twentieth century:

> Many persons, most prominently social and economic leaders and social reformers, grasped the uses of schooling and the vehicle of literacy for the promotion of values, attitudes and habits considered essential to the maintenance of social order and the persistence of integration and cohesion.
>
> (Graff 1987: 7)

The role of the teaching of English in promoting success or creating failure in working-class pupils is still an important issue, although it is often ignored. What follows is a preliminary exploration of the topic – a longer, in-depth study would have to address issues of gender and race, but to do so here would result in their trivialisation.

Social class and educational policy makers

State education and the importance of English were 'advocated in a hard-headed way as a means of social control' (Gossman 1981: 82). Poet and HMI, Matthew Arnold (1869: 105), saw the 'raw and half developed' working class living 'amidst poverty and squalor' as a threat to social stability: a threat that would be averted by a high cultural, pure-English-as-civilising-agent approach to education. 'Pure English is not merely an accomplishment, but an index to and a formative influence over character' (BoE 1910: para. 2).

The first major report into *The Teaching of English in England* was published in 1921 and it is suspicious of the growing working class. It is sympathetic to elementary school teachers who 'fight against evil habits of speech contracted in home and street'. Pupils' spoken English is considered 'disfigured' (BoE 1921: para. 67). The report's hostility to working-class children is confirmed, when it describes the teacher's battle, which is 'not with ignorance but with a perverted power' (BoE 1921: para. 59).

For the members of the Newbolt Committee, not only were working-class children perceived as potentially dangerous, so too were members of 'organised labour movements', because they 'were antagonistic to, and contemptuous of literature ... a subject to be despised by really virile men'. The report states that, 'a large number of thinking working men' not only believe literature to be as useful and relevant to their lives as, 'antimacassars, fish-knives and other unintelligible and futile trivialities of middle-class culture', but also believe that it is taught in schools only 'to side-track the working movement' (BoE 1921: para. 233).

Early twentieth-century policy makers espoused a moral, and almost evangelical, approach to the teaching of 'Great Literature'. It was believed that nothing was more valuable or indeed more civilising than pupils connecting with the great minds of the past. Pupils were to be brought into the presence of the great works of Milton, Wordsworth, Coleridge, Swift and the like, in order to 'appreciate' the 'divine nature' of such texts (Davison and Dowson 1998: 22).

Popular culture

Educationists unequivocally denigrated popular culture. The adverse effects of cinema were deplored by headteachers: 'the mental effect upon the children was to make them more fond of noise, ostentatious display, self-advertisement and change. The pictures excited their minds and created a love of pleasure and disinclination for steady work and effort' (*Times Educational Supplement* 1915). Such attitudes can be found in official education documentation throughout the century: 'The pervading influences of the hoarding, the cinema, and a large section of the public press, are (in this respect as in others) subtly corrupting the taste and habits of the rising generation' (BoE 1938: 222–3). This antipathy to the indulgence of children in popular culture can be traced to the present day in educational documents: from cinema through radio, television and video, to computer games. Although the Bullock Report, *A Language for Life* (DfES 1975), helped to pave the way for media education, it contains the same attitudes displayed by the dominant social groups half a century earlier:

> Between them, radio and television spread the catch-phrase, the advertising jingle, and the frenetic trivia of the disc-jockey ... it is clear that the content and form of much radio and television utterance makes the teacher's job a great deal more difficult.
>
> (DfES 1975: para. 2.8)

Twenty years later, at the Conservative Party conference on 7 October 1992, Secretary of State for Education, John Patten, railed against '1960s theorists', 'the trendy left' and 'teachers' union bosses', who were destroying 'our great literary heritage'. In a speech that attacked not only the trades unions but also popular culture, he warned: 'They'd give us chips with Chaucer. Milton with mayonnaise. Mr Chairman, I want William Shakespeare in our classrooms, not Ronald McDonald' (Patten 1992).

Discourse

Dominant social and cultural groups have been able to establish their language, and their knowledge priorities, learning styles, pedagogical preferences, etc. as the 'official examinable culture' of school – their notions of important and useful knowledge, their ways of presenting truth, their ways of arguing and establishing correctness and their logics, grammars and language as institutional norms by which academic and scholastic success is defined and assessed (Lankshear 1997: 30).

Colin Lankshear goes on to say that the determination of 'the official examinable culture of the school' by dominant social and cultural groups is not necessarily a conscious process and far less a conspiracy:

It is simply what tends to happen, with the result that Discourse and discourses of dominant groups become those that dominate education, and become established as major legitimate routes to securing social goods (like wealth and status). As a result, educational success is patterned along distinct lines of prior discursive experience associated with membership of particular social groups.

(Lankshear 1997: 30)

For most of the twentieth century and into the twenty-first century, dominant views about 'notions of important and useful knowledge' and 'ways of arguing and establishing correctness' have formed the basis of school curricula, examination syllabuses and the National Curriculum. Furthermore, assessment methodologies established the 'institutional norms by which academic and scholastic success is defined and assessed'.

With the passing of time, the reiteration of a dominant view leads to the belief that the status quo is the natural order of things by some universal right. Particular curricular content, attitudes, values and practices are accepted rather than interrogated to determine the underpinning value systems: 'A particular set of discourse practices and conventions may achieve a high degree of *naturalisation* – they may come to be seen as simply "there" in a common-sense way, rather than socially put there' (Fairclough 1992: 9).

Schooling and under-achievement

In the latter half of the twentieth century a variety of aspects of school life have been examined in order to identify the causes of pupil under-achievement: access, institutional structures and the nature of school knowledge. It is well documented that, despite the intentions of Education Acts from 1944 to 1988, children from the working class have continued to under-achieve at school. Floud *et al.* (1966) exposed massive under-representation of working-class boys at grammar schools. Douglas (1964) showed how working-class pupils with the same IQ scores as middle-class children were failing to gain grammar school places, because of the bias of teachers in primary schools. IQ tests themselves were shown to have a middle-class bias in their content. It is also now known that the 11+ examination scores of girls were adjusted down because they were far outstripping boys' achievement. (See *The Report of the Task Group on Assessment and Testing* (TGAT) (DfES 1987: 40–53) for a discussion of these issues in relation to the establishment of the National Curriculum.)

Hargreaves (1967), Lacey (1970) and Ball (1981) have cited the institutional structures of schools, such as streaming and banding, as influential in determining the performance of working-class pupils, a disproportionate number of whom were found to be represented in the lower streams and bands. For others, such as Brown (1973), Bourdieu (1973) and Bowles and Gintis (1976), it is the stratification of school knowledge that reproduces inequalities in 'cultural capital'.

This is not to say that working-class pupils are simply passive recipients of a dominant culture. Studies by Gaskell (1985) and Willis (1977, 1981), for example, have shown how pupils resist school culture – although Abraham's (1993) study reveals that resistance comes more from 'anti-school' pupils, whatever their social background. Abraham further argues that: 'the organising and processing of school knowledge provides a setting which is not sufficiently critical of social class and gender divisions to discourage their reproduction in further schooling and out into the occupational structure' (1993: 136).

Conclusion

The central metaphor of the National Curriculum is 'delivery'. Eisner (1984) reminds us that the metaphors we use shape our understanding of the concepts we study. A curriculum to be 'delivered' by a teacher is disempowering of pupils and teachers alike. It is a view of knowledge that is hierarchical, top-down and characterised by prescription and direction. Consequently, it is unsurprising that the 'official examinable culture' of school – the language, knowledge priorities, learning styles and pedagogical preferences – is that of dominant social and cultural groups. It is also well documented that children from the working class under-achieve disproportionately.

The close of the twentieth century was marked by a Conservative prime minister announcing that *Society* did not exist and a New Labour prime minister announcing that we are now all members of the middle class. In recent years it has become unfashionable to discuss social class and education. There appears to be an under-lying assumption that it is now passé to do so: the debate has moved on; social class is an irrelevance. However, it could be argued that the issue has never been properly tackled. In the early 1980s the Inner London Education Authority launched its 'Sex, Race and Class' initiative. While the ILEA did much work relating to the first two, for all its egalitarian zeal it shied away from grasping the nettle of class.

Government figures produced in 1992 showed that only 5 per cent of children from skilled manual home backgrounds attended university (Central Statistical Office 1992). Despite a claimed 30 per cent increase in access to university, in 1998 only approximately 5 per cent of those at university came from the poorest post-code areas (Halsey 1998) – a fact that the introduction of top-up fees in 2005 is unlikely to reverse. Despite the inception of the National Curriculum, designed to ensure equal curricular entitlement for all pupils, and despite Widening Participation rhetoric, children from working-class backgrounds are under-achieving. OECD (1998) statistics declare eight million adults in the UK to be 'functionally illiterate'. Proposals in October 2003 to split Key Stage Four into academic and vocational streams will further widen the gulf between pupils and adults along social-class lines. In Willis (1971) terms, working-class kids will continue to get working-class jobs.

The work of Gee (1992), Mercer (1995), Lankshear (1997) and others offers teachers the possibility of empowering pupils through developing powerful literacies: through participation, collaboration and negotiation; by making discourses visible; and by exposing the ground rules, the underpinning values and beliefs. As a result, pupils and teachers are more likely to recognise, critique and value aspects of their primary discourses and less likely to uncritically take on the language and attitudes of secondary discourses they encounter:

> Learning should lead to the ability for all children . . . to critique their primary and secondary discourses, including dominant secondary discourses. This requires exposing children to a variety of alternative primary discourses and secondary ones (not necessarily so that they acquire them, but so that they learn about them). It also requires a realising explicitly that this is what good teaching and learning is good at.
>
> (Gee 1992: 27)

References

Abraham, J. (1993) *Divide and School: Gender and Class Dynamics in Comprehensive Education*, London: Falmer Press.
Arnold, M. (1869) *Culture and Anarchy*, London: Penguin (1969 edn).
Ball, S. (1981) *Beachside Comprehensive: A Case Study of Secondary Schooling*, London: Cambridge University Press.
Board of Education (BoE) (1910) *Circular, 753*, London: HMSO.
Board of Education (BoE) (1921) *The Teaching of English in England* (Newbolt Report), London: HMSO.
Board of Education (BoE) (1938) *Report on Secondary Education* (Spens Report), London: HMSO.
Bourdieu, P. (1993) *The Field of Cultural Production*, Cambridge: Polity Press.
Bowles, S. and Gintis, H. (1976) *Schooling in Capitalist America: Education and the Contradictions of Economic Life*, London: Routledge & Kegan Paul.
Brown, R. (ed.) (1973) *Knowledge, Education and Cultural Change*, London: Tavistock.
Central Statistical Office (1992) *Social Trends*, no. 22, London: HMSO.
Davison, J. and Dowson, J. (1998) *Learning to Teach English in the Secondary School: A Companion to School Experience*, London: Routledge.
Department for Education and Science (DfES) (1975) *A Language for Life* (Bullock Report), London: HMSO.
Department for Education and Science (DfES) (1987) *The Report of the Task Group on Assessment and Testing* (TGAT), London: HMSO.
Douglas. J. (1964) *The Home and the School*, London: MacGibbon & Kee.
Eisner, E. (1984) *Cognition and Curriculum*, London: Longman.
Fairclough, N. (1992) *Critical Language Awareness*, London: Longman.
Floud, J., Halsey, A. and Martin, F. (1966) *Social Class and Educational Opportunity*, Bath: Chivers.
Gaskell, J. (1985) 'Course Enrolment in High School; The Perspective of Working Class Females', *Sociology of Education* 58: 48–59.
Gee, J.P. (1992) *The Social Mind: Language, Ideology and Social Practice*, New York: Bergin & Harvey.
Gossman, L. (1981) 'Literature and Education', *New Literary History* 13: 341–81.
Graff, H.J. (1987) *The Legacies of Literature: Continuities and Contradictions in Western Society and Culture*, Bloomington, IN: Indiana University Press.
Halsey, A.H. (1998) 'Leagues Apart', *The Times Higher Education Supplement*, 6 February.
Hargreaves, D. (1967) *Social Relations in the Secondary School*, London: Routledge & Kegan Paul.
Lacey, C. (1970) *Hightown Grammar*, Manchester: Manchester University Press.
Lankshear, C. (1997) *Changing Literacies*, Buckingham: Open University Press.
Mercer, N. (1995) *The Guided Construction of Knowledge*, Clevedon: Multilingual Matters.
Organisation for Economic Co-operation and Development (OECD) (1998) *Literacy Skills for the Knowledge Society: Further Results from the International Adult Literacy Survey*, Paris: OECD.
Patten, J. (1992) Speech to Conservative Party Annual Conference, 7 October.
Times Educational Supplement (1915) Report on Lancashire Headteachers' Report, London: Times Newspapers.
Willis, P. (1971) 'Cultural Production is Different from Cultural Reproduction . . .', *Interchange* 12(2–3): 48–67.
Willis, P. (1977) *Learning to Labour: How Working Class Kids Get Working Class Jobs*, Sheffield: Saxon Press.

Key readings

Freire, P. (1985) *The Politics of Education: Culture Power and Liberation*, London: Macmillan.
Gee, J.P. (1992) *The Social Mind: Language, Ideology and Social Practice*, New York: Bergin & Harvey.
Lankshear, C. (1997) *Changing Literacies*, Buckingham: Open University Press.

Mercer, N. (1995) *The Guided Construction of Knowledge*, Clevedon: Multilingual Matters.
Shannon, P. (ed.) (1992*) Becoming Political: Readings and Writings in the Politics of Literacy Education*, Portsmouth, NH: Heinemann.

Focus question

To what extent do you think that the notion of the 'delivery' of knowledge in any subject is a political one, the use of which disadvantages working-class pupils?

CHAPTER 16

THE SUBJECT OF SPIRITUALITY

Mike Radford

The Education Reform Act 1988 (ERA) states the requirement of schools to provide a 'balanced and broadly based curriculum which promotes the spiritual, moral, cultural, mental and physical development of the pupil' (ERA Sect. 1 (2a)). Although religious education does not appear in the National Curriculum, it is nevertheless a requirement that schools provide an 'act of collective worship' and, unless parents apply for their children to be excused, this should be for all pupils. Religious education continues to be a statutory part of the curriculum as required by the 1944 Education Act (HMSO: 2003).

Given the religious diversity and the predominant secularity of the UK population these provisions have given rise to substantial discussion, but this has seen limited development in our understanding of the nature of spiritual development and the role of religious education (NCC 1993; Best 1996; SCAA 1996). There is still a tendency to conflate the spiritual with the personal, emotional, social and moral development of the child (Grainger and Kendall-Seatter 2003) while failing to address its central quality, that is, our human relationship with God. The atheist will retort that many people show no sign of believing in the existence of God, so how can we talk of a relationship in this context. Education may yet deal with religion from a social, cultural or anthropological perspective, but it would be indoctrinatory to teach children about God as a fact when most believe that he is an illusion. The problem is, that to say one believes or does not believe in God is to assume that we know what God is – that there is some shared concept upon which we are all agreed and that forms the basis for our acceptance of denial of his existence.

Religion is the process whereby many people, though by no means all, experience and give articulation to that experience of God. Therefore it might be argued that a central question for religious educators is that of the nature of this experience and the ways in which it is variously articulated. From the point of view of the spiritual development of pupils, the question is that of how this experience relates to themselves, religious or otherwise, in their everyday lives. Has the experience and the concept of God any meaning at all for the secularly minded pupil in contemporary schooling and if so what?

Spiritual development and religious education

The 'natural' home of spiritual development, it might be argued, is in religious education, but what is religious education? Theology is a recognised discipline, an identifiable form of knowledge containing content in the form of texts and employing its own forms of analytical enquiry. Religious education on the other hand may be regarded as a 'field' of knowledge (Hirst 1974: 127) – a region in which different forms of knowledge come together including philosophical, moral and social as well as the study of the world's religions as cultural phenomena. One might be left in this context asking what are its objectives in terms of spiritual development. Given the difficulties associated with this concept, the problem of differences of belief and the predominantly secular and materialist nature of society, it is perhaps natural to find the notion of spiritual development submerged under claims that religious education is about tolerance, multi-cultural perspectives and moral education.

Clearly many human beings have a sense of God as a real presence, as listening to them when they pray and being with them in their daily lives. Comparative studies of religious practice however do not help in conveying this sense to our young atheists. Some devout beliefs and practices manifest themselves in what may appear as strange and eccentric, and others in what might appear distasteful, such as the ritual sacrifice of animals or the mutilation of the human body in circumcision or ritual scarring. God must be a curious form of being in that he is worshipped and confirmed in his existence in so many different ways. Teaching our pupils about such practices poses problems for teachers when religious practices seem to conflict with contemporary Western values and might be more likely to draw derision than respect on the part of our pupils. The notion of God as having relevance to their lives is put even further beyond reach.

Alternatives?

There may be three courses of action open to us. The first and most commonly practised is to tend towards the secularisation of worship and to argue that spiritual education (as required by the ERA) is adequately contained in the moral, social and emotional development of pupils, identified in personal, social and health education and in the social and moral ethos of the school community. Religious Education has a place as a form of social and cultural studies, its importance deriving from the presence of religion as a powerful force in shaping human societies. From scriptural works, as from other forms of literature, we may draw moral teachings. Teaching about religion also complements pupils learning in history, literature, the arts and also about contemporary global society. In so far as it reduces ignorance, it might help dispel prejudice and intolerance. This approach seems to be broadly compatible with the requirements that Ofsted makes of its inspection teams when it comes to the evaluation of this aspect of provision (Ofsted 1995: sect. 5.3).

An alternative course of action is to induct pupils into some form of religious faith within a faith-based school. We may teach them how to worship and encourage the development of what we may term 'a sense of God' (Bowker 1995). Religious Education then becomes a much more enlivened subject in so far as it encourages reflection on a part of the pupils' daily experience of worship. Belief in God is taken for granted – an accepted part of the common understanding of both staff and pupils. We can discuss the nature of God, but prayer as well as discussion is considered important in terms of pupils' understanding. Experiencing the 'presence of God' through prayer and other actions is regarded as the most important and fundamental experience in our lives, and is a foundational assumption in the practice of the school. But this is not without its costs. Such schools tend to be exclusive and to channel spiritual development along what may be considered indoctrinatory lines. It may be argued that this denies children the opportunity to a more creative and open form of spiritual development.

The third approach to this problem of developing a 'sense of God' in a 'godless society' is to seek to deconstruct the experience and see if we can find any basic points of principle that underlie it – principles that might have relevance in the lives of our pupils. There are some key questions that may be relevant to the start of any such enquiry. These are 'why me?', 'what is of ultimate importance to me?' and 'how do I stand in relation to the material order of things?' The first question dwells in the wonder that we might have at our own existence and our distinctive ability among other animals to reflect on that. The second question looks towards the fragility of material existence and the third to the relative unimportance of my life in relation to the unity that I may perceive within the universe of which I am a part.

The question 'why me?' grows out of what has been termed an 'existential angst' (Richmond 1999: 31) that is the tension that I may feel between myself as an isolated centre of consciousness within finite body and the infinite nature of the universe that I inhabit. It may arise in the context of our sense of 'awe and wonder' at both the great and small universes uncovered by science or from the sheer puzzle articulated in the question of what is the ultimate reason or purpose of my life. A possibly more sophisticated articulation might come in the form of the question, 'how can I as a limited and confined individual come to have a conception of myself, a reflective self-consciousness that recognises myself as a limited entity within a limitless world and universe?' The sense of wonder expressed in this question may be more or less keenly felt by different people (Nagel 1986: 214).

For the religious believer there is a sense of resolution that is achieved through realisation of a relationship with God. This relationship consists of an experience of unity between the self and the experienced other. The question 'why me?' is answered by the statement, 'Because God wills it', and my experience of God's presence makes this response sufficient. But what relevance or meaning has this way of thinking and feeling about the question for the non-believer? Is there any resolution to the puzzle or is he destined to forever suffer the 'existential angst'?

Literary and aesthetic possibilities

The closing scenes of the film *American Beauty* (Ball 1999) feature the dying moments of the central character, Lester Burnham. In these moments he describes a sense of timelessness – of his life as both instantaneous and as extending forever. He also describes an intense feeling for the beauty of the world and of his own unimportance within the broader context of the reality within which he exists. There is a sense of reconciliation and an ability to let go of the material world in a way that is both ultimately fulfilling and final (Ball 1999: 144–9). Somerset Maugham writes in a similar way when he has his character, Larry Darrell in *The Razor's Edge*, describing a sunrise in the mountainous forests of southern India. As with Lester Burnham, Larry senses his own detachment from the beauty that surrounds him. In Darrell's experience there is a letting go of his own materiality and of reconciliation, 'so that everything that had been confused was clear and everything that had perplexed me was explained' (Maugham 1998: 298).

Both these experiences are undoubtedly aesthetic in nature but they also have a spiritual dimension in so far as they address the question of the relationship between the reflective consciousness and that being conceived. In each instance there is a letting go of the materially defined part of our lives, a realisation of release and a sense of distance from the mundanity of the world. In both instances the writer records the possibility of a sense of unity as the self dissolves, becoming a part of that which is being perceived, and a sense of resolution of the tension implicit in human existence. These literary realisations reach back to the literary tradition of the early Romantics, in particular the poetry of William Wordsworth and John Keats, and there is much more to be said about the spiritual dimension that is implicit in our capacity to experience beauty (Radford 2001).

The point that may be made here is that the experience of the self – the sense of purpose and the tension experienced in our existence – is, to some extent, dissolved by the experience of beauty wherever this is achieved, including through acts of love and human kindness. I am not sure how far this will address the problem of the spiritual development of our atheistic pupils, but at least it offers a possible opportunity to focus attention and address this quality in human experience, outside the context of conflicting forms of religious articulation. If we can bring pupils to this point of realisation then we may be in a much stronger position to bring them to the religious texts that try to describe this sense of being in contexts other than the contemplation of beauty.

References

Ball, A. (1999) *American Beauty*, London: FilmFour Books.
Best, R. (ed.) (1996) *Education, Spirituality and the Whole Child*, London: Cassell.
Bowker, J. (1995) *The Sense of God* (2nd edn), Oxford: Oneworld.
Grainger, T. and Kendall-Seatter, S. (2003) 'Drama and Spirituality: Reflective Connections', *International Journal of Children's Spirituality*, 8(1): 25–32.
Hirst, P. (1974) *Knowledge and the Curriculum*, London: Routledge & Kegan Paul.
HMSO (2003) *Education Reform Act 1988*, available at www.hmso.gov.uk/acts/acts1988/ Ukpga_19880040_en_2.htm (accessed 16 September 2003).
Maugham, S. (1998) *The Razor's Edge*, London: Mandarin.
Nagel, T. (1986) *The View from Nowhere*, Oxford: Oxford University Press.
NCC (1993) *Spiritual and Moral Development : A Discussion Paper*, London: NCC.
Ofsted (1995) *The Ofsted Handbook*, London: HMSO.
Radford, M. (2001) 'Aesthetic and Religious Awareness Among Pupils: Similarities and Differences, *British Journal of Music Education* 18(2): 151–9.
Richmond, J. (1999) 'Reconsidering Aesthetic and Religious Experience: A Companion View', *Journal of Aesthetic Education* 33(4): 28–41.
SCAA (1996) *Education for Adult Life: The Spiritual and Moral Development of Young People*, London: SCAA.

Key readings

Anderson, J. (1980) 'Religion in Education', in *Education and Inquiry*, Oxford: Basil Blackwell.
Best, R. (ed.) (1996) *Education, Spirituality and the Whole Child*, London: Cassell.
SCAA (1996) *Education for Adult Life: The Spiritual and Moral Development of Young People*, London: SCAA.
Wright, A. (2000) *Spirituality and Education*, London: Routledge.

Focus question

How far do you think there should be an emphasis on the value of 'spirituality' in schools? Shouldn't schooling, like education, be secular?

CHAPTER 17

WHO IS THE GOOD CITIZEN?

Simon Hughes

This essay seeks to challenge and reopen the debate about what constitutes a good citizen. Since the year 2000 all schools have been bound to inculcate their pupils with a set of values that have been determined at the very heart of government under the label 'Citizenship'. On the one hand this appears to be a liberal and modern way of encouraging young people to participate in the democratic processes. For some, though, it represents a form of creeping totalitarianism predicated on a contested set of values and which could be seen more as an exercise in social control and the subtle delimitation of freedoms.

The project of Citizenship education is potentially vast, so a systematic analysis of the concept of *political literacy* has become the focus for this essay; the hope is that others will 'pick up the baton' and critique other aspects. The method used is biographical as it examines the response of some key figures to the challenge of being a *good* citizen. Inevitably questions are asked of these people, such as:

Nelson Mandela – global citizen or enemy of the state?

Central to the controversy is disagreement about the attitudes, values, beliefs and behaviours of people in the practice of their citizenship, since there will always be debate about the philosophical term 'good'.

The National Curriculum for Schools (QCA 2000) sponsors the teaching of Citizenship education, drawing on the work undertaken by Sir Bernard Crick and the team of people commissioned to look into education for Citizenship and democracy (Crick 1998). There are three strands within the orders:

- education about what it means to be a citizen;
- social responsibility;
- political literacy.

For many the introduction of Citizenship education characterised thus is not contentious; rather, it is to be applauded because it will enable schools to focus on training pupils for life in consensus-driven adult society. Pupils will be encouraged to exercise relational propriety, financial responsibility, community care and social praxis. Philosophically however it remains problematic, because the actions by which pupils' citizenship is judged might be prescribed by persons with no understanding of their context and whose preconceptions about being a 'good citizen' might be prejudiced by their culture, class or belief system.

One answer to these questions is that a good citizen is 'politically literate' (Crick 1998). In other words they know, understand and are able to exercise informed judgements about political matters. They can evaluate political activity and behaviours and can engage with the tools of democracy. Taken at face value this is admirable and such a view is reinforced upon an examination of a unit of work that derives from this thinking:

> They understand the importance of human rights, and recognise why the Universal Declaration of Human Rights and later conventions like the UN Convention on the Rights of the Child were adopted and endorsed by nations across the world.
>
> (DfES 2000)

There is, however, an alternative perspective. The fundamental premise of the Citzenship agenda is that UK parliamentary democracy was not only the beginning but is the end of the debate about political representation and engagement. Clearly it follows then, in the minds of those who promote the agenda, that no other political system needs to be considered and that Citizenship teachers have the simple task of demonstrating to pupils the importance of exercising their democratic rights, the need to avoid apathy in and towards politics at all costs and the compunction to make informed choices about the party political alternatives available.

This is, however, disingenuous because true political literacy would necessarily expose learners to the full range of political theories and ideologies that have found historical voice and expression, even if their learning might threaten the stability of the present political system. For example, a person could not be said to be politically literate if they had not had the opportunity to examine Marxist political thought and theory and to study the many countries that have or are governed by a regime with this as its ideological base; nor indeed would it be *good* education if a learner had not had the chance to examine National Socialism. It would be possible, therefore, for someone to be an accredited 'good citizen', under the terms of the National Curriculum, but never engage in thoughts or actions that were political or (party) Political.

A further problem, noted by those on the right wing of this debate, is that pupils in UK schools are subjects, not citizens. Her Majesty may abrogate responsibility for government to her Prime Minister and her/his cabinet, but her people are subject to her laws and her taxes and are policed by her agents. Those who commit crimes against society or the nation are tried in a *Crown Court*. For example, Pat Magee, the so-called Brighton Bomber, was convicted and jailed for his attack on the Grand Hotel during the Conservative Party Conference in September 1984. Had his attack been made against the Queen he would have been tried for treason. That he attempted to assassinate the Prime Minister, and in the process killed four others, is beyond question, but his crime in British law was murder not treachery. At the time the IRA were engaged in what they termed an 'armed struggle' against an occupying nation and that violence was the justified last resort of a people to whom access to the democratic process had been denied. Given the clarity of his thought and the accuracy of his assessment of the political conditions in which he was operating, he could well be described as being politically literate. Presumably he would have achieved a National Curriculum level 8 had his Citizenship been examined.

Clearly there is an equation between political literacy and activism that can be defined as the enactment of political dogmas, doctrines and ideologies. Historically it can be seen that activism is related to political struggles or struggles for participatory politics: the Tolpuddle Martyrs sparked the modern right to association; the Trades Union Movement won the right for the working person to exercise the powerful political tool of the withdrawal of labour and the Suffragettes drove, through non-violent direct action, the then government to extend the right to vote to women. Demonstrations, hunger-strikes, leafleting, rallies, sit-ins, picketing and so on have all become legitimate tools for exerting political pressure on issues of injustice. An understanding of these facets of activism ought to form a part of a mature syllabus in political literacy. A National Curriculum for Citizenship that did not teach these as means to achieve political ends would be like a National Curriculum for Chemistry that did not teach about Bunsen burners. Interestingly they do not appear in the prescribed curriculum, which can therefore be charged with encouraging not participation but conformity, collusion and complicity.

Could it be that the traditions of British activism outlined above are to be denied or omitted as education becomes tasked with increasing participation? Or worse, might someone only be described as a 'good' citizen if they were to renounce activism and seek only to maintain the status quo? It has been argued that the reasons for apathy lie not in the assumed consensus described above but rather in the death of politics itself. For school-age children activism has been reduced to working in and around environmental issues. *Good* citizens recycle, save whales, use Body Shop products, picket livestock carriers in Dover and occasionally attack battery farms or GM plantations. At maturity, however, few convert this into a Green vote (16.6 per cent of PGCE Secondary initial teacher trainees at Canterbury Christ Church University College were prepared to report their support for the Green Party in 2001 General Election). The use of animals for sport, pleasure or cosmetics is just about the only issue that divides classrooms as weary teachers attempt to engage debate and stimulate discussion. Despite what the Countryside Alliance might say there is only a small minority who convert their opinions into activism. Frequently the majority ask the rhetorical question, 'What's the point [of politics or political involvement]?' Occasionally they might ask the more cynical question, 'What's in it for me?'

Research points to a complexity of reasons for this, including the increasing levels of material comfort that most young people experience, the stupefying effect of mass media penetration into homes, increased mobility and the solipsistic outcomes of much contemporary education. In short, young people have become depoliticised. There is a diminishing number of issues over which they are prepared to take action. For instance, the most common student response to the uncapping of tuition fees in universities is to secure part-time work. Such responsibility is applauded by parents and politicians increasingly freed of the financial burden of the human right to education, but it serves not to increase political literacy. It could be argued that the present student population is not politically *illiterate*, rather it is non-literate in that it does not even possess the tools for engagement with political 'stuff'.

In reality the Citizenship project could be conceptualised as an attempt to inculcate those values most often associated with white, middle- and upper middle-class power structures and the kind of patriarchy that has underpinned western hegemonic expressions of Christianity. Indeed, the New Labour project that has embraced Citizenship education derives much of its conceptual framework from the Christian Socialist agenda, which the politically literate could characterise as centrist, hierarchical and exclusive. In the new millennium being a good citizen cannot just be about going to a Christian place of worship, doing 'good' deeds and belonging to a neighbourhood watch scheme. In any case, recourse to Christian doctrine as a justification for this approach to political literacy and engagement is misplaced too. There is no doubt that Jesus was a great prophet, and for some people he was and is the Son of God, but he was also an enemy of the state and was tried, convicted and executed as such by the government of his time. He was a victim of the political system, though his death has been theologised into the great work of salvation.

An honest approach to Citizenship education *should* therefore include teaching that encourages activism and an appraisal of systems that can both enable and liberate but also enslave or oppress. Mandela was enslaved and incarcerated for his activism and for his participation in political life; few would argue, however, that he exhibits now political literacy on a global scale. That he was a terrorist is a time-bound historical fact; that he has become one of the most famous and celebrated citizens of the global community is also fact. Put together, these two facts serve to demonstrate that the question of what constitutes a *good* Citizen remains an area for considerable debate.

References

Crick, B. (1998) *Education for Citizenship and the Teaching of Democracy in Schools. Final Report of the Advisory Group on Citizenship*, London: QCA, 98/245.
Qualifications and Curriculum Authority (QCA) (2000) *Citizenship at Key Stages 3 and 4*, London: QCA/00/581.

Key readings

Character Education Partnership, http://www.character.org/.
Citizenship Foundation, http://www.citizenshipfoundation.org.uk/.
Crick, B. (1998) *Education for Citizenship and the Teaching of Democracy in Schools. Final Report of the Advisory Group on Citizenship*, London: Qualifications and Curriculum Authority, 98/245.
DfES (2000) www.standards.dfes.gov.uk/schemes2/ks4citizenship/cit01/428871?view=get.
Gutierrez, G. (1970) *A Theology of Liberation*, New York: SCM.
Initial Teacher Training Citizenship, http://www.ittcitized.info/index.pl.
Mandela, N. (1994) *Long Walk to Freedom*, New York: Little Brown & Company.

Focus question

How can citizenship be more than a concern with 'green' and other single issues when there are no political movements in which young people can be active?

CHAPTER 18

CITIZENSHIP EDUCATION
Reflecting a political malaise

Kevin Rooney

> We aim at no less than a change in the political culture of this country both nationally and locally.
>
> (Crick 1998: 7)

Sounding more like something you would find in a political party's manifesto, this ambitious statement is actually to be found in the final report of an influential advisory group on citizenship education, the new compulsory subject being taught in our schools.

But can citizenship education succeed where our political leaders have failed in creating a new generation who will engage with the political process and espouse a new set of moral values?

As citizenship education gathers ever more momentum, it is time to challenge some of the claims made by the influential advocates of this new subject. As one of the new band of citizenship teachers, I speak as someone who thoroughly enjoys citizenship lessons, but who has become increasingly sceptical about the motives behind its introduction into our schools. More than anything I seek to stimulate debate among educationalists about the underlying assumption that citizenship education will help create a new generation of young people prepared to engage more actively with the political system.

What is citizenship education?

From August 2002 citizenship entered the National Curriculum as a statutory subject at key stage levels 3 and 4. There are three strands involved:

- Social and Moral Responsibility – defined as morally responsible behaviour both inside and beyond the classroom, towards those in authority and to each other.
- Community Involvement – learning through community involvement and service to the community.
- Political Literacy – an understanding of Britain's political institutions, parties and civil society.

The course itself reflects a variety of contemporary themes including multiculturalism, human rights and 'global community'. The stated aim of studying the subject is not so much acquiring a body of knowledge, but acquiring the enquiry and communication skills needed to encourage participation in society (QCA 2000: 14).

Why the need for a new subject?

The stated aim of introducing this new subject into the education system is to reverse the decline in young people's participation in public and political life in the UK. The influential Crick Report, which effectively gave birth to citizenship education, argued that research revealed 'an historic political disconnection. In effect an entire generation has opted out of party politics' (Crick 1998: 22).

The debate about the alienation of young people from politics has absorbed many academics and policy makers around New Labour for some time. Reports published by influential think-tanks like the Institute of Public Policy Research (IPPR) and DEMOS have acknowledged that the British political system is facing a crisis of legitimacy and all the political parties have lost their social base and find it particularly difficult to connect with young people (Wilkinson and Mulgan 1995; Hallgarton 2000). While some commentators are reassured by the new forms of political engagement displayed by environmental campaigns or the anti-globalisation protests, research from the British Youth Council shows that less than 2 per cent of young people got involved with any kind of direct action campaign over the previous year.

Citizenship education is certainly not the only government-sponsored initiative to tackle this malaise. A government known for its almost obsessive stream of new initiatives has come up with a variety of proposals to get young people to start voting, including polling booths in shopping malls, internet and postal voting, and even lowering the voting age to 16. But few suggestions have been as radical and far-reaching as introducing an entire new compulsory subject for all 11–16-year-olds in the UK.

Lack of debate

One of the most striking things about citizenship education is the speed with which it has moved from the theoretical musings of 'policy wonks' to the school classroom. While the wheels of change may grind slowly in many areas of education, this could never be said of the rapid integration of this new subject into the curriculum. Bernard Crick himself acknowledges the speed with which the government 'moved so quickly on citizenship ... probably for very much the same reasons stated in the group's report' (Crick 2000: 11). While in the past educationalists might have challenged the notion that teachers are to be made responsible for teaching moral values and reducing crime, what is striking about citizenship education is the lack of controversy around its introduction. Teaching unions, exam boards, political parties and pressure groups have all welcomed the new subject and endorsed the idea that it could play a positive role in combating youth apathy (Lawton *et al.* 2000).

That is not to say there is no discussion over what and how students should learn (Kerr 1999) and concerns have been expressed by Ofsted about managing the introduction of citizenship to a satisfactory standard. But what is lacking is any real philosophical or political debate over the introduction of this new subject. The goal of this chapter is to incite such a debate. I believe that educationalists and policy makers alike need to address a number of fundamental questions about citizenship education.

Will it work?

The obvious answer to the question 'Will citizenship education work?' and one that will be offered by advocates of citizenship is 'Only time will tell'. And of course nobody is arguing that a year of citizenship lessons will transform young people into budding community activists. However, the international examples don't bode well for the UK experiment.

There has long been an acceptance within the United States that responsibility for preparing students to be effective democratic citizens rests with the education system. Yet despite the well-established 'civics programme' in American schools, the young electorate seems even more reluctant to vote than its UK counterpart. According to US expert Morris Janovitz (1993), two decades of civics education have failed to achieve the enhanced levels of civic engagement that they openly seek to promote. France and Australia also have well-established civics programmes and voting trends that continue on the downward slope. The international context provides little to instil confidence in citizenship education programmes, but citizenship enthusiasts in the UK have an answer to that – it's the style of teaching. According to this view citizenship education is failing in the US only because of its 'didactic teaching and passive learning' (Conover *et al.* 1991).

My answer would be rather different. Even without sufficient evidence from the UK experiment, I would argue that citizenship education is doomed to fail. I believe that what the international examples are telling us is that voter apathy is a result of a stale political climate rather than poor teaching. I have seen nothing to convince me that political illiteracy produces voter apathy or vice versa. Indeed my own experience after many years of teaching politics A Level is of highly literate students who understand the political systems but still choose not to vote.

If the reality is that the current political culture is failing to inspire or engage young people, it follows that there is little that can be done in the classroom to rectify this.

Of course most citizenship supporters acknowledge that there is more to creating active citizens than teaching a new subject (Addison 2001). However, they would argue that it is one key measure that, if introduced alongside other government attempts to connect with young people, can help stem the tide of apathy.

On one level it would seem fatuous to argue with this, and if the fact that citizenship is unlikely to deliver on its ambitious goals was the only area of concern, we could just wait around for a few years and see whether the UK evidence proves me right. But it is not the only concern.

Is it a teacher's job to create active citizens?

Many educationalists and commentators now believe that teachers do have a role to play in turning young people into active citizens who use their vote and participate in civil life: 'Citizenship is a positive step forward in challenging voter apathy . . . as political illiteracy and ignorance can breed a nation of alienated citizens' (Addison 2001: 26).

For many of those involved in this debate the failure of the education system has been a major factor in creating the current crisis. As Morely and Rassool point out, people are quick to equate poor education with political illiteracy and voter apathy: 'Teachers are held responsible for alleged falling education standards, plus a range of social ills such as youth crime, violence, young people's alienation and disaffection' (cited in Lawton *et al.* 2000: 7).

Citizenship teachers are encouraged to emphasise the historic importance of voting and remind pupils that the suffragettes and others died to win the vote. Within course materials for citizenship, the act of voting is presented as a heroic gesture. People who vote are presented as having a higher moral value than those who casually forget the historic battles of their forefathers.

We are even told to emphasise the political differences between the current arrays of political parties – something of a challenge at a time when the ideological differences between parties seem to be lost on most of their own members.

But blaming the education system for failing to produce 18-year-olds who are bursting to vote in local, national and European elections is an outrageous cop-out by politicians and policy makers. It also misses the point as to where real responsibility lies for the current malaise.

In my view no amount of moralising about the need to vote will inspire enthusiasm in young people who find nothing in the current political culture to inspire or enthuse them.

Like many of my contemporaries, I didn't need lessons in citizenship to teach me the importance of the vote. Growing up in Belfast in the 1960s and 1970s, I eagerly awaited my eighteenth birthday and the opportunity to cast my vote. While I certainly wouldn't recommend conflict as a way of increasing the vote, what inspired many in my generation in Belfast and others throughout Britain was the battle of ideas represented by elections. Voting mattered because different parties laid out contrasting visions of the future and the kind of society you could be a part of. It is the total failure of today's political leaders to provide a vision of the future or a battle of ideas that is responsible for young people's lack of interest in politics.

While I have some sympathy with the idea that poor education leads to disaffection, I would argue passionately that citizenship education is not the right response. If anything the complete lack of intellectual rigour and educational value of the subject is in many ways itself a symptom of falling standards. My argument would be that the role of teachers is to provide the best possible liberal education, which equips students with the knowledge and skills to become all-rounded, critical thinking individuals.

The task of the political class is to re-establish points of contact with young people through creating a dynamic political environment where ideas and beliefs are openly contested.

For me, one of the most disturbing aspects of the embracing of citizenship by educationalists is the way that it has allowed politicians to shift the blame for a political problem on to teachers.

Is it possible to teach firm moral values in a society that struggles to define them?

For many advocates of citizenship education the actual act of voting is less important than the urgent need to instil a new set of moral values in today's young generation. They acknowledge that almost all the institutions that once represented the moral arbiters of our times – the Church, the family, trades unions, political parties and scientists – can no longer be relied on to inspire the necessary trust and respect to impart morality to the nations youth. Citizenship education holds out the hope of offering future generations the kind of moral compass now sadly lacking in society. Nick Tate, the former Chief Executive of the Qualifications and Curriculum Authority, clearly thought that citizenship education is about promoting and transmitting 'values'.

This is a common view. Being interested in politics is seen to be tightly bound up with being a moral being and where there exists political apathy there must exist moral apathy. But is it possible for teachers to transmit a common standard of moral values at a time when society appears to have such difficulty in defining what those common values are?

This was a challenge that even the most passionate advocates of citizenship failed to meet. The National Forum for Values in Education – the body charged with contributing a set of common values into the Crick Report – struggled to reach agreement on what constitutes a common set of values in today's society. To avoid a split and after a series of threatened walkouts, its final report was a banal compromise of views which could mean all things to all people. One commentator on citizenship has pointed out that replacing traditional morality in an age of moral uncertainty leads to a rather fluid concept – what might be called a 'virtual morality' (Beck 1998).

One way that citizenship education has sought to overcome this moral vacuum is by redefining morality and introducing new values more closely linked to personal behaviours. At first glance the citizenship curriculum may look like it's promoting the same old traditional values of honesty, fairness and so on. However, closer inspection reveals that alongside these goes a set of personal behaviours recast as moral values. For example, 'community' is now a value, as is participation (voting), voluntary work and caring for the environment. It's also worth taking a look at the list of prescribed values in the overview of essential elements to be reached by the end of compulsory schooling (Crick 1998: 14).

Whose values are we teaching?

This redefining of personal behaviours into moral values leads to the question of whose values are we teaching?

While volunteering and concern for the environment may be desirable, should they be prescribed as values? And where is the space for intellectual debate about these activities? In the past the education system was asked to produce well-educated young people capable of making independent decisions about what to do with their lives. Now teachers are meant to produce people with a particular set of views repackaged as moral values.

And what of those young people who may reject the prescriptive values taught in citizenship lessons. Official guidelines emphasise that students must demonstrate a concern and commitment for the values laid out in order to achieve a good assessment. So what marks will be awarded to the young man who has concluded that there is no point in voting, or the young woman who feels that 'sustainable development' may be robbing the developing world of the most advanced technology, or the pupil who has decided to get involved in party politics – with the British National Party?

It is understandable that a government that is desperate to re-engage young people would like to see young people regarding volunteering and voting as moral values, but using education as a tool of social engineering is a dangerous move and one that teachers should question.

Conclusion

Advocates of citizenship may argue that my critique offers no alternative solutions to the crisis of alienation and apathy among the nation's youth. They point out that my vision of a good all-round liberal education system feeding young people into a dynamic political culture with strong moral values is all well and good in an ideal world – but we don't have an ideal world and something must be done.

No one would agree more than me that something must be done when an entire generation appears to have turned its back on the political system. But I would strongly argue that citizenship education is the wrong response and one which brings new problems in its wake.

By transforming the act of political participation into a subject that can be taught, the proponents of citizenship have trivialised and undermined the whole concept of political activity.

A striking example of this trivialisation is the way that many advocates of citizenship believe that young people can be encouraged to acquire the 'habit' of political participation. The widespread establishment of new forms of school councils and youth parliaments are intended to turn the school into some kind of participation factory that will churn out students who are used to participating.

But this reduces the essence of political activity to the utterly banal. The truth is that no amount of practising will perfect the art of active involvement in society. Throughout history people have become involved in politics when they believe they can make a real difference and effect real change. Relying on the education system to revitalise a stagnant political culture is not only doomed to failure, it is also a dangerous attempt to shift the responsibility from where it really lies – with the political leaders who have completely failed to inspire our young people with a vision of a society worth engaging in.

Despite the enthusiasm of those behind the introduction of citizenship, the reality is that this new subject is more a reflection of the current malaise than a recipe for it. It says a lot about our political leaders' lack of confidence in their own system that they now feel their best chance of persuading people to take part is by putting it alongside maths and English as a compulsory subject.

References

Addison, B. (2001) 'Teaching Citizenship', in Association of Citizenship Teaching (eds), *Turning the Tide*, Birmingham: Questions Publishing.

Beck, J. (1998) *Morality and Citizenship in Education*, London: Cassell.

Conover, P.J., Crewe, I. and Searing, D. (1991) 'The Nature of Citizenship in the United States and Great Britain: Empirical Comments on Theoretical Themes', *Journal of Politics* 53(3): 800–32.

Crick, B. (1998) *Education for Citizenship and the Teaching of Democracy in Schools*, London: QCA.

Crick, B. (2000) *Essays on Citizenship*, London: Continuum.

Hallgarten, J. (2000) *Tomorrows Citizens*, London: IPPR.

Janovitz, M. (1993) *The Reconstruction of Patriotism: Education of Civic Consciousness*, Chicago, IL: University of Chicago Press.

Kerr, D. (1999) *Re-examining Citizenship Education: The Case of England*, Slough: NFER.

Lawton, D., Cairns, J. and Gardiner, R. (2000) *Education for Values*, London: Kogan Page.

Qualifications and Curriculum Authority (QCA) (2000) *National Curriculum: Key Stages 3–4 Citizenship*, London: QCA.

Wilkinson, H. and Mulgan, G. (1995) *Freedom's Children*, London: DEMOS.

Key readings

Gearon, L. (2003) *How Do We Learn To Become Good Citizens?*, BERA Professional User Review, Southwell: British Educational Research Association.

Halpern, D., John, P. and Morris, Z. (2002) 'Before the Citizenship Order: A Survey of Citizenship Education Practice in England', *Journal of Education Policy* 17(2): 217–28.

Wilkinson, H. and Mulgan, G. (1995) *Freedom's Children*, London: DEMOS.

Focus question

Should it be the task of educators to solve what is in effect a political problem of disaffected and disengaged young people?

PART IV

CHANGING TIMES? CHANGING EDUCATION

CHAPTER 19

GREENING EDUCATION

Dominic Wood

Since environmentalists emerged in the 1960s they have focused on education as being both a contributing factor to environmental problems and a possible solution to them: 'The ecological crisis . . . is a crisis *of* education, not one *in* education' (Orr 1996: 7). They have presented radical critiques of existing educational practices (Bowers 1993; 1995; 2001) as well as suggesting alternative approaches to ensuring that education produces environmentally responsible citizens. The argument I wish to present is that achieving environmental responsibility as an educational goal represents a retreat from education. It is important educators recognise this and, no matter how serious environmental problems are, and no matter what society deems to be an appropriate political response to these problems, educational principles should not be sacrificed in order to produce an environmentally aware populace.

The imperative nature of a green perspective leads to ambivalence towards democracy

An immediate concern for educationalists is that calls to green education represent an ambivalence towards democracy. This is a concern for educationalists because education is founded upon the open and democratic spirit of disinterested inquiry. Green attitudes towards democracy are not straightforward and simple; however, a number of reasons why greens are ambivalent towards democracy have been noted. First, it is argued that this ambivalence arises from the nature of what Bonnett (1999: 315) refers to as 'ecological imperatives'. He makes reference to the incompatibility of democracy and ecological sustainability to argue that, if we accept that 'nature has intrinsic value, giving it priority over things that have contingent, instrumental value', we remove an increasing number of ecological imperatives from the democratic arena of debate. From this, he argues, the democratic process is determined by, and reduced to being a means of achieving, ecological imperatives: democracy is thus reduced to being a peripheral and 'contingent value'.

Second, this ambivalence is said to reflect environmentalists' concerns with the impending doom scenarios of environmental catastrophe. Dobson (2000: 117) illustrates this second aspect by asking rhetorically, 'if getting the right thing done is more important than how it gets done, why should greens not endorse authoritarian means to green ends?'.

Dobson is sympathetic towards those who are impatient with the slow pace of democratic responses to urgent matters. However, he argues that greens are not generally authoritarian by nature and that it is wrong to present greens as being anti-democratic: green thought, he argues, opposes *liberal* democracy, not democracy per se. Dobson goes on to suggest a number of reasons why greens should support democracy and extend it beyond its liberal interpretation. Eckersley (1996; 1999) also insists that an ecological perspective promotes a stronger form of democracy in which there is greater representation of other species, future generations, etc. She has argued that the green movement emerged as part of the civil rights movement – what she calls the 'environmental problematic as a crisis of participation' (Eckersley 1992: 8) – pointing out that greens were concerned with what was happening to the environment *and* the fact that people had no control over why this was happening.

In other words, it might be true to say that greens do not give democracy unconditional support, but who does? Indeed, Dobson (2000) argues that liberals are also ambivalent towards democracy when illiberal consequences arise from democratic processes. We favour pupils coming to understand the world themselves, but we are horrified when this understanding does not conform to a liberal perspective. So does the greening of education pose a new threat or is it merely a different form of the same educational concern that has always existed between the processes and products of education?

The green dilemma

On the one hand green ambivalence towards democracy is not that different from liberal concerns with balancing openness, with the possibility of getting it wrong, and a commitment to rational inquiry, where it is assumed that there is only one correct conclusion. However, at the same time, this green ambivalence is an exaggerated form of the liberal ambivalence towards democracy. The 'green dilemma', i.e. the tension between allowing people choice and recognising that they might choose the wrong thing, represents an extension and exaggeration of the 'liberal dilemma'. On the one hand, greens are committed to extending the democratic franchise further than liberals have been willing to. On the other hand, the potentially dire repercussions of choosing a non-green option as a consequence of greater openness, i.e. what happens when voters 'make ecologically bad decisions' (Eckersley 1996: 212), are seen to be so much more catastrophic than illiberal choices.

It is the exaggerated nature of the green dilemma that should be a concern to educationalists because despite greens' desires to extend democratic and open debate, the severity of environmental concerns leads to the 'ecological imperatives' that undermine the open, democratic nature of education.

The imposition of green values upon education

Greens believe that we require a transformation in our attitudes and values. An example is Orr (1992), who contrasts the relatively peaceful and harmonious lifestyles of 'indigenous' peoples with the barbaric ventures of 'educated' people, particularly throughout the twentieth century. He has suggested that there is something wrong in the way we educate at present and he proposes a reorganising of education with a different curriculum and reading list. Others too have stressed the need for us to re-educate ourselves. Schumacher (1993 [1973]: 79), in his seminal book *Small is Beautiful*, saw the responsibility of his generation as being 'one of metaphysical reconstruction'. There are more 'pragmatic' approaches that are critical of what they see as 'idealist' green views on education, but the overall focus within green thought has been on how education can bring about a change in people's attitudes and values in favour of an environmental perspective.

It is these kinds of arguments about attitudes and values that have influenced government thinking on environmental education in the UK. In the late 1980s and early 1990s there were discussions about how environmental education could be incorporated into the educational system in the UK. There was a debate as to whether environmental education should be 'about', 'through' or 'for' the environment and it was primarily the 'education *for* the environment' view that gained the support of the government. Environmental education was introduced into the school curriculum as a 'cross-curricular theme' rather than as a core subject (NCC 1990) and the Toyne Report (DoE 1993) and its *Review* (DfEE 1996) promoted achieving environmental responsibility as a core aim within further and higher education.

Bonnett (1997) has discussed these developments as representing environmental education as 'an approach to learning'. In other words, it is a way of perceiving education in general rather than being a disciplinary sub-set of the curriculum. It involves more than studying environmental issues; it involves adopting an environmental perspective on all matters concerning education, including administrative and organisational aspects of educational institutions. It also promotes the view that everyone needs to be environmentally educated – that everyone 'has some scope for doing his or her job in a more environmentally responsible way' (DoE 1993: 5). Likewise, Shirley Ali Khan, who has been a key player in the environmental education policy agenda in the further and higher education sector, speaks of 'getting people motivated and activated in the pursuit of sustainability' (Ali Khan 1996: 222).

What these quotations express is a political commitment to the environment, which people may or may not agree with. However, what is of concern to educationalists is the extent to which it represents an imposition upon educational practice.

The need to defend academic space

Montefiore (1975), in his defence of a liberal university education, emphasises the importance of separating the political and the academic. He argues that at times in history political views impose themselves upon education and make it difficult for educational principles to be realised. I believe that we are now living at a time when political concerns for the environment have been imposed upon education. The consequences of this imposition are expressed by Kwong (1997), who refers to the 'literature of despair' used in American schools with sarcastic admiration for the authors' abilities to continually produce new combinations of 'save' and 'earth' in environmental book titles. Kwong criticises the impression that the continued message of despair has upon children, arguing that, while doomsday scenarios attract attention, they also undermine educational initiatives because feelings of despair overwhelm children's inquisitive nature. Kwong (1997: 97) argues that children have a natural interest in the environment and 'can spend hours on their bellies examining an ant hole' and her concern is that, instead of engaging with this interest, 'environmental education programmes often start right in with "issues" teaching'.

A second concern raised by Kwong (1997: 99) is that the focus on values is often at the expense of factual accuracy. She presents a tension between getting children to feel responsible for the environment and teaching them scientific facts about the environment, and she argues that environmental education is producing an 'Eco-kid movement' in which children 'are told explicitly what to do, not how to think'.

Reducing the 'educational footprint'

The demand upon education to produce environmentally responsible citizens is potentially far greater than other demands because it represents more than a practical compromise of academic ideals; its significance is the extent to which it challenges educational principles because they are not desirable, rather than simply because they are not achievable or practical. For example, Alabaster and Blair (1996: 98) see the *political* needs of society, in terms of producing 'a more environmentally literate workforce and citizenry', as being more important than academic concerns about what the greening of education means.

To illustrate what I mean further, consider the notion of an 'educational footprint'. I use this term to convey the extent to which educational principles are compromised by external considerations in the same way that the concept of an 'ecological footprint' is used to measure the impact that human activity has upon the natural world (see Wackernagel *et al.* 2000). The ecological footprint is greater the more diversity of life is reduced, pollution of renewable resources is increased and non-renewable resources are depleted. With the concept of an educational footprint I take the most significant measures to be open, free and disinterested inquiry. These three interrelated features of a liberal education will always tend to be compromised practically. The extent to which they are compromised is measured by the concept of an educational footprint. The educational footprint is greater, the more that these educational principles are compromised.

Greening education increases the educational footprint by raising ecological imperatives over and above educational ones. Just as greens feel the need to reduce the ecological footprint in the world of politics, in education we need to always be aware of the educational footprint and protect the space allowed in society for open and disinterested inquiry. We need to defend the educational imperative that the pursuit of knowledge and the engagement with ideas must be free from ideological and political impositions of any kind. This educational imperative must take precedence over the 'ecological imperative' within educational settings, which is why we should see the calls to green education as an imposition upon, and retreat from, education.

References

Alabaster, T. and Blair, D. (1996) 'Greening the University', in J. Huckle and S. Sterling (eds), *Education for Sustainability*, London: Earthscan, pp. 86–104.
Ali Khan, S. (1996) 'A Vision of a 21st-century Community Learning Centre', in J. Huckle and S. Sterling (eds), *Education for Sustainability*, London: Earthscan, pp. 222–7.
Bonnett, M. (1997) 'Environmental Education and Beyond', *The Journal of the Philosophy of Education* 31(2): 249–66.
Bonnett, M. (1999) 'Education for Sustainable Development: A Coherent Philosophy for Environmental Education?', *Cambridge Journal of Education* 29(3): 313–24.
Bowers, C.A. (1993) *Critical Essays on Education, Modernity, and the Recovery of the Ecological Imperative*, New York: Teachers College Press.
Bowers, C.A. (1995) 'Toward an Ecological Perspective', in W. Kohli (ed.), *Critical Conversations in Philosophy of Education*, London: Routledge, pp. 310–23.
Bowers, C.A. (2001) 'How Language Limits Our Understanding of Environmental Education', *Environmental Education Research* 7(2): 141–51.
DfEE (1996) *Environmental Responsibility: A Review of the 1993 Toyne Report*, London: HMSO.
Dobson, A. (2000) *Green Political Thought* (3rd edn), London: Routledge.
DoE (1993) *Environmental Responsibility: An Agenda for Further and Higher Education* (the Toyne Report), London: HMSO.
Eckersley, R. (1992) *Environmentalism and Political Theory Towards an Ecocentric Approach*, London: UCL Press.
Eckersley, R. (1996) 'Greening Liberal Democracy: The Rights Discourse Revisited', in B. Doherty and M. de Geus (eds), *Democracy and Green Political Thought*, London: Routledge, pp. 212–36.

Kwong, J. (1997) 'An American Perspective on Environmental Literacy: A New Goal for Environmental Education', in B. Aldrich-Moodie and J. Kwong, *Environmental Education*, Studies in Education No. 3, Studies in the Environment No. 9, London: Institute of Economic Affairs, pp. 87–126.

Montefiore, A. (ed.) (1975) *Neutrality and Impartiality: The University and Political Commitment*, London: Cambridge University Press.

National Curriculum Council (NCC) (1990) *Curriculum Guidance 7 Environmental Education*, London: HMSO.

Orr, D.W. (1992) *Ecological Literacy Education and the Transition to a Postmodern World*, Albany, NY: SUNY.

Orr, D.W. (1996) 'Education for the Environment: Higher Education's Challenge of the Next Century', *Journal of Environmental Education* 27(3): 7–10.

Schumacher, E.F. (1993 [1973]) *Small is Beautiful*, London: Vintage Edition.

Wackernagel, M., Chambers, N. and Simmons, C. (2000) *Sharing Nature's Interest: Ecological Footprints as an Indicator of Sustainability*, London: Earthscan.

Key readings

Bonnett, M. (1999) 'Education for Sustainable Development: A Coherent Philosophy for Environmental Education?', *Cambridge Journal of Education* 29(3): 313–24.

Dobson, A. (2000) *Green Political Thought* (3rd edn), London: Routledge.

Palmer, J. (1998) *Environmental Education in the 21st Century: Theory, Practice, Progress and Promise*, London: Routledge.

Focus question

Variations on 'green' ideas such as the 'precautionary principle' and 'sustainable development' are widespread in education. Do they limit or enhance the search for knowledge?

CHAPTER 20

EDUCATION AS ENTERTAINMENT

James Woudhuysen

At first sight there ought to be nothing contentious about the idea of education as entertainment. Who, after all, has not been entertained, at least once in their life, by a great teacher – has not been diverted by the teacher's wit, enthusiasm, bearing, tone of voice, turn of phrase or use of eye contact? And who has not learned something profound from a great entertainment – from a brilliantly performed Shakespearean play, for example? Yet underneath such common ground lurks another idea that ought to be very contentious: the idea that education, to be truly *modern* and therefore *accessible*, should nearly always be *entertaining*, for otherwise it may not be *inclusive*.

This view condescends. It is an attempt to sugar what is obviously thought to be a bitter pill. The *struggle to learn* is, in this conception, not valued for what it is: an active struggle, with the potential that such an activity has to build character among the millions of pupils and students who are prepared to engage in it. No, since the struggle to learn is, very probably, perceived as *painful*, so it is felt that entertainment – a less active, strenuous pursuit of *leisure* – must take some or all of that struggle's place.

In the current culture, education as entertainment marks the final stage in a broader *démarche* from the substantive business of education. That much is confirmed by the specially exalted role given to different forms of play within education.

The role of play in education

Today, influenced both by the spread of information technology (IT) in schools and elsewhere, and by a loathing for what is held to be the authoritarian pedagogy of the past, experts believe that education should not be a one-way exercise in teacher 'chalk and talk' (Woudhuysen 2002a, 2002b, 2003). Despite or perhaps because of the couch-potato implications of recasting education as entertainment, its advocates in the world of education are firm that they want teaching to be interactive and 'student centred'. In a significant borrowing from American management theory and its cult of user delight in new products, they hope that education can prompt awe, wonder, excitement, laughter and exhilaration. In short, educationalists believe that education should be entertaining in the sense that the pupil or student is able to *play with ideas*.

In ancient Greek philosophy, a clear distinction was made between the teacher and the entertainer. In Roman times, a sound body, promoted in part through participation in sport, was seen as useful for the preservation of a sound mind. However today's liberal educationalists take the Romans a step further. They intend that the catchphrase of the Early Learning Centre retail chain – 'Playing to Learn, Learning to Play' – should be understood not just by parents of pre-school children, but by teachers everywhere.

Government policy is to have more and more very young children supervised in formal play sessions at British primary schools. It is sympathetic to the speculation that computer games can provide a model for e-learning, the online school and the corporate university. Importantly, too, government reserves a special place in the curriculum for *sport*.

The Qualifications and Curriculum Authority's chief executive during 2000–1, David Hargreaves, argued that physical education and school sport were 'a vital part of pupils' learning experience, enhancing attainment in other subjects' (O'Leary 2001). Then, announcing a £450 million programme of investment in school sports in October 2002, Tony Blair committed the government to recruiting nearly 16,000 new school sports coordinators and teachers, as well as to a guarantee that all 5–16-year-olds in the UK would receive a minimum of two hours a week of phys-ical education and sport by 2006 (DCMS 2002). Sport is seen as a means of keeping young people engaged and out of trouble (DCMS 2002). Most recently, *chess* has been revived as an excellent means of assisting child development.

It is a short step from here for government to see adult attendance and partici-pation in playful entertainments as a fitting arena for state education. Both junior and senior audiences, after all, were the target of the Millennium Dome (McGuigan and Gilmore 2000), which might best be considered a giant induction of millions into the Blairite conception of citizenship (Lewis *et al.* 1998). Following in the foot-steps of the San Francisco Exploratorium and the Science Museum's Launch Pad, 'hands on' is the philosophy at science museums in Bristol, Cardiff, Edinburgh and Glasgow. Playful interactivity also characterises many exhibits at many Lottery-funded museum developments.

What play means in the classroom

Since the early 1950s and the pioneering work of the Swiss psychologist Jean Piaget, the idea has grown that child development is strongly assisted by a particular activity: play. Play and its effect on schoolchildren have been the concern of key post-war educationalists in both America (Jerome Bruner, Brian Sutton-Smith) and Britain (Peter and Iona Opie). Yet if we build upon the seminal Dutch author on play, Johan Huizinga (Huizinga 1938), we can perhaps sketch those aspects of play that particularly lend themselves to today's educationalists.

Though the attribute of beauty does not attach to play as such, play has a profoundly aesthetic quality about it, and assumes marked elements of beauty. Thus playful classrooms are a matter of ornament and decoration. They are festive.

Play builds social cohesion around rules, order and finite boundaries of time and space. It is a form of discipline in class, but a politically correct one. There are no dunces in the ludic framework for education; there are only those pupils who do not want to be team players.

In play one dis-plays to win admiration. In play we deliberately and enjoyably suspend rationality. Not for nothing are the clownish interpersonal skills of David Beckham the subject of many vacuous studies in class.

Because today's schools frown on competition and want no more risks than are already felt to be present, aspects of play that involve winning, losing and chance are not too prevalent in British education. But playful pedagogy does rely on *new tricks*, in the sense of exploration and improvisation, and it also favours *role play*. Many schoolchildren, for example, are invited to do projects that invite them to imagine they are children of Stone Age people, the subjects of racial attack and so on.

Play as retreat

In play today there is rarely thoughtful experiment, but all too often a relentless trend towards public exposure and disclosure. Play only rarely lives up even to its promise of real mastery and self-development, because it only rarely embraces sustained contemplation, reading or intimate tutorials.

The argument that playful, interactive forms of education are a basic good is misleading. It begins in 1975 with the influential psychologist Mihaly Csikszentmihalyi and his book on leisure, significantly titled *Beyond Boredom and Anxiety* (Csikszentmihalyi 1975). The argument values playful, interactive entertainment not in its own right, but, as Fox and Walker have pointed out, instrumentally. Leisure and entertainment within it are really only celebrated in so far as they reinforce:

- a sensation-based, 'optimal experience' of 'flow', the means to happiness (Csikszentmihalyi 1992); and
- self-esteem, the economy and 'the normalized values of productivity, achievement, challenge, action, and worthiness to dominant societal standards' (Fox and Walker 2002: 18, 23).

Active, public and open though they may appear to be, classroom play and the 'flow' it is based on lead not to education and the liberation of the Self, but to a bogus ecstasy and the diminution of Self. Csikszentmihalyi argues that flow is 'autotelic', in that the autonomous Self makes its own teleology, or goal-directed activity, into something in which 'the doing itself is its own reward' (Csikszentmihalyi 1992: 67). In the flow of Csikszentmihalyi's dancer, rock climber and chess player, all the 'psychic energy' of each is, in a 'spontaneous, almost automatic' manner, focused on the task in hand. Significantly, then, flow stops people being aware of themselves as separate from the actions performed. Indeed, 'in flow there is no need to reflect, because the action carries us forward as if by magic' (Csikszentmihalyi 1992: 53, 54).

In this conception and in many practical ways, too, classroom play becomes not education, but its antithesis. Yet early in New Labour's first administration, it was reported that Cabinet ministers and policy advisers had 'adopted' Csikszentmihalyi as the 'high priest of our future wellbeing' (Chittenden 1997).

In many translations, for a mass audience of youth workers worldwide, *Gamesters Handbook*, written by Donna Brandes and Howard Philips, further popularised Csikszentmihalyi's instrumentalist approach to play. The *Handbook* gathered together scores of games 'for developing self-awareness, confidence, decision-making skills, trust, assertiveness, and just for fun' – in that order (Brandes and Philips 1977, 1982). The *Gamesters* manifesto is worth quoting in full to bring out the therapeutic dimensions of play as it has come to be interpreted today:

> Games can be used constructively and not as pointless activities ... can help sort out problems, the kinds of problems found in inter-personal relationships. They can help social inadequacy by developing co-operation within groups, develop sensitivity to the problems of others through games needing trust, and promote interdependency and a sense of personal identity.
> ... By helping people to relax in groups, games can promote the flow of communication between complete strangers – particularly important with shy people who need additional encouragement.

The 'role playing' aspects of many games provide the security which enables group members to develop their ideas and express themselves. The enjoyment which can be generated by games does more than anything to develop a group identity . . . .

Sitting in a circle . . . gives the same status to everyone, including the leader, and allows a much greater degree of eye contact.

(Brandes and Philips 1982: 7)

In a similar vein, Rice and Yaconelli wrote, more than a decade later:

Winning should be either irrelevant or anticlimactic, never the focus of game playing.

Just as enjoyment is more important than competition, participation is more important than performance . . .

. . . After a game is over, players should be better friends than when the game started.

(1993: 10–11)

Ultimately, education as entertainment turns a noble profession into a relentlessly upbeat and communitarian kind of social work. At the end of the class, everyone has enjoyed playing with each other . . . even if they have learned nothing.

Conclusion

The claims that are now made for play in education are dishonest. Play in that domain today is not about expanding minds, but about what James Heartfield has analysed as the death of the active, conscious Subject (Heartfield 2002). It is a kind of therapeutic mental massage that is fundamentally restrictive and conservative. To give a lurid but telling example: toys have been pressed into service, with no public outcry, to try to cut down on America's unrivalled world lead in teenage pregnancies. No fewer than 40,000 'infant simulators', in the shape of $250 Baby Think It Over electronic dolls that come in five different ethnicities, have been delivered by Federal Express to US high schools since 1993, in the hopes of convincing young girls of the burdens of parenthood (Bax 1999: 121).

Everyone likes to play. But the tasks facing British education are more serious than ever.

References

Bax, P. (1999) 'Pauline Thinks It Over', in J. Abrams (ed.), *If/Then*, Amsterdam: Netherlands Design Institute.

Brandes, D. and Philips, H. (1977) *Gamesters Handbook*, Cheltenham: Stanley Thornes Publishers, 1990.

Brandes, D. and Philips, H. (1982) *Gamesters Handbook Two*, London: Hutchinson Education.

Bruner, J., Jolly, A. and Sylva, K. (eds) (1976) *Play: its Role in Development and Evolution*, Harmondsworth: Penguin Books.

Chittenden, M. (1997) 'Labour's Guru Puts "Flow" Before Sex', *The Sunday Times*, 21 December.

Csikszentmihalyi, M. (1975) *Beyond Boredom and Anxiety*, San Francisco, CA: Jossey Bass.

Csikszentmihalyi, M. (1992) *Flow: The Psychology of Happiness*, London: Rider Books.

DCMS (2002) 'School Sport Investment to Triple in Next Three Years', Press release 11/2002, 2 October, London: Department of Culture, Media and Sport.

Fox, K. and Walker, G. (2002) 'Reconsidering the Relationship between Flow and Feminist Ethics: A Response', *Leisure Studies* 21 (January): 18–23.

Heartfield, J. (2002) *The 'Death of the Subject' Explained*, Sheffield: Sheffield Hallam University Press.

Huizinga, J. (1938) *Homo Ludens: A Study of the Play Element in Culture*, Boston, MA: Beacon Press.

Lewis, P., Richardson, V. and Woudhuysen, J. (1998) *In Defence of the Dome*, London: Adam Smith Institute.

McGuigan, J. and Gilmore, A. (2000) 'Figuring out the Dome', *Cultural Trends* 39: 39–83.

O'Leary, J. (2001) 'Fitter Pupils Go to Top of the Class', *The Times*, 27 March.

Opie, P. and Opie, I. (2001) *The Lore and Language of School Children*, New York: NYRB Classics.

Rice, W. and Yaconelli, M. (1993) *Play It! Over 150 Great Games for Youth Groups*, Grand Rapids, MI: Zondervan Publishing House.

Sutton-Smith, B. (1972) *Folkgames of Children*, Austin, TX: University of Texas Press/ American Folklore Society.

Sutton-Smith, B. (1979) *Play and Learning*, New York: The Gardner Press.

Woudhuysen, J. (2002a) 'The Online Campus', in D. Hayes and R. Wynyard (eds), *The McDonaldization of Higher Education*, Westport, CT: Bergin and Garvey.

Woudhuysen, J. (2002b) 'E-learning Joins the Class Struggle', *IT Week*, 8 March, available at http://www.itweek.co.uk/Analysis/1129890.

Woudhuysen, J. (2003) 'Play as the Main Event in International and UK Culture', *Cultural Trends* 43 and 44: 95–145, www.psi.org.uk/docs/2003/news-CT-Woudhuysen-play.pdf.

Key readings

Csikszentmihalyi, M. (1992) *Flow: The Psychology of Happiness*, London: Rider Books.

Huizinga, J. (1938) *Homo Ludens: A Study of the Play Element in Culture*, Boston, MA: Beacon Press.

Woudhuysen, J. (2003) 'Play as the Main Event in International and UK Culture', *Cultural Trends* 43 and 44: 95–145.

Focus question

'Making learning fun' is the aim of many schools and colleges. What does this tell us about how educationalists view young people?

CHAPTER 21

ICT

Don't believe the hype

Toby Marshall

Many people believe that the growing use of ICT in schools and colleges will radically change education for the good. Others maintain that it could seriously undermine the position of teachers. Both reactions tend to overstate the importance of this technology and underestimate those factors that are central to the raising, or indeed the lowering, of educational standards.

Can we discuss ICT without the hyperbole?

The dominant response, that of the key decision makers and opinion formers, is overwhelmingly positive. This technology, we are told, could bring about an educational revolution by putting 'learners in the ICT driving seat' (Foresight 2000). In doing so, it might also change the role of teachers. Where once we hoped that they would be inspirational sages on the stage, now we will expect them to work as guides on the side. The new role of the teacher, we are told, is to be a facilitator, who helps students to navigate the knowledge that ICT makes available (Selinger 2001).

At the same time a smaller and perhaps less influential body of critics has expressed concerns over the risks associated with this technology. Excessive exposure to ICT in schools, they argue, could arrest children's physical and psychological development (Alliance for Childhood 2001). It might also limit opportunities for shared experiences in classroom and in doing so encourage greater individuation among pupils (Hatcher 2001), while the growing use of commercially produced software could assist in the corporate takeover of schools (Klein 2001).

If we took all of this too seriously we could be forgiven for concluding that ICT will shape, and maybe even govern, the ways in which forthcoming generations are schooled. If this were true, then we might have sufficient cause to join the ranks of the pessimists, as no self-respecting teacher would want to be a peripheral in the classroom of the future. Fortunately, there are two good reasons to believe that teachers will remain at the centre of education for some time to come.

First, ICT itself has no fixed, hard-wired, educational agenda. Rather, it is our educational thinking that structures the ways in which we use ICT. If we want, we can always use it in ways that differ from those predicted by the advocates and detractors. Either way, the critical educational issue is the quality of the thinking that underlies our application of this technology. If we get this right, everything else will fall into place. Equally, if we get it wrong, then this technology will do no more than express our errors. Whatever outcome, we can't hold ICT responsible.

Second, it seems highly unlikely that the introduction of ICT into the classroom will result in the sidelining of practitioners. For better or worse, pupils most often engage with their subjects through a relationship with their teachers. And the more committed the teachers, the more engaging the subjects. CD-ROMs, databases and the Internet can make curriculum content available to pupils, but there is no evidence to show that they can engage pupils more effectively, and consistently, than other human beings. For this reason we should not fear for our jobs or for the impact of ICT. If we find that it gets in the way, we can always pull the plug.

New Labour, for its part, has positioned itself as the lead advocate of this technology and it is at this level that the real problem exists. Providing schools with access to ICT was one of its six education pledges in the 1997 General Election and also formed a key component of its 2001 manifesto. On this issue it has been true to its word. Since New Labour took office over £1 billion has been invested in teacher training, software and infrastructure for schools, colleges and libraries (DfES 2003a).

In some respects this is to be welcomed. Teachers should expect access to the latest information technologies as a matter of course, just as they should expect funding for professional development and the most recent publications in their field. But for New Labour providing access to ICT has been far more than a routine resource issue.

In its first term in office New Labour argued that the provision of ICT in schools would 'transform' education provision in this country (DfEE 1997), a term that suggested that they had bought too much of the hype. ICT does indeed make possible new learning activities, but its use does not, in itself, transform either the goals, or to any great extent the content, of education, as these express our social and cultural priorities.

More recently, New Labour has adopted a more measured tone. While Education Secretary Charles Clarke, for example, still talks about a digital revolution, government documentation has noted that ICT can augment established teaching methods (DfES 2003b) and that it should be not viewed as an end in itself (DfES 2003c). At the same time, it has been claimed that, by increasing pupil motivation, and enabling the greater personalisation of teaching methods, ICT can dramatically improve examination results (DfES 2003c).

Yet the findings of large-scale studies of school performance, conducted by the government's own agencies, suggest a more complex picture. One showed that primary schools with good ICT resources do generally obtain better examination results than those with poor ICT resources. But at the same time it also showed that schools with less able pupils sometimes performed better in Maths and English if they had fewer ICT resources (BECTA 2001).

A second more recently produced set of studies examined the impact of ICT in terms of pupil performance within a wide range of disciplines at primary and secondary level. Again, the results indicated that there is no simple correlation between the use of ICT and pupil performance. In some subjects and at some levels there was indeed a positive effect of a significant order, yet in many others it was shown that the use of ICT had no major effect on examination results. Indeed, many schools in this study performed well in spite of their low levels of ICT usage (BECTA 2002).

In sum, these studies show that, while high levels of ICT access are often associated with positive examination results, it can also correlate with negligible or even negative performance and many schools and teachers do well by other means.

These findings could be interpreted in one of two ways. One could argue that teachers have not been adequately trained in the use of the technology and that if only they could be compelled to used it more consistently and expertly then the promised transformation of pupil performance would materialise.

Alternatively, one might argue that we might have placed too great an emphasis on the educational potential of ICT and that any strategy for raising standards should begin and end by addressing how the professional commitment and capacity of teachers might be raised.

If we were to follow this second approach – if we were to put teachers first – then it does not follow that we should argue against further investment in ICT, as it has already and will continue to provide teachers with range of valuable and exciting new teaching options.

However, given the uneven impact of ICT, we might conclude that teachers should be left to decide for themselves if, and to what extent, this technology should be used. Professionals, most would agree, should be judged by their results, not the means, digital or otherwise, by which they are achieved. To suggest otherwise limits their scope for creative decision-making – a process that in fact engages teachers in their work and, by extension, their pupils.

Unfortunately, the hyping of ICT has resulted in its over-zealous promotion. Too often teachers who decide that ICT is not for them are dismissed as dinosaurs or even wreckers. Indeed, the Qualifications and Curriculum Authority has made the use of ICT compulsory in the core curriculum subjects at Key Stage 1, and in all subjects, with the exception of Physical Education, from Key Stage 2 upwards (DfEE 1999). It is this typically heavy-handed and dogmatic approach that in fact undermines the professionalism and morale of teachers and is likely to promote the indiscriminate, and ineffective, application of this technology.

References

Alliance for Childhood (2001) *Fool's Gold: a Critical Look at Computers and Childhood*, available at http://www.allianceforchildhood.net, 29 January 2001.

BECTA (2001) *Primary Schools of the Future: Achieving Today*, Coventry: BECTA.

BECTA (2002) *The Impact of Information and Communications Technologies on Pupil Learning and Attainment*, London: Department for Education and Skills.

Department for Education and Employment (DfEE) (1997) *Connecting the Learning Society*, available at http://www.dfee.gov.uk, 7 October 1997.

Department for Education and Employment (DfEE) (1999) *The National Curriculum for England: Information and Communication Technology*, London: Department for Education and Employment.

Department for Education and Skills (DfES) (2003a) *Press Notice 2003/0003*, available at http://www.dfes.gov.uk, 10 October 2003.

Department for Education and Skills (DfES) (2003b) *Towards a Unified e-Learning Strategy: Consultation Document*, London: Department for Education and Skills.

Department for Education and Skills (DfES) (2003c) *Fulfilling the Potential: Transforming Teaching and Learning through ICT in schools*, London: Department for Education and Skills.

Foresight: The Learning Process in 2020 Task Force (2000) *Point and Click: Learners in the ICT Driving Seat*, London: Department of Trade and Industry.

Hatcher, R. (2001) 'Privatisation and Schooling', in C. Chitty and B. Simon (eds), *Promoting Comprehensive Education in the 21st Century*, Stoke-on-Trent: Trentham Books.

Klein, N. (2001) *No Logo*, Flamingo, London.

Selinger, M. (2001) 'Can ICT Improve the Recruitment, Retention and Morale of Teachers?', in M. Selinger and C. Yapp, *ICTeachers*, London: IPPR, pp. 8–17.

Key readings

Alliance for Childhood (2001) *Fool's Gold: A Critical Look at Computers and Childhood*, available at http://www.allianceforchildhood.net, 29 January 2001.
Department for Education and Skills (DfES) (2003) *Fulfilling the Potential: Transforming Teaching and Learning Through ICT in Schools*, London: Department for Education and Skills.
Selinger, M. (2001) 'Can ICT Improve the Recruitment, Retention and Morale of Teachers?', in M. Selinger and C. Yapp, *ICTeachers*, London: IPPR.

Focus question

Does the use of ICT make you a good teacher?

CHAPTER 22

VIRTUAL LEARNING OR REAL LEARNING?

Mike Blamires

Many education professionals believe in the potential of ICT to enable the voice and increase the inclusion of learners experiencing barriers to learning due to physical and/or learning disabilities. For example, adults with learning difficulties have created accounts of their experiences using symbols with a talking word processor, thus overcoming the barrier of print-based systems (Detheridge and Detheridge 2002). Equally, a learner without speech and limited movement may be able to communicate and even write using switches and scanning software.

Nind (2003) has suggested that teachers need to feel competent and confident in dealing with the demands of including a range of learners with diverse needs. However, awareness of a lack of confidence and competence can lead to anxiety and even hostility. In the context of ICT usage in education the requirements of the Teacher Training Agency (TTA) in relation to ICT competencies may have created a professional hostility to the potential of ICT. Recently, the DfES has attempted to rectify this situation by issuing consultative documents and guidance on the development of 'e' confidence in pupils, staff and schools (DfES 2003a; 2003b). But the potential of ICT is still being squandered for a variety of reasons.

Shovelware: where content is king

First, the TTA 'competency' model of ICT capability for professional development led to training based upon a deficiency model of professionalism. Built into the model was an industrial assumption of how ICT would change practice through improvements in the efficiency of the education factory. Without providing rich conceptual frameworks, models and examples, this often created an antagonism to ICT at worst and a misconception of ICT as a discrete set of skills relating to eye candy web dressing consisting of links to other collections of links. The terms 'browser' and 'download' are indicative of the superficial engagement with models of teaching and learning that can allow us to exploit the technology in an educational fashion. A recent report in *The Guardian* noted a preference for use of word files rather than 'pdf' as the latter took longer to download and print. This raises the issue of transfer in teaching and learning. Are print materials of more value to teachers than 'e' materials?

Chalking and talking into the new millennium

Second, the emphasis on 'e' learning is often seen as a technical thing, as with recent developments in 'e' teaching that provide new technical aids for traditional 'chalk and talk'-based approaches. It may be a good thing for teachers to extend their skills through their use of technologies such as the interactive white board and projectors that present dynamic content to the whole class. However, the 'e' learning revolution promised by the edu-tech gurus of the last century (Papert 1982) is unlikely to occur when the teacher is still in control of the mouse and keyboard. That the teacher will no longer be the 'sage on the stage' but a 'guide on the side' (Cochrane 2003) has been a mantra for ICT revolution advocates, but this may not hold with what is known about learning and teaching. The assumptions that schools will change from 'teaching factories' to community hubs for learning and network centres for negotiated curricula ignore the social control function of education, which needs activities to keep children and young people occupied and the ongoing educational impetus for school to compete. One of the aims of the DfES ICT strategy is 'more effective tracking of pupils' performance, attendance and behaviour, and of children at risk' (DfES 2003a: 15).

A curriculum is not delivered: it is negotiated and engaged with

Third, the concept of curriculum delivery through the use of a computer (or rather a teaching machine) undermines aspirations for learners as future members of an 'e' society to go beyond learning as the passive accumulation of facts and skills. In their review of evidence and theory on how people learn, John Bransford and colleagues state that the purpose of education should move beyond fact accumulation towards being able to find information and then work with it (Bransford *et al.* 1999). They also note the importance of development of meta-cognition in this process and the implications that experts will organise and contextualise their knowledge in different ways to those of novices. This has implications for the 'guide on the side' model of teaching in that the guide really does need to have some expertise. It also has ramifications for increasing use of classroom assistants, who frequently work by the side of learners experiencing difficulties in learning. Perhaps the growing ability of software to elicit and map different understandings of difficult concepts may be an important area for development in education. This potential to make schemas and knowledge explicit and dynamic may appeal to educationalists who are concerned with curricula that require active involvement of the learner rather than passive delivery.

The digitally divided

Fourth, the potential is not there for everyone. In the United States, the *Report to the President on the Use of Technology* (PCAST 1997) recognised the importance of developing a workforce that could locate rich and relevant information and harness it to solve problems and this was linked to a constructivist model of teaching and learning involving access to networked computers rather than traditional programmed learning. This aim is mirrored in the DfES consultation. Both documents note a lack of equity in access to technology. The DfES document states that 80 per cent of learners now have access to technology at home with many having Internet access. The advantages of this access are outlined in the same document as 'enabling learning to take place more easily beyond the bounds of the formal school organisation and outside the school day – and of enhancing the quality of such experiences' because it is essential for participation in today's society and economy.

   This means that there is digital divide between the technologically rich and poor learners, which could become a growing factor of educational and social exclusion.

The US report also noted that, where learners from socio-economically impoverished areas did gain access to technology for learning, it tended to be in activities of a drills and skills nature rather than in tasks using rich meaningful information in problem-solving. This situation is not unique to the United States. The National Council for Educational Technology (now BECTA) supported the use of ironically named 'Integrated Learning Systems' such as Success Maker$^{(TM)}$ with an emphasis on progress through basic skills for low achievers (NCET 1986). At its worst, the digital divide is manifest here as groups of learners are selected to learn redundant skills and knowledge using a second curriculum delivered in a box.

Towards 'e' confidence

Is there a way of moving forward? The DfES guidance on *Transforming Teaching and Learning Through ICT in Schools* provides a renewed emphasis on ICT's potential to change educational thinking and practice, where:

- ICT makes a significant contribution to teaching and learning across all subjects and ages, inside and outside the curriculum;
- ICT is used to improve access to learning for pupils with a diverse range of individual needs, including those with SEN and disabilities;
- ICT is used as a tool for whole-school improvement;
- ICT is used as a means of enabling learning to take place more easily beyond the bounds of the formal school organisation and outside the school day; and
- ICT capabilities are developed as key skills essential for participation in today's society and economy.

(DfES 2003a: 1)

This indicates a move in policy and practice from the National Grid for Learning initiative that was focused on networking and connectivity towards an emphasis on ICT pedagogy and whole school improvement to develop 'e' confidence among all stakeholders. In the DfES vision 'e' confidence includes high bandwidth networking technologies, a range of ICT including more mobile devices, readily available whole class displays, managed learning environments incorporating assessment and curriculum content across the school and potentially the community, and creative technologies to manipulate digital content and access technologies with 'intelligent deployment' for learners with communication difficulties and/or disabilities. Implicit throughout the document is a welcome invitation to be creative and inclusive.

But there is also the challenge of harnessing the support infrastructure of advisory staff and web-based resources to ensure the digital divide is narrowed or crossed. This clearly has implications for the whole school management of change. The National College of School Leadership has responded with short courses and conferences for Head Teachers, but it will be longer accredited HE-based courses that use 'e' learning as the medium of the message that will enable schools to fully engage with the implications of these educational changes. Teachers need to be supported in the exploration of different models, theories and practice so that 'e' learning is not merely bolted on but has shared impact across the school system.

Supporting the change to 'e' confidence

If there is to be a change from 'e' competence to 'e' confidence then this change needs to be managed appropriately. Perhaps the most important is an acknowledgement of the emotional nature of change. To overcome these potential emotional difficulties it is important that teachers and other staff are enabled to have some purchase on these changes. This process may be encouraged by locating the benefits for learning and teaching that can accrue from 'e' teaching and learning.

Evaluating the benefits of 'e' teaching and learning

The DfES consultation document privileges pedagogy in the future development of ICT in learning, but it is, perhaps deliberately, vague in describing its actuality. Kennewell (2003) identifies the difficulty in evaluating the impact of new technologies on teaching and learning using traditional approaches, whereas school effectiveness advocates would have no such difficulty, as they would enter into post hoc models correlating educational achievement with ICT usage. Such approaches rely upon traditional assessment tools that may not be sensitive to potential learning gains that relate to 'e' learning. Kennewell suggests a 'progressive improvement model' closely related to action research methodology that focuses upon what he terms 'affordances' and constraints within teaching and learning activities. 'Affordances' are the features of a learning activity that provide potential for action, while constraints are the conditions and relationships among the features of the learning task which structure and guide the course of actions. Basically put, Kennewell is focusing on the interaction between the learner(s) and the task demand.

Towards a pedagogical infrastructure for 'e' learning and teaching

From Ofsted's (2002) review of ICT usage, it could be argued that a closer consideration of learner interaction within 'e' teaching and learning is well overdue even if Kennewell's language is not adopted. A focus upon pupil–teacher interactions, however, might lead to parochial and anecdotal theory-building that does not take into account the growing body of theory and guidance in this area. So CPD has a role to play here according to the strategy document in creating 'online communities of practice' by bringing learners, teachers, specialist communities, experts, practitioners and interest groups together to share ideas and good practice through the Internet.

Features of the model of learning underpinning Wenger's (1998) concept of communities of practice include meaningful learning, activities to support learning, a sense of belonging and identity projects that have an emphasis on learning as becoming. Such a model has important implications for teachers engaged in the identity project of becoming an 'e' confident teacher. Such requirements may mean that previous mistakes have been learned from, and that teachers engage in shared professional development focused on the development of their subject or specialism rather than isolated tasks often unrelated to their professional interests.

Conclusion

The promised jam tomorrow of a developing 'e' confidence among teachers and learners that exploits the potential of ICT in learning needs to be based upon a sound infrastructure that interlinks pedagogy and technology resulting from appropriate professional development that increases the equity of engagement with education of an increasing diversity of learners.

Yet, there is a multi-faceted digital divide in education with many teachers achieving competence but not always confidence in their use ICT. Some homes and educational settings are poorly resourced and connected so that the potential of ICT to enable a wide diversity of learners is not realised. The government vision of ICT transforming education implies a significant change in the capability and versatility of schools. This will require the development of a clearly articulated pedagogy that is not currently present in the guidance.

References

Bransford, J.D., Brown, A.L. and Cocking, R.R. (eds) (1999) *How People Learn: Brain, Mind, Experience, and School*, National Research Council, Commission on Behavioral and Social Sciences and Education, Committee on Developments in the Science of Learning, available at http://www.nap.edu/html/howpeople1/.

Cochrane, P. (2003), interviewed by Jack Schofield in 'How their Kids will Learn', available at http://www.education.guardian.co.uk/cof/story/0,13893,1047449,00.html.

Detheridge, T. and Detheridge, M. (2002) *Literacy Through Symbols: Improving Access for Children and Adults*, London: David Fulton Publishers.

DfES (2003a) *Fulfilling the Potential: Transforming Teaching and Learning Through ICT in Schools*, Nottingham: DfEs Publications.

DfES (2003b) *Towards a Unified e-Learning Strategy: Consultation Document*, Nottingham: DfES Publications, DfES/0424/2003.

Kennewell, S. (2003) 'Developing Research Models from ICT-Based Pedagogy', in McDougall, A., Murname, J.S., Stacey, C. and Dowling C. (eds) *ICT and the Teacher of the Future – Selected Papers*, Melbourne: ACS, pp. 73–4. Available online at: http://www.crpit.com/confpapers/CRPITV23Kennewell.pdf.

National Council for Educational Technology (NCET) (1986) *Evaluation of Open Learning Systems*, Warwick: NCET.

Nind, M. (2003) *Curriculum for Inclusion*, Maidenhead: Open University Press.

Ofsted (2002) *ICT in Schools: Effect of Government Initiatives*, Progress Report, London: Ofsted.

Papert, S. (1982) *Mindstorms*, Brighton: Harvester Wheatsheaf.

PCAST The President's Committee of Advisors on Science and Technology (1997) *Report to the President on the Use of Technology*, available at http://www.whitehouse.gov/WH/EOP/OSTP/NSTC/PCAST/k-12ed.html.

Wenger, E. (1998) *Communities of Practice: Learning, Meaning and Identity*, New York: Cambridge University Press.

Note: Successmaker is available from rm plc, www.rm.co.uk.

Key readings

Blamires, M. (ed.) (1999) *Enabling Technology for Inclusion*, London: Paul Chapman/Sage.

DfES (2003) *Fulfilling the Potential: Transforming Teaching and Learning Through ICT in Schools*, Nottingham: DfEs Publications.

Ofsted (2002) *ICT in Schools: Effect of Government Initiatives*, Progress Report, London: Ofsted.

Focus question

To what extent does the use of 'e' learning and teaching resources enable teachers to engage a wider range of learners?

CHAPTER 23

THE SHATTERED MIRROR

A critique of multiple intelligences theory

David Perks

The protagonists in the field of human intelligence often give the distinct impression that they already know the answer and are just searching around to find evidence to back up their points of view. Psychologists use arguments about intelligence much like most of us use a mirror. They bring to debates about intelligence the aspirations and prejudices of society at large, just as we do when we look at ourselves in the mirror. The end result is that psychology's portrayal of intelligence tends to reflect society's view of itself. This leaves our understanding of intelligence subject to change and reinterpretation. In the past, theories of intelligence reflected the view that it was acceptable to believe that different races or classes of people were innately inferior to others. However, it would be unacceptable for psychologists to present us with such an image of ourselves today. Elitism in all its forms is distinctly out of fashion. This makes discussing natural differences between individuals problematic. In educational terms, innate differences in intelligence run counter to the philosophy of opening up education to the broadest possible cross-section of society. In the government's own words we are striving for 'excellence for all'. This creates a dilemma for psychology. If the psychologist's mirror is brought up to face humanity should it still see the differences between us?

Dealing with this dilemma has remained problematic. The American educational psychologist Howard Gardner, in his book *Frames of Mind*, came up with his own answer (Gardner 1993). He told psychologists to break the mirror. Instead of seeing intelligence as a single universal characteristic all of us possess, he suggested that intelligence was fragmented. In his view, our intellectual capacity is derived from multiple intelligences (MI). So, instead of one central intellectual capacity or general intelligence, Gardner suggests each individual possesses up to eight separate intelligences, such as linguistic or musical intelligence. By insisting that each of these intelligences is treated separately and independently, Gardner is insisting that psychology cannot provide us with a single mirror with which to compare humanity. Instead, we only have the fragments of a shattered mirror with which to look at each other. He focuses our attention on the different intellectual capacities of the individual rather than between different individuals.

Gardner's work has come to prominence, not because of its explanatory power, but more because it was adopted by New Labour just as they came to power in 1997. Just prior to the election Michael Barber, then at the Institute of Education in London, published *The Learning Game* (Barber 1996). The book amounted to an education manifesto for New Labour and its themes still reflect the government's agenda. The prioritising of education by the government was part of its anti-elitist attack on what it continues to see as old institutions with vested interests opposed to its own outlook. From the opening up of access to university to the scrutinising of schools' examination bodies, any institution perceived to be a bastion of privilege or unaccountable power has been drawn into question. However, despite co-opting Barber into Blair's inner circle, by initially making him Head of the government's Standards and Effectiveness Unit and later Head of the Prime Minister's Delivery Unit, New Labour still lacked a broader theoretical basis with which to arm itself in the fight against those who objected to reform.

It was Geoff Mulgan, the founder of Demos and later a government adviser, who discovered Gardner and published him in an influential book at the start of New Labour's first term (see Mulgan 1997). Mulgan correctly identified MI as a tool that could be used to push through educational reform. MI challenges the orthodox understanding of education – the one size fits all approach. Instead, MI insists that pupils need to be educated in a way that suits the individual profile of intelligences each child posseses. Using MI as a lever, Mulgan and later Tom Bentley at Demos have questioned everything from the inflexibility of the classroom to the validity of written examinations (Bentley 1998). Each aspect of education challenged is portrayed as an elitist echo of a past era, unreflective of the challenges of living in an information society.

But what is the substance of the case Gardner makes for MI theory? Gardner developed his ideas while facing up to the problem that theories of intelligence up until the 1980s had given general intelligence a privileged position above any other account of separate cognitive abilities. This meant that intelligence quotient or IQ testing was still seen as a valid measure of a person's educational potential. Used widely in the United States, IQ testing was criticised as elitist especially as it related to theories of racial difference. The controversy surrounding Arthur Jensen's work on twin studies, which he used explicitly to challenge educational reform programmes for black children in the United States, provoked considerable unease within academia (Jensen 1969). The controversy was reignited with the publication of *The Bell Curve* 25 years later, which restated the case that blacks have on average a lower IQ than whites in the United States (Herrnstein and Murray 1994). The reaction against this perspective, as Gardner admits in the introduction to *Intelligence Reframed*, spurred him on to find a way round the dilemma of having a single universal scale of intellectual ability against which everyone is judged (Gardner 1999: 1–25). Although Gardner was not the first psychologist to suggest that different cognitive abilities could be identified, he was the first to call for a decisive break with the notion of general intelligence. By insisting that general intelligence did not exist and that instead we posses eight different intelligences he was able to paint a completely different picture of the individual.

From the point of view of psychology, Gardner's claims rest on his insistence that he based MI on 'marshalling biology to explain human intelligence' (Gardner 1993: 31). He compares himself to Franz Joseph Gall, the nineteenth-century originator of the study of phrenology, in an attempt to give himself credibility. However, the comparison is apt but not for the reason Gardner supposes. It illustrates that Gardner uses science as Gall did, to confirm an answer he already knew he wanted to find. Gall used crude empirical techniques, measuring the size and shape of skulls to determine personality types, whereas Gardner uses an eclectic collection of scientific approaches to confirm his own ideas. The problem for both figures was that scientific advance quickly left their ideas behind.

The strength of Gardner's case at the time of the publication of *Frames of Mind* was that it coincided with Jerry Fodor's thesis of the modular structure of the mind

(Fodor 1983). Fodor insisted that it might be possible to construct a model of intelligence based on autonomous information-processing modules designed to process specific and independent types of information in the brain. This idea was adopted by evolutionary psychologists like Stephen Pinker who added the emphasis that each module was a product of evolutionary pressure and was as a result fitted to particular evolutionary demands. The central thesis of modularity was the biological independence of each module. Each module corresponds to what Gardner called a psychobiological potential or intelligence.

For Gardner the consequences of MI are dramatic. It no longer makes any sense to teach every pupil the same curriculum. Each individual needs to be taught according to his or her own profile of intelligences. In an interview he gave recently, Gardner explains this in terms of one of his favourite intelligences, musical intelligence. 'So you and I do not have the same musical potential raised in the same environment. . . . One of us becomes much more accomplished than the other. That is the genetic contribution of the potential'. He goes on to explain, 'If we aren't exposed to music, it's never going to get expressed' (Larsen 2002). As far as Gardner is concerned, schooling has over-emphasised our linguistic and logico-mathematical intelligences as opposed to the other intelligences he identifies. So for many individuals their psychobiological potentials are never realised.

It is worth noting three points of confusion about MI. First of all, even though Gardner rejects the idea of a universal scale of ability by dismissing IQ, he does not reject a natural basis to intellectual capacities. Implicit within his work is an acceptance of the biological foundation of each psychobiological potential, by which he ultimately means genetics. During the period Gardner has been writing on multiple intelligences, support for the idea that intelligence is heritable has grown. Gardner acknowledges this by tacitly accepting a genetic limit to the intellectual capacities he identifies.

Second, within British education it is a common mistake to believe that MI theory refers to learning styles. Gardner suggests we need to teach to different intelligences not because that is the way we learn best but because that is what we can learn. Gardner does not suggest we can learn mathematics via music – he says there is no point studying mathematics if you don't have the biological capacity to do so. Gardner's theory is much more in line with the government's current notion of matching education to pupils' aptitudes rather than the learning styles approach preferred by most teachers.

Third, MI is largely discredited within academic circles. The concept of the modular mind has been qualified significantly in recent years. Its author, Jerry Fodor, has made it clear that as far as he is concerned his thesis was a challenge to those involved in computer modelling to see how far they could go in writing programs to mimic the operation of the mind. As he later wrote, *'the mind doesn't work that way'* (Fodor 2000). According to Fodor, his 'informationally encapsulated' modules would require non-modular cognition in order to work. This means he acknowledges the need for a general processing unit or homunculus. Fodor's qualification of his original idea fundamentally undermines Gardner's case for separate biologically determined modules.

Apart from the loss of computer modelling as a basis for his ideas, analysis of twin studies has shown that, if genetic inheritance is to operate to determine differences between the intelligence of individuals, then it can only be understood as an influence on general intelligence as no evidence of separate intelligences has been found (Plomin 2003). On top of that there is practically no direct evidence for a genetic basis to individual differences in intelligence in the first place. Even the idea of one gene causing one type of behaviour has been significantly drawn into question by the work of developmental psychologists like Annette Karmiloff-Smith, Professor of Neurocognitive Development at University College London. She suggests that the outcome of genetic faults in the development of the brain is far more widespread than previously thought and behavioural outcomes depend significantly on the process of development itself (Karmiloff-Smith 1998).

In terms of Gardner's own perspective on intelligence, there is a more fundamental problem. In undermining the case for IQ testing he has undermined the case for general intelligence. If this is accepted then instead of viewing human beings as each capable of excelling in any area of human achievement he puts biological limits on our potential to develop in different areas of intellectual ability. This degrades our view of ourselves to a far greater extent than the old elitist notion of intelligence. The idea of general intelligence expresses at least the notion of universal human qualities. It carries with it the sense that at least a few of us can aspire to be as good as the best in any field of human endeavour. It is still worth pursuing a universal curriculum that gives us all a taste of the achievements of humanity in all of the fields of human endeavour. Gardner's theory on the other hand supports a view of humanity that describes the individual as limited biologically to never be able to achieve in some areas of human achievement irrespective of our efforts.

The consequence of accepting MI as a way of looking at human intelligence is to reinforce the separation of different spheres of human activity and to encourage the idea that we have no common language with which to talk to each other as we all have separate intellectual potentials in different frames or fields of intellectual activity. If education is reorganised around this principle it will have a far more damaging effect than any so-called elitist examination of each individual against a common scale, be it IQ or any other set of tests. By denying the possibility of testing individuals against a common scale we refuse to push people beyond their starting position. Education just becomes a confirmation of who we are, celebrating the differences between us. There is and can be no sense of aspiring to what is universal about humanity.

In attempting to move us away from Gardner's fragmented view of intelligence, I am suggesting that we can only make progress if we consider the human intellect as a unified whole. While biology may have something to say about the limits to our intellectual capacities as individuals, it should not be the basis for education. I am suggesting that our starting point should return to what we have in common between us – our ability to learn in the broadest possible sense. Put into the context of the history of the intellectual achievements of humanity, the education of an individual appears entirely different. In learning from the history of human achievement, in order to go one step further and add to the sum total of our knowledge, education is given a qualitatively different purpose. Even when we express the differences between us, we can do so in a way that celebrates our common humanity. Education should, after all, be a platform from which any individual can aspire to be the best in their field of enquiry. We don't need to break the psychologist's mirror in order to see ourselves as fragmented and limited individuals. Instead, we need to point our mirror higher at the best that humanity has achieved and see in it a glimpse of what we might become.

References

Barber, M. (1996) *The Learning Game: Arguments for an Education Revolution*, London: Victor Gollancz.

Bentley, T. (1998) *Learning Beyond the Classroom: Education for a Changing World*, London: Routledge.

Fodor, J. (1983) *Modularity of Mind*, Cambridge, MA: MIT Press.

Fodor, J. (2000) *The Mind Doesn't Work That Way: The Scope and Limits of Computational Psychology*, Cambridge, MA: MIT Press.

Gardner, H. (1993) *Frames of Mind: The Theory of Multiple Intelligences*, 2nd edn, London: Fontana Press.

Gardner, H. (1995) *The Unschooled Mind: How Children Think and How Schools Should Teach*, New York: Basic Books.

Gardner, H. (1999) *Intelligence Reframed: Multiple Intelligences for the 21st Century*, New York: Basic Books.

Herrnstein, R. and Murray, C. (1994) *The Bell Curve*, New York: Free Press.

Jensen, A. (1969) 'How Much Can We Boost I.Q. and Scholastic Achievement?', *Harvard Educational Review* 39(1), February: 1–123.

Karmiloff-Smith, A. (1998) 'Development Itself is the Key to Understanding Developmental Disorders', *Trends in Cognitive Sciences* 2(10): 389–98.

Larsen, S. (2002) 'An Interview with Howard Gardner Conducted by Steen Nepper Larsen', (*Project Zero*), available at http://www.pz.harvard.edu/PIs/HG_Larsen.pdf (accessed 29 September 2002).

Mulgan, G. (ed.) (1997) *Life After Politics: New Thinking for the Twenty-First Century*, London: Fontana Press/Demos.

Plomin, R. (2003) 'Genetics, Genes, Genomics and G', *Molecular Psychiatry* 8(1): 1–5.

Key readings

Gardner, H. (1999) *Intelligence Reframed: Multiple Intelligences for the 21st Century*, New York: Basic Books.

Mulgan, G. (ed.) (1997) *Life After Politics: New Thinking for the Twenty-First Century*, London: Fontana Press/Demos.

Focus question

To what extent do you think that stressing individual differences in intelligence means that access to a broad curriculum will not be possible for everyone in the future?

CHAPTER 24

AN IMPOVERISHED EDUCATION FOR ALL

Jennie Bristow

The continuous policy churn of new educational reforms and initiatives set in motion by the current UK government purports to be about education. But the role of education is now seen explicitly in terms of social engineering. So far as the government is concerned, the primary function of education is to compensate somehow for society's failings towards the category of people it deems to be socially excluded.

Two major reforms announced during one week in January 2003 provide a useful case study of this process. The first was the government's response to the consultation on the February 2002 Green Paper on 14–19 education, announced by schools minister David Miliband at a conference of the Secondary Heads Association, the Association of Colleges and the National Association of Head Teachers on 21 January 2003. The second was a reform of higher education funding, proposed by education secretary Charles Clarke in a statement to the House of Commons on 22 January 2003. As these reforms indicated, even the pretence that education has something to do with intellectual development or academic achievement has been lost – to the extent that educational criteria cease to matter at all.

'Our task', said David Miliband, 'is to . . . reach our shared vision of a coherent 14–19 phase of education' (Miliband 2003). You do not have to be a teenager struggling through the bewildering mess of vocational GCSEs, specialist schools, modern apprenticeships, accusations of grade inflation and the 2002 A-levels scandal that brought down Estelle Morris as education secretary to know that coherence is sorely lacking in current 14–19 education. But how does the government propose to stabilise things? Through shaking it up further. Reaching a 'shared vision' of 14–19 education means 'responding to individual need, offering choice to the young people but also promoting progression at every stage' (Miliband 2003). This is not a coherent vision – it is more of the all-things-to-everybody approach that we have already. Bereft of a clear idea about what secondary education should do, increasing importance is placed on more variety, more choice, more criteria to judge 'progression'.

In fact, the current government has only one firm, unshakeable principle about 14–19 education – and that is that more people should be involved in it for longer. Towards the end of his speech, Miliband criticised 'an old English curse' which 'underlies many debates in education': the curse being 'that "more will mean worse"' (Miliband 2003). This, he said:

> is a credo suited to the nineteenth century and not the twenty-first, a credo of weeding people out of education rather than supporting them to succeed. Our challenge is to show that the potential of our young people – all our young

people – can be realised. They will not all achieve the same. But they can all achieve their potential.

(Miliband 2003)

Of course, this is true. It is also a truism. If one rejects the notion that education is about one thing – developing children's academic ability, for example – and relies instead on flabby, easily manipulated notions of individual potential, it is quite easy to make the argument that more and more young people should be in education just because it is somehow good for them to be involved. When the primary goal is simply inclusion of more young people in education, the content of what they are taught can keep changing, and the assessment criteria can keep shifting – because what pupils are learning or doing matters far less than the fact that they are there at all.

Shifting goalposts was the spirit behind a new set of secondary school league tables, also published in January 2003 – which, rather than looking at schools' performance per se, employed 'value added' measures to show the progress children have made through different levels of their schooling. In other words, these aimed to show not how good the children's education was, but how good it was for them. Genuine 'progression', in terms of young people having their minds developed, their ideas challenged and their horizons raised through education, does not seem to matter much to those in the government's education department. What matters is that young people are in the system for longer, doing something more constructive than vandalising cars: and if 'progression' means that they have gone from being illiterate to only semi-literate, this is apparently something to be celebrated.

In New Labour's world of learning, the phrase 'education for education's sake' takes on a whole new meaning. What used to be a defence against notions that academic learning must be justified in terms of economic benefit now seems to mean that getting young people into education is justifiable even when they learn nothing, because at least they are included and are in a relationship with an institution. This is the grim philosophy that links Miliband's 14–19 proposals with Charles Clarke's higher education reforms.

Most of the debate about HE reform – in January 2003, and in subsequent months – has centred on the decision to allow certain universities to charge top-up fees. However, the real question is surely not whether students should pay, but what are they paying for? Charles Clarke's presentation of his reforms did little to enlighten us. Like Miliband, Clarke's core principle when it comes to HE is to get as many young people into university as possible. In his January 2003 speech, he confirmed the government's commitment 'to increase participation in higher education towards 50 per cent of those aged 18–30 by the end of the decade', and set out his vision for making this happen: namely, by turning universities into outreach projects for the socially excluded (Clarke 2003).

Universities, claimed Charles Clarke, 'have to extend the opportunities of higher education to all of our population, irrespective of their personal and economic background' (Clarke 2003). Of course, allowing access to university 'irrespective of economic background' is a laudable goal, and not so very long ago was one of the great features of British higher education: linked to the grammar school system and the existence of maintenance grants, both of which, up to a point, enabled universities to select on the basis of academic achievement and students from working-class backgrounds to afford their years of study.

It was in this spirit that Clarke's cautious reintroduction of the maintenance grant was received. 'From September 2004 students whose families will earn under £10,000 will receive a £1,000 grant, with a proportion of that paid up to family income of

£20,000', stated Clarke (Clarke 2003). But there's a lot more to Clarke's proposal than giving young people from low-income backgrounds some much-needed spending money. When he talked about the need for young people to have higher education opportunities 'irrespective of their personal and economic background', the clear implication is that selecting on the basis of academic ability, bolstered by financial support, is not enough to compensate for social inequalities. What is needed, apparently, is a system of positive discrimination – to get young people in not 'irrespective' of their background at all, but *because* they come from poor families.

This is why, said Clarke, the government intends to raise the 'postcode premium', which gives 'extra money to universities who teach and support students from disadvantaged backgrounds' (Clarke 2003). Furthermore, all universities will be subject to the eagle eye of an 'access regulator', 'who will ensure that any university that wants to increase its tuition fee has rigorous admissions procedures, provides bursaries and other financial support and works directly with schools in every part of the country to promote the aspiration of a university education'. In case anybody is in any doubt about where Clarke is going to get the students to meet his 50 per cent target, and whether the access regulator will have anything to do, the education secretary has done the maths. 'We believe that the bulk of the increase in degree student numbers, from its current proportion of 43 per cent of the cohort, should come from two-year vocational foundation degree courses' – many of which are to be provided by further education colleges.

We are not looking, then, at aspirational youngsters being given greater opportunities to study Classics, or any such romantic nonsense. We are looking at teenagers who have been clawed off the streets and put into further education colleges, to do something vaguely manual or creative. And if they live in an area with a dodgy postcode, so much the better. For Clarke sets another target: '30 per cent of students will get the full £1,000 grant' (Clarke 2003). This seems to mean that Clarke's vision of higher education is that 50 per cent of young people will be in university, of whom 30 per cent come from families earning under £10,000 – which, we can surely agree, is very little money for a family income. Taken in the context of Clarke's prioritisation of the 'postcode premium' above all else, there is a clear implication here: that the role of universities should be to seek out large sections of the poorest of the poor, because they are poor. This is not about access to higher education. It is about social engineering on a despicable scale.

Of course young people from deprived backgrounds should not be prevented from going to university because of their financial circumstances. But at every level, Clarke's proposal patronises these would-be undergraduates and sells them short. By forcing universities to hand-pick them from the community because of their impoverished state, the government absolves itself from responsibility for educating schoolchildren to the level where they could get into university based on academic merit. By making the admissions process a proactive one on the part of admissions departments, and a passive one on the part of young people, the proposal assumes that certain groups of young people have no will to study, and nor should they need one. And by turning universities into glorified secondary schools for the 'socially excluded', the proposal is another blow to the very idea of a higher education.

References

Clarke, C. (2003) *Statement to the Commons*, 22 January.
Miliband, D. (2003) *Excellence and Opportunity From 14–19*, speech given to a conference of the Secondary Heads Association, the Association of Colleges and the National Association of Head Teachers, 21 January.

Key readings

Mulgan, G. (ed.) (1997) *Life after Politics: New Thinking for the Twenty-First Century*, London: Fontana Press/Demos (the section on 'Learning').
Woodhead, C. (2002) *Class War: The State of British Education*, London: Little & Brown.

Focus question

What is the purpose of getting so many people into school and university, if they learn so little while they are there?

PART V

LIFELONG LEARNING – LIFELONG DEPENDENCE

CHAPTER 25

THE RISE OF LOW SELF-ESTEEM AND THE LOWERING OF EDUCATIONAL EXPECTATIONS

Kathryn Ecclestone

A further education college principal argued at a conference in 2002 that lifelong learning should enable us to 'search for the hero inside ourselves', quoting a song by M People that accompanied an advertisement about the freedom offered by a certain French car. But her vision of educational heroism was not about challenge, risk-taking and empowering others, or even the open road. Instead, teachers and students are heroic if they can confess their mutual vulnerability in the face of a scary future where 'there are no experts'.

The rise of low self-esteem

A rising tide of concern about people's psychological fragility, fears and vulnerability is reflected in the idea that education plays a fundamental role in remedying the apparently growing problem of low self-esteem. Some random examples illustrate the point: researchers claim that school tests damage self-esteem and cause anxiety (Assessment Reform Group 2002). The Socialist Education Association and other socialist groupings regard the building of self-esteem as schools' fundamental social role (Hayes 2003; SEA 2003), while the National Institute of Adult and Continuing Education regards low self-esteem as one of the most significant barriers to educational achievement for adults (James 2003). Closer to home, a growing number of the students I teach, all of whom are education practitioners, cite their lack of self-esteem as a problem for speaking in a group, receiving feedback on their work or being challenged by others.

It is difficult, initially, to see problems with a humane concern that many adults and young people are disaffected by education, have fears and uncertainties caused by low self-esteem and that the future is indeed scary and uncertain. New Labour has successfully created a consensus that educational achievement leads to social and individual benefits, including the building of self-esteem (Kennedy 1997; DfES 2002). Prime Minister Blair regards low self-esteem as the most destructive cause and effect of social exclusion, making it important for the welfare state to confer recognition and make people feel valued (Blair 1997).

A crucial motif in this consensus is the idea of 'equal worth' and 'recognition' for people deemed to be disadvantaged, marginalised and excluded. Notions of 'hard to reach' people, locked in cycles of personal and social deprivation, excluded, but also *self-excluding*, emotionally damaged and lacking confidence and skills permeate initiatives like the SureStart early years initiative for young mothers and the Connexions guidance and careers service (see, for example, SEU 1998). Interest in the measurable benefits of education lends credibility to such concerns by suggesting that confidence, self-esteem and a positive self-image are tangible outcomes of education in the form of 'identity capital' (see www.learningbenefits.net).

Some researchers and professional educators regard awareness of identity formation and social capital as counters to the individualistic, instrumental idea that education should create human capital (Baron *et al.* 2000). In pedagogy, exploring identity and developing psychological capital offer both immediate therapeutic recognition and a politicised understanding of personal circumstances. In this scenario, life experience, emotion and identity are a legitimate focus for learning, enabling students to confront the oppression of broader forces shaping personal identity, and the effects of institutions, teachers and the curriculum.

Merging radical pedagogy and humanist psychology

It seems that there is a shift from demands that education should promote equality and useful forms of cultural capital to the goal of self-esteem and conferring recognition. There seem to be few heartfelt calls from liberal and radical educators for education to promote equality, redistribution of wealth, social progression or genuinely useful forms of cultural capital. Indeed, questions about class have all but disappeared from debate about public policy and education. It is important to explore why this is happening now, particularly in areas of adult and community education that were once seen as radical alternatives to formalised, mainstream education. Some critics argue that policy makers moralise about an 'underclass' through negative stereotypes about deprivation and dysfunction (Colley and Hodkinson 2002). Other critics argue that emphasising individuals' problems and self-esteem overlooks structural causes of deprivation and inequality and their effects on collective self-esteem (see Griffiths 2003). Others argue that the concept of self-esteem has little theoretical coherence and that evidence for its impact is inconclusive (Emler 2001).

From these perspectives, low self-esteem enables policy makers to blame people for their own fate. But the essentialist, pseudo-psychological tone in ideas about low self-esteem is also problematic because it infects progressive educational goals and practices by extending processes and ideas associated with guidance, mentoring, therapy and counselling into pedagogy. Appeals to self-esteem and understanding of identity resonate with older calls for education to promote personal and social change.

Current interest in people's psychological fragility and vulnerability as a basis for curriculum and teaching has strong progressive credentials. One heritage is a set of goals and processes from social movements, radical community and working-class education aiming for social change, individual emancipation and subversion of existing systems. The radical adult educator Paulo Freire is perhaps the most influential exponent of these ideas and his book, *Pedagogy of the Oppressed*, is required reading on many post-16 teacher education courses (Freire 1999). The other heritage is liberal humanist psychology, particularly the work of therapist Carl Rogers, which was influential in British and American adult education throughout the 1980s. His influential books, *On Becoming a Person* and *Freedom to Learn*, are also on many post-16 reading lists (Rogers 1961, 1983).

Although these influences emerge from very different educational traditions for promoting individual and social change, processes such as 'creating safe spaces', 'privileging the learners' voice', recognition and 'positive, unconditional regard' appear in current manifestations of therapeutic pedagogy (see Ecclestone 2003). They fit well with interest in the psychological and emotional minutiae of people's learning identities, their learning biographies and narratives.

Yet, these ideas are now turning educational goals inwards and moving debate from moral questions about the fundamental purpose of education. Instead, concerns about individuals' psychological fragility erode such questions as well as those about deeper inequalities. In the light of this analysis, it is telling that concerns about the effects of testing focus on self-esteem and anxiety rather than the more fundamental social function that testing plays in rationing opportunities for work and education.

The rise of a therapeutic ethos

Further insight into why preoccupation with people's psychological well-being is taking hold emerges from recognising a broader therapeutic ethos that blurs differences between welfare and education. For example, a therapeutic ethos which uses the language and mindset of disorder, addictions, vulnerability and dysfunction is prevalent in American culture and is now seeping into media, popular culture and politics in Britain (Nolan 1998; Furedi 2003). A therapeutic ethos is not merely the extension of therapeutic processes into new areas of life. Instead, it is the subtle ways in which the language, codes and symbols of therapy change our idea of what it means to be human. According to Nolan, notions of the Rogerian self, which is positive, optimistic and naturally disposed to improve, grow and learn, are giving way to a more negative, dysfunctional view of self and an acceptance of weakness caused by 'being only human'.

New tendencies to see people as 'victims' of everything from genetics, to childhood experience and life experiences generally, as being 'at risk' or having 'fragile identities', all resonate with a broader cultural de-moralisation. Fevre argues that de-moralisation has two meanings: one is its everyday meaning as pessimism and loss of morale and the other is a deeper stripping of moral literacy and discourse from life (Fevre 2000). Both meanings are relevant to ideas here. De-moralisation and a therapeutic ethos intertwine, enabling us to feel more comfortable with weakness, victimhood and what Furedi characterises as the 'diminished self' (Furedi 1999).

These trends both reflect and create pessimism about the idea of human agency, namely the aspiration and ability to control one's own life and optimism about social progress (Malik 2001). De-moralisation and pessimism about agency also make people nervous about moral debate, reducing moral questions to questions of ethics, rights and recognition and, eventually, to simple questions about value and emotional preferences (Fevre 2000).

Low educational expectations

It is difficult to see how low expectations of human agency and depictions of people at risk can form the basis for respect, challenge and risk-taking in education. Once adults and young people regard themselves as marginalised and vulnerable or are encouraged to see education as a source of self-esteem, it is difficult to offer challenging experiences that may threaten them further. And, once psychological deficiency, risk and vulnerability become embedded in beliefs about people, educators could find themselves offering comforting interventions or probing into people's life histories and identities.

Yet, a therapeutic ethos appears to legitimise activities and interventions offered by state agencies and institutions. For example, exploring the effects of biography and identity enables professionals to bond with demotivated, disaffected people (Gordon 2002). But therapeutic education carries huge dangers. Not only does therapeutic government make it legitimate for people's emotional states to be a matter of public concern and part of the responsibilities of citizenship (Pupavac 2001). A pessimistic view of human agency also undermines beliefs that people have a moral capacity and that they can act on or develop it. Despite the radical rhetoric that 'understanding the personal' is a springboard for a politicised consciousness, there is a danger that therapeutic pedagogy starts where learners are – and leaves them and their teachers in the same 'safe space'.

From negative to positive liberty

Profound problems could arise if a therapeutic ethos takes hold. Instead of education to promote what Isaiah Berlin called 'negative liberty', namely the resources for people to take responsibility for their own freedoms, a therapeutic ethos produces 'positive liberty', namely the political and professional power to confer freedom and protection on the vulnerable and powerless. In a de-moralised educational climate, safe spaces that were once genuine springboards for critical autonomy end up as low-risk comfort zones. In addition, formulaic affirmations of esteem and recognition through institutional processes place people in the role of supplicants for professional and bureaucratic recognition. One side-effect is to marginalise informal networks, community aspirations and social capital by formalising them through state-sponsored interventions.

So what is to be done? Critics might see arguments here as an attack on therapy and radical pedagogy and, instead, attribute a therapeutic ethos to well-meaning attempts to soften instrumental goals for education. Others might see arguments here as overstating a problem or as too pessimistic. Others might ask what front-line educators who deal with people suffering from profound individual and social disadvantage should do instead.

Moving debate on

These questions make it important to seek more empirical evidence of therapeutic pedagogy and its effects, as well as evidence of counter-trends. The concept of de-moralisation is useful because it counters an impoverished understanding of social action and the deep pessimism evident in educational and social debates about the future. It also enables new ideas about cultural and social trends to be constructed across different domains (see Fevre 2000).

More immediately, the chapter suggests that humanist goals for education to challenge, to take us into new worlds, ideas and cultures and to permit criticism, hopes, fears and aspirations have never been more necessary. Instead, a de-moralised humanism is one of the most pressing problems facing educators committed to social justice and to the transforming power of education. Educators committed to humanist aspirations should therefore reject the building of self-esteem as an educational goal and challenge therapeutic pedagogy disguised by radical rhetoric.

References

Assessment Reform Group (2002) *Testing and Motivation*, Cambridge: University of Cambridge.
Baron, S., Field, J. and Schuller, T. (eds) (2000) *Social Capital: Critical Perspectives*, Oxford: Oxford University Press.
Blair, T. (1997) Speech given at Stockwell Park School, Lambeth, December.
Colley, H. and Hodkinson, P. (2002) 'Problems with "Bridging the Gap": The Reversal of Structure and Agency in Addressing Social Exclusion', *Critical Social Policy* 21(3): 337–61.

DfES (2002) *Education: Breaking the Cycle of Deprivation*, DfES Research Conference, Institution of Civil Engineers, Great George Street, London, 12 November.

Ecclestone, K. (2003) 'From Freire to Fear: The Rise of Low Self-esteem as an Educational Concern', paper given to the British Educational Research Association Annual Conference, Herriott-Watt University, September, and to the European Educational Research Annual Conference, University of Hamburg, September.

Emler, N. (2001) *Self-esteem: The Costs and Causes of Low Self-worth*, York: Joseph Rowntree Foundation.

Fevre, R. (2000) *The Demoralisation of Western Culture: Social Theory and the Dilemmas of Modern Living*, London: Continuum.

Freire, P. (1999) *Pedagogy of the Oppressed*, revised 20th anniversary edition, New York: Continuum.

Furedi, F. (1999) *The Culture of Fear: Risk Taking and the Morality of Low Expectation*, London: Cassell.

Furedi, F. (2003) *Therapy Culture: Cultivating Vulnerability in an Uncertain Age*, London and New York: Routledge.

Giddens, A. (1998) *Third Way: The Renewal of Social Democracy*, Oxford: Polity Press.

Gordon, J. (2002) *Beyond the Classroom Walls: Ethnographic Enquiry as Pedagogy*, London: RoutledgeFalmer.

Hayes, D. (2003) 'New Labour, New Professionalism', in J. Satterthwaite, E. Atkinson and K. Gale (eds), *Discourse, Power and Resistance: Challenging the Rhetoric of Contemporary Education*, London: Trentham Books.

James, K. (2003) 'How Low Self-esteem Affects Adult Learners', *Adults Learning* 24 (January): 24–6.

Kennedy, H. (1997) *Learning Works: How to Widen Participation*, Coventry: Further Education Funding Council.

Malik, K. (2001) *Man, Beast and Zombie: What Science Can and Cannot Tell Us About Human Nature*, London: Phoenix Books/Weidenfeld & Nicholson.

Nolan, J. (1998) *The Therapeutic State: Justifying Government at Century's End*, New York: New York University Press.

Pupavac, V. (2001) 'Therapeutic Governance: Psycho-social Intervention and Trauma Risk Management', *Disasters* 25(4): 358–72.

Rogers, C. (1961) *On Becoming a Person*, Boston, MA: Houghton Mifflin.

Rogers, C. (1983) *Freedom to Learn for the 1980s*, New York: Merrill.

Social Exclusion Unit (1998) *Bridging the Gap: New Opportunities for 16–18-year-olds Not in Education or Training*, London: HMSO.

Socialist Education Association (SEA) (2003) *Excessive Testing is Bad for Children*, newsletter, Summer, available at www.SocialistEducation.org.uk.

Key readings

Ecclestone, K. (2004) 'Learning or Therapy?: the Demoralisation of Education', *British Journal of Educational Studies* 29(2): forthcoming. (This is an extended version of the arguments in this chapter.)

Fevre, R. (2001) *The Demoralisation of Western Culture: Social Theory and the Dilemmas of Modern Living*, London: Continuum.

Freire, P. (1999) *Pedagogy of the Oppressed*, revised 20th anniversary edition, New York: Continuum.

Furedi, F. (1999) *The Culture of Fear: Risk Taking and the Morality of Low Expectation*, London: Cassell.

Focus question

Do you consider that the therapeutic ethos is beneficial in that it softens instrumental approaches to education or does it de-moralise people by making them dull and comfortable?

CHAPTER 26

THE TROUBLE WITH LIFELONG LEARNING

Linden West

Lifelong learning is the flavour of the times, beloved of governments, policy makers and corporations. In a foreword to a Green Paper, *The Learning Age: A Renaissance for a New Britain* (DfEE 1998), the then Secretary of State for Education and Employment in England suggested that lifelong learning offered the means, no less, to a new renaissance, for a new century. Lifelong learning, the argument proceeded, represented the acquisition of knowledge and skills over the life cycle, encouraging the creativity and imagination of all people. The vision and values, on the surface at least, appeared to be more than narrowly utilitarian and vocational: there was talk of learning for citizenship while the Fryer Report (Fryer 1997) on lifelong learning noted the significance it had for spiritual as well as democratic health.

However, as many commentators have observed, the main discursive thrust in government pronouncements is economistic rather than to do with renaissance or the human spirit (Field 2000). The preoccupation is with worklong learning and a perpetual updating of knowledge and skills in that context. This includes individuals' capacity to adjust (under the impact of globalisation, technological and scientific innovation) to a constantly changing work environment. The emphasis is on adaptability to the market and the need, in effect, for people to constantly reinvent themselves as marketable products. Frank Coffield (1999), an enthusiastic proponent of lifelong learning, questions the term, and associated values, when it entails shifting responsibility for learning on to individuals to ensure employability or the modernisation of education becomes primarily a matter of servicing employer needs. Most official policy literature, as indicated, presents lifelong learning as a means to ensure a more productive and efficient workforce. Notions of renaissance, individually or collectively, get lost.

But there is a broader, more humanistic, holistic as well as democratic and critical discourse too. One core idea here has to do with the increasingly central role of learning, or reflexivity, in a diverse range of contexts, including composing biographies in a more fragmented, individualised, constantly changing culture (Field 2000); or of the role of lifelong learning in processes of professional development as well as, at a very different level, in struggles to reinvigorate democratic processes and active citizenship. Lifelong learning, in these different horizons, has also moved centre stage.

Too vague?

Lifelong learning, however, begs many questions of meaning. It can be considered too vague for serious analysis: learning is what we do all the time, often without knowing it. We learn from relationships (or not), from conversations with friends, from the media, from everyday encounters at work or in communities as well as in cyberspace. We may learn, at a deeper level, from experience of failure, loss and death, or from the birth of a child or when taking on a new role. But we may fail to learn too and life can become a series of traps, dead ends or a source of overwhelming anxiety from which there is no escape. Learning, in these terms, may amount to little more than survival (Williamson 1998). The notion of learning at the heart of this chapter is more proactive than this and has to do with the quality of an individual's response to new experience, which can range from the merely adaptive, or even pathological, to a more creative, emotionally open and generative response (West 2001).

The basic argument is that the concept can and should be reclaimed for more humanistic and democratic ends. It represents a potentially important way of thinking about how people can best negotiate a range of biographical, professional and collective discontinuities, uncertainties and challenges in the contemporary world. The biographical learning imperative is strong, for instance, in our more fragmented and individualised culture. Whereas in previous agrarian and industrial societies people lived, inter- and intra-generationally, according to more or less clearly inherited scripts, economic change means these can quickly unravel or are made redundant. The new global economic order involves fund managers, banks and corporations, as well as millions of individual investors, transferring immense sums of money from one part of the globe to another at the flick of a switch. Traditional economies, communities and shared biographical expectations can be destabilised overnight (Giddens 1999). Processes of economic liberalisation and individuation, as well as the collapse or marginalisation of many of the informal mechanisms by which working-class communities historically supported themselves (trades unions, churches, etc., as well as the extended family), mean that people, like it or not, are forced to take greater responsibility for the circumstances, rules and direction of their lives.

The point made by various theorists (Beck 1997; Giddens 1999) is that composing a biography in a world of unpredictability requires the capacity, and resources, to make meaningful choices and reorientate oneself afresh and on a recurrent basis. We are all perpetually confronted with new knowledge, or rather competing versions of how we should live or behave, including as professionals. We cannot escape making choices and the need to learn our way through and beyond confrontations with different knowledge claims in situations in which there are no easy answers. The range of the confrontation is extraordinary, from the banal – what is currently fashionable – to the deeply complex, surrounding, for example, what it means to be a man or woman or for that matter a doctor (Field 2000; West 2001). But the scope and meaning of learning implied is far broader than what happens in universities or more formal settings. Informal, tacit, subjective and emotional learning moves centre stage while the struggle for agency, authenticity and the capacity to live with uncertainty becomes key. Such learning challenges the traditional paradigms of learning, which assumed a Cartesian split of mind and body, with the former as the prime locus and motor of learning. It also challenges the privileging of propositional knowledge as well as of notions of certainty and of the idea of learning as linear progression best engaged in earlier life. There is a basic challenge too to an overly individualistic model of learning.

Recomposing a biography

Some of my own in-depth and longitudinal biographical research has focused on struggles to compose lives – and to build more confident reflexivity and agency – in conditions of pervasive insecurity (West 1996); among working-class men, for instance, living in communities where historic occupational structures and biographical predictabilities have fractured. Men, in such contexts, can easily become trapped in the pretence of coping and psychological defensiveness. They can struggle to handle the emotional aspects of lost status, given their relative investment in public roles and how they have been socialised into repressing anxiety and denying vulnerability. They can end up feeling trapped, at a complete loss and clinically depressed.

In my research, what was interesting in the narratives of particular men who were managing to recompose their lives relatively successfully was the central place of informal and emotional learning in their struggles. Even when learning took place in formal contexts, for example in an Access programme, the space provided for experiment in composing a new identity was, on reflection, as important as the formal curriculum. A turning point was frequently the feeling that one could successfully meet the academic requirements of the programme and thus, in effect, confirm a new identity as a student in higher education, with all that that might entail. But this depended on forging new and positive relationships with a range of other learners, teachers and significant others. This was learning of a deeply emotional, biographical as well as intellectual kind, in which letting go of a past identity and perceiving self in a new, more positive light was central (West 1996).

The creative struggle to become a more effective professional has many parallels to the above. In a biographical and longitudinal study of GPs working in inner London, what was frequently crucial to being a more effective and contented doctor, in their narratives, had to do with learning emotional and self-awareness, as much as clinical technique or formal knowledge. This included the ability to transcend the omnipotent, omniscient myth – often imbibed in training – that the doctor ought to know and be able to cope. Many doctors, especially when working in marginalised communities, can struggle with large numbers of distressed and disturbed patients. Disturbance can disturb a doctor and s/he has to learn to handle the emotional distress and sense of inadequacy this can evoke. The capacity to engage creatively and openly with patients (similar points might be made for other professions) stemmed from their own, often painfully won subjective and emotional learning, as much as from formal training, including from experiences of mental illness and depression in themselves as well as of from being silenced and marginalised in their own lives, because of a particular identity, like many of their patients (as gay or a woman, for instance) (West 2001).

Finally, lifewide as well as lifelong learning may be central to developing successful popular education programmes, and the active forms of engagement these require. In my work on family learning in marginalised communities, success in particular projects often appeared to depend on the extent to which vulnerable and disaffected parents could experience greater agency, and thus hope, in their lives. In one project, for example, young single mums learned to be advocates in relation to housing for single parents, while, in another, parents were active and creative in its governance, despite initial terrors and resistance. But such openness to new possibility was heavily dependent on the quality of relationships with particular workers and the personal attributes, insights and values they brought to interactions. Good projects had a learning as well as democratic culture in which power was shared and parents were enabled to take risks and move from the periphery towards the centre of the community of practice. Emotion and relationships were at the heart of these change processes: the development of relationships in which there could be greater honesty, openness, space for reflection and even anger without fear that all would disintegrate, was vital in enabling parents to take risks.

In fact, for all these different, diverse groups of people – men undergoing major change and struggling to rebuild careers, doctors working in the inner city or marginalised parents engaging in community projects – success in learning seemed to depend on the quality of relationships in which they were embedded and significant others, who, the learners felt, understood and could accept them without reservation, yet who also challenged them to take risks. Success also depended on having secure space for imaginative play and experiment with identity, for storytelling and trying out new ideas, whether in a women's group, or in case study-based learning for doctors (in which they could be open about their feelings and explore different management options). In fact the capacity to tell and experiment with stories – or what I term narrative repertoire – seems essential to life spacing of the kind described above. Generating stories, on more of our own terms, is the means by which we create meaning and direction in a life (that is, learn) and is also essential to psychological health.

We have moved a conceptual distance from the narrow notion of lifelong learning as adaptability to the supposed imperatives of the market and of the value placed on a perpetual remarketing of self as commodity. We have moved instead towards a notion of lifelong learning as central to the struggle we all share, to create a life on more of our own terms, however constrained and difficult this may be; a process acutely dependent on others and the quality of our relationships. Learning, in this holistic, psychosocial perspective, moves centre stage in a late or postmodern world where we are forced to make choices, and to compose a life, without confident reference to inherited templates, established knowledge or undisputed authority. Such learning is lifewide as well as lifelong when viewed through the lens of biographical research. It is about learning to be more of an author in our own lives, with the help and support of others and their stories, rather than feeling overwhelmed, stuck and powerless.

References

Beck, U. (1997) *The Reinvention of Politics: Rethinking Modernity in a Global Social Order*, Cambridge: Polity Press.
Coffield, F. (1999) 'Breaking the Consensus: Lifelong Learning as Social Control', *British Journal of Educational Research* 25(4), September: 479–99.
DfEE (1998) *The Learning Age: A Renaissance for a New Britain*, London: DfEE.
Field, J. (2000) *Lifelong Learning and the New Educational Order*, Stoke-on-Trent: Trentham Books.
Fryer, R. (1997) *Learning for the Twenty-first Century*, London: DfEE.
Giddens, A. (1999) *Runaway World*, London: Profile.
West, L. (1996) *Beyond Fragments: Adults, Motivation and Higher education. A Biographical Analysis*, London: Taylor & Francis.
West, L. (2001) *Doctors on the Edge: General Practitioners, Health and Learning in the Inner-city*, London: Free Association Books.
Williamson, B. (1998) *Lifeworlds and Learning: Essays in the Theory, Philosophy and Practice of Lifelong Learning*, Leicester: NIACE.

Key readings

Field, J. (2000) *Lifelong Learning and the New Educational Order*, Stoke-on-Trent: Trentham Books.
Giddens, A. (1999) *Runaway World*, London: Profile.
Williamson, B. (1998) *Lifeworlds and Learning: Essays in the Theory, Philosophy and Practice of Lifelong Learning*, Leicester: NIACE.

Focus question

How far is the current interest in lifelong learning about pressurising individuals to take more responsibility for worklong learning and employability, or about our need to find meaning in an unpredictable, constantly changing world?

CHAPTER 27

FE CANNOT SAVE THE ECONOMY

Jon Bryan

There is an increasing tendency for solutions to the economy to be sought in the sphere of education. While this is not a new idea – in 1874 Disraeli said 'Upon the education of the people of this country, the fate of this country depends' – it is an idea that is gaining in popularity with both writers and politicians. The *21st Century Skills* White Paper DfES 2003) is recent evidence of the government's belief that a strong link needs to be built between the education system and the economy to boost productivity and competitiveness. Unveiled in July 2003, the White Paper gave particular prominence to the role that further education can play in reviving the economy. It seems that the government sees a key role for colleges and other training providers in helping to overcome the skills gap.

There are two concerns that I have about this notion that FE can save the economy. First, it is largely unchallenged and unproved that economic activity and productivity will increase if we can improve the links between colleges and employers. Second, I believe that it is undesirable to have colleges in such a direct link with the business community. If college curricula are written to satisfy the needs of industry, FE will cease to be about furthering education and more about training for jobs.

The rise of vocational education

Although there is a long history to this debate (as illustrated by the quotation from Disraeli), today's emphasis on vocational education has a starting point in the 1970s rather than the 1870s. We can trace recent discussions back to James Callaghan's speech at Ruskin College in 1976. Callaghan was Prime Minister at the time and he argued that the education system needed to adapt to meet the needs of British industry. The vocational initiatives in the 1980s, such as the Technical and Vocational Education Initiative (TVEI) and the Certificate for Pre-Vocational Education (CPVE), can be seen as reactions to the ideas espoused by Callaghan, even though they were introduced by a different government. Tony Blair's cry for 'Education, education, education' can also be seen as a continuation of this stress on improving the skills and qualifications of the nation to help the economy.

As the term of office of the present government has continued, the momentum for these ideas has increased. It is evident from both their policies and the ideas that are expressed by Ministers that the linking of education and the economy has become firmly embedded in New Labour ideals.

John Healey, one of the many Ministers that Tony Blair has charged with responsibility for FE, explained how he saw his role when he was appointed as Adult Skills Minister in 2001: 'First and foremost it's an economic policy area. It's a question of employability, it's a question of productivity and competitiveness' (Kingston 2001).

Healey went on to explain that colleges had a key part to play in this. When asked about the role of FE in this process of economic regeneration, he explained that it had 'A central role. It can't be done without further education' (Kingston 2001).

This is part of the problem with educational thinking in British political life. Rather than perhaps leave economic policy to the Chancellor of the Exchequer and concentrate on educational matters, the Minister responsible for FE argues that his first priority is the economy.

Eighteen months later, John Healey was in a different role in the government, but still keen to promote the role of FE in helping to improve competitiveness and productivity. He argued that, 'Better skills among the workforce mean greater productivity for the economy', and he threw down a challenge to FE stating that 'Colleges and other suppliers have to interact with local employers and employees to ask: "What skills training do you need to succeed in your business and progress in your workplace? How best can we meet that need?"' (Healey 2002).

As with many critiques of education, Healey argues the current college curriculum is irrelevant to employers and argues the need for change. The danger here is that FE ceases to be further education if it is merely a reaction to the needs and whims of employers. Unfortunately, the views espoused by Healey are not unpopular, even among those who work in colleges. A group of writers associated with Bilston Community College (now part of Wolverhampton College) illustrates this last point.

The Bilston College fallacy

At the end of the 1990s, a collection of writers associated with Bilston Community College put forward a set of arguments about the role that FE can play in revitalising the economy. Their aim was to look at the various ways in which FE colleges can help in the economic regeneration of the country.

Defining economic regeneration as, 'the process of renewal and reinvigoration of the relations of production, distribution and the consumption of goods and services' (Reeves 1997: 1), the Bilston College collective believe there are various ways that FE can help the economy. From basic skills to international partnerships, these writers share the belief that the key to economic progress lies in further education.

There is an optimistic theme running throughout the book as they believe that their work in and through the college can increase the skills level of individuals, create more opportunities for employment, provide a boost for small businesses and improve the productivity and competitiveness of the economy.

However, one of the main failings of this book is the assumption on which it is based. As the editor states, 'This book does not attempt to address the more fundamental questions of whether and in what way national economic performance is related to educational level' (Reeves 1997: 4). Ultimately, this means that their arguments remain unsubstantiated.

Can FE save the economy?

Are Healey and the Bilston collective correct in their argument about colleges being able to increase productivity and competitiveness and help in economic regeneration? Let's examine the arguments.

The idea that the problems of the economy can be solved by further education rests upon two false premises: that the reason that people are unable to obtain work is because of a lack of skills; and that productivity can be improved by raising the skills level in society. It is not that the workforce is unskilled, far from it. This country has a large number of individuals with high-level qualifications. That many graduates now have to work in employment for which a degree is not necessary is proof that the problem lies not with the workforce and the supply of labour, but with the supply of jobs and the operation of the market.

One writer who has challenged the necessity for a more skilled/qualified workforce is John Philpott. Philpott is chief economist at the Chartered Institute of Personnel and Development and he argues that the fault lies not with the workforce, but with the way that businesses use their employees. He claims that too few employers make the most of the skills on offer, stating that 'there is no guarantee that increasing the supply and level of qualifications will translate into higher productivity. At worst, skilled people simply end up performing tasks for which they are overqualified' (Philpott 2003).

The thrust of his argument is that what must change is what happens in the workplace: 'Unless and until this improves, increasing the supply of qualifications will have no more than a limited impact on productivity' (Philpott 2003).

For Philpott, the emphasis on FE and skills is misplaced. Rather than see the solution to the economy in the supply of skilled/qualified labour, he argues that it is the way that labour is used that is more important. Economic issues of competitiveness and productivity cannot be solved through concentrating on just one aspect of the production process.

This is the main failing of Healey, the Bilston collective and those who share the similar basic premise about the need to raise skills to improve the economy. Their arguments express a one-sided view of economics as they only address one aspect of the economy – the supply of labour. There is an assumption that other aspects of the economy are either of no concern, or cannot be influenced in any way. Changing the supply of labour by increasing the skills and qualifications in the country, while leaving other aspects of the economy untouched, is not a guarantee of economic success.

For example, jobs are not created simply by increasing the level of skills. The opposite could be true as a skilled worker could perhaps perform the work of two unskilled workers. Employment is created where profits are able to be made, regardless of the skill level of the workforce. Therefore, to argue that FE can save the economy is to misunderstand the nature of business and of capitalism. It is the ability to make a profit that determines the creation of employment opportunities, not the skill levels of the workforce.

However, this is not the only problem with the idea of increasing the links between the economy and the education system. What role do we see for FE in society?

What type of further education do we want?

For those of us who work in FE, a key consequence of this debate is what do we want to be teaching? Those who want to see FE being used to save the economy assume that the focus of courses should be on what students will need in the world of work. To oppose this is to argue that colleges should not focus on the skills that are going to be needed for work. While this would seem a strange proposition, we do have to ask what we want further education to be about. Do we see it as furthering the education of others, or do we see it as entirely vocational – simply training students for employment?

There is a need for vocational education in colleges and there is certainly a demand for it. However, there also needs to be space for education for its own sake. Education is not solely about preparing us for work. It is about broadening our understanding of society and developing our critical faculties so that we can understand, analyse, interpret and assess. These are skills that are useful to everyone and help to make us who we are. FE offers people the ability to think, communicate, discuss, evaluate and be more than just a cog in the machine.

Colleges have always been about providing an arena for 16–19-year-olds and adults to have an educational experience that is different to the one provided by schools. There is still a large demand for academic studies in FE, as the popularity of subjects such as Psychology and Sociology demonstrates. Moreover, there is a need for students to study purely for educational value, rather than solely for the exchange value of being able to gain employment at the end of studying.

The skills agenda devalues what education should be about. FE is just that – furthering our education by continuing to broaden the minds of those who are above school age. Challenging the skills agenda can help us to restate what FE is about, so we can produce individuals for society who are educated for life, not just trained for a job.

References

DfES (2003) *21st Century Skills: Realising Our Potential*, London: HMSO.
Healey, J. (2002) 'Filling the Gaps', *The Guardian*, 3 December.
Kingston, P. (2001) '"It's the Economy, Stupid"', *The Guardian*, 26 June.
Philpott, J. (2003) 'The Critique of Qualifications', *The Guardian*, 2 September.
Reeves, F. (ed.) (1997) *Further Education As Economic Regeneration: The Starting Point*, Wolverhampton: Bilston College Publications.

Key readings

Ashton, D. and Green, F. (1996) *Education, Training and the Global Economy*, Cheltenham: Edward Elgar.
DfES (2003) *21st Century Skills: Realising Our Potential*, London: HMSO.
Reeves, F. (ed.) (1997) *Further Education As Economic Regeneration: The Starting Point*, Wolverhampton: Bilston College Publications.

Focus question

If further education has no role in relation to the skills agenda, what is its function? Should its role be solely to educate?

CHAPTER 28

TAKING CONTROL

Fashioning the new citizen

Jerome Satterthwaite and Lyn Martin

Contemporary discussion of citizenship in the UK must start with Bernard Crick, David Blunkett's guru and former tutor (as the Campaign for Real Education (CRE 2000) recently described him). Crick chaired the Citizenship Advisory Group (see CAG 1998), and the subsequent Advisory Group on Citizenship for 16–19 year-olds (see FEFC 2000). Crick is an old-fashioned republican drawing on a vision of citizenship originating in classical Greece, a vision most perfectly articulated in the funeral oration of Pericles reported by Thucydides:

> our ordinary citizens, though occupied with the pursuits of industry, are still fair judges of public matters; for, unlike any other nation, ... we Athenians are able to judge at all events if we cannot originate, and, instead of looking on discussion as a stumbling-block in the way of action, we think it an indispensable preliminary to any wise action at all. ... It was by courage, sense of duty, and a keen feeling of honour in action that men were enabled to win all this, and ... no personal failure in an enterprise could make them consent to deprive their country of their valour, but they laid it at her feet as the most glorious contribution that they could offer.
>
> (Peloponnesian War, Book 2.34–46)

This inspirational statement of (male) democratic citizenship will be as familiar to Crick as it has been to generations of public school boys. But not all Greek thinkers shared this vision. Aristotle (in *A Treatise on Government*, Book III, chapter IV) made citizenship depressingly simple – a matter of obedience and control: 'A citizen is one who obeys the magistrate'; and Plato in *The Republic* famously dismissed democracy as merely the third stage in the degradation of the body politic, beyond which the final step was mob rule. For Plato democracy was 'an agreeable form of anarchy'. His democratic citizen was in the grip of '*unnecessary and expensive appetites ... subject to no order or restraint*' (viii.558). There is, then, a central dilemma in classical thinking about citizenship, which has dogged discussion ever since: on the one hand, the ideal is celebrated of free citizens, heroically sacrificing themselves for the common good; on the other there is the more sceptical view, that the people are unfit for political responsibility. It is this view which leads to the conclusion that the state works best when citizens do what they are told: that, in practice, democracy does not work.

Rousseau's struggles on this issue are instructive. In *Émile*, commenting on the approach to education of eighteenth-century France – in our own day so mercilessly analysed by Foucault (Foucault 1987) – the natural state, before the intervention of civilising education, is innocent:

> The literature and learning of our day tend rather to destroy than to build up. We find fault after the manner of a master; to make proposals we must adopt a different style, a style less in accordance with the pride of the philosopher. ... We know nothing of childhood; and with our mistaken notions the further we advance the further we go astray. ...
> Nature provides for the child's growth in her own fashion and this should never be thwarted. ... Let us lay it down as an incontrovertible rule that the first impulses of nature are always right; there is no original perversity in the human heart. ... Reading is the curse of childhood.
>
> (Mason 1979: 182)

But in *The Social Contract* (Cole 1955) he speaks of the 'very remarkable change in man' brought about in the passage 'from the state of nature to the civil state, ... substituting justice for instinct in his conduct, and giving his actions the morality they had formerly lacked'. It all depends, for Rousseau, on the quality of the political regime. But his argument is circular: we get the good political regime when the people take control; and when they do, their morality will improve and they will be free. Deviant individuals must learn to conform. They must be 'forced to be free' (Cress 1987: 150).

Notwithstanding the strained and somewhat casuistic thinking exemplified in Rousseau, the view has consistently been, ever since Plato, that the way to resolve the dilemma of good citizenship is by education. It was Robert Lowe, some 23 centuries after Plato, responding with dismay to the extension of the franchise in 1867, who gave this view its most memorable (and most often misquoted) expression, urging that it would now be necessary to 'compel our future masters to learn their letters' (Briggs 1962: 521). He doubted the soundness of judgement of the new voters: they needed education so as to know how properly to make political and moral judgements. Lowe was here making the comfortable assumption that the members of his own social group knew best: that their point of view was, as if by axiom, the one the masses should be educated to adopt. Crick has his sights on the young; but he is contributing to a long tradition in so far as he aims to correct, through education, the assumed moral imbecility of the people (the δεμος), so as to enable them properly to handle their democratic responsibilities. Among the 17 values and dispositions listed as learning outcomes of citizenship education (CAG 1998: 44) are 'judging and acting by a moral code ... determination to act justly ... concern for the common good ... civility and respect for the rule of law.'

Citizenship education in schools is thus unashamedly concerned with ethics. What is not confronted is the stubborn question of who knows best what makes a good citizen, and how we should decide who knows best, and upon what criteria. These questions, so fundamental to ethics and civics alike, are evaded. In the void left by their absence, hegemonic convention is quietly endorsed. Ultimately, it seems, young people, like the luckless citizens of Rousseau, had better do as they are told. When this is the argument for promoting citizenship education, it should be no surprise if it is greeted with scant enthusiasm.

We need a more powerful reason than the patrician logic of the likes of Robert Lowe, to motivate the development of a citizenship education which can effectively challenge the lacklustre response in the UK and elsewhere (Park 1995, 1999, 2000; Russell *et al.* 2002) of the electorate, particularly the young, to their responsibilities as citizens. It is notable that, in the subsequent report, *Citizenship for 16–19-year-olds in Education and Training*, values and dispositions are not listed as learning outcomes; the focus of attention now is on skills and knowledge. The presumption is that, by the age of 16, young people have learned the values and dispositions they need for good citizenship. Thinking on citizenship may now make progress; we can begin to ask the real-politik questions about why it matters.

Citizenship education matters because, as Paul Gelderd argues:

> The citizenship agenda is part and parcel of a wider agenda about social inclusion. Citizenship education seeks to give to members of socially excluded groups the skills to be more effective as people in the workplace, to engage in their communities and have a voice: it is, in the jargon, Capacity Building. It is not about telling them what is right and wrong, what they should believe, what values they should uphold; it is about enabling them to contribute to the community and through that to their region and society. Citizenship education is about preventing people being marginalised in society through lack of communication skills and giving them the skills to be active in the community, increasing their confidence, their sense of self worth. In the end it is about people having a stake in society, being valued.
>
> (Gelderd 2003)

How can this be done? Crick has rather vaguely warned readers of *The Guardian* (30 April 2002) that 'many existing practices in government and education will need challenging hard', if young people are going to start taking citizenship seriously. More pointedly, the Children and Young People's Unit (CYPU 2002a) responding to the initiative of John Denham, Minister for Children and Young People, has taken the simple and most obviously democratic step of asking young people themselves what can be done to make citizenship an issue they think it worthwhile to discuss. The young people's responses were heavily focused on the need for better, more accessible and more immediately relevant (i.e. local) information. They did not want to be told what to think; equally, they did not want politicians to assume they knew in advance what young people were thinking. They reminded government and media of the diversity of young people's views: that there were no safe generalisations about 'what young people think'. It was all about making the issues clearly known, so that young people (young citizens) could think for themselves from a well-informed position:

> Talk to us in language we can understand – simple, clear, basic, understandable, keep us informed.

> Talk to us directly, regularly, and in our environments – not just at election times, not just when we're old enough to vote, and face to face, not through a leaflet.

> Listen and respond to our concerns – don't lecture us and don't assume we have no opinions or you know what we think.

> Respect our diversity – and recognise that you need to find new ways of reaching out to different groups of young people.
>
> (CYPU 2002a: 8)

Our own small-scale research has reinforced the view that young people want to be taken seriously and included in the processes of democracy. In July 2003 we asked members of the sixth form at Torpoint Community School to talk about citizenship.

They had no specific standpoint on citizenship issues, except an understandably impatient sense that the adult world should relax its control and trust them to think for themselves. Instead, their response was to focus on control:

> You can do what you want but you get chucked out of the sixth form.
>
> Yeah because there are so many rules.
>
> I think the rules here are quite petty.
>
> Like you're not allowed to dye your hair and stuff like that ... you're not allowed to play music ... you're not allowed to go home. ... It's silly that you're not allowed to go home when there are no lessons.
>
> If you make rules for good people they'll stick to them but if you make too many rules then they're just going to ignore them.
>
> You don't really realise how many laws there are. And the government's bringing in more and more and you don't really know. ... You're getting to the stage where everything that isn't compulsory is banned. When you're out and about there's age restrictions like drinking. But when you're over 16 you don't need other people to make decisions for you. Like the drinking thing. Like having sex ... I don't think the sex law is really that important. I think it sort of makes people do it more (Yeah). I think there's too much control in some places. ... It's like stupid things like drinking. If there wasn't a law against drinking young people wouldn't be that interested in doing it. Because drugs are illegal it creates this whole 'Oh I'm going to go out and take drugs'. If there was less control for things like that it would kind of reduce it.

These young people are asking to be left alone to decide for themselves. They trust their own judgement and see no need to have their opinions shaped for them. Rules imposed by their elders are little more than a nuisance; they believe that they do not restrain young people's behaviour and may produce the very practices they seek to control. For these young people, issues of citizenship have to do with taking responsibility for themselves. It seems that the wider issues of citizenship – those well-informed interventions in the community which Gelderd speaks of and which the citizenship agenda is intended to promote, will remain of secondary concern to young people while their freedom to act as they see fit is being restricted by a more powerful group – the adult world – whose opinions, spelled out in what they see as often frivolous regulation, they are unwilling to respect.

References

Briggs, A. (1962) *The Age of Improvement*, London: Longman.
Campaign for Real Education (CRE) (2000) *Newsletter*, Winter.
Children and Young People's Unit (CYPU) (2002a) *Upfront – YVote?/YNot? Young people tell Government, politicians and the media what they think and what they need*, http://www.cypu.gov.uk/corporate/downloads/CYPU_Upfrontdoc.pdf.
Children and Young People's Unit (CYPU) (2002b). *Young People and Politics: A Report on the YVote/YNot Project*, available at http://www.cypu.gov.uk/corporate/search_cypu.cfm.
Citizenship Advisory Group (CAG) (1998) *Education for Citizenship and the Teaching of Democracy in Schools*, London: Qualifications and Curriculum Authority.
Cole, G. (1955) *Jean-Jacques Rousseau: The Social Contract*, London: Dent.
Cress, D. (ed.) (1987) *Jean-Jacques Rousseau: The Basic Political Writings*, Indianapolis, IN: Hackett.

Crick, B. (2000) *Essays on Citizenship*, London: Continuum.

Crick, B. (ed.) (2001) *Citizens: Towards a Citizenship Culture*, Oxford: Blackwell.

Crick, B. (2002) 'Mobilising Youth and Democracy: Voter Antipathy Must Be Countered by Sixth-form Citizenship', *The Guardian*, 30 April.

FEFC (2000) *Citizenship for 16–19-year-olds in Education and Training: Report of the Advisory Group to the Secretary of State for Education and Employment*, London: FEFC.

Foucault, M. (1987 [1977]) *Discipline and Punish: The Birth of the Prison*, London: Penguin.

Gelderd, P. (2003) Personal interview with the authors.

Mason, J. (ed.) (1979) *The Indispensable Rousseau*, London: Quartet Books.

Park, A. (1995) 'Teenagers and their Politics', in Jowell, R., Curtice, J., Park, A., Brook, L. and Ahrendt, A. (eds), *British Social Attitudes: the 12th Report*, Aldershot: Dartmouth.

Park, A. (1999) 'Young People and Political Apathy', in Jowell, R., Curtice, J., Park, A., Thomson, K. and Jarvis, L. (eds), *British Social Attitudes: the 16th Report*, Ashgate: Aldershot.

Park, A. (2000) 'The Generation Game', in Jowell, R., Curtice, J., Park, A., Thomson, K., Jarvis, L., Bromley, C. and Stratford, N. (eds), *British Social Attitudes: the 17th Report*, London: Sage.

Russell, A., Fieldhouse, E., Purdam, K. and Kalra, V. (2002) *Voter Engagement and Young People*, London: Electoral Commission.

DfEE and QCA (1999) *The National Curriculum for England: Citizenship*, London: DfEE and QCA.

Key readings

Children and Young People's Unit (CYPU) (2002) *Young People and Politics: A Report on the YVote/YNot Project*, available at http://www.cypu.gov.uk/corporate/search_cypu.cfm.

Crick, B. (ed.) (2001) *Citizens: Towards a Citizenship Culture*, Oxford: Blackwell.

FEFC (2000) *Citizenship for 16–19-year-olds In Education and Training: Report of the Advisory Group to the Secretary of State for Education and Employment*, London: FEFC.

Focus question

How far are the responses of the sixth-formers quoted in this chapter concerns about real freedom or restrictions on their personal lifestyle?

CHAPTER 29

LABOUR'S FUEL

Lifelong learning policy as labour power production

Glenn Rikowski

Like mother's apple pie or peace in our time, lifelong learning sounds like a surefire good thing. The notion that people should learn new information and skills throughout their lives borders on common sense. Increasingly, the UK government has encouraged us all to become lifelong learners, with a succession of reports, initiatives and programmes on lifelong learning emerging over the last 10 years.

Lifelong learning is a highly contested concept (Smith and Spurling 1999). Rather than attempting yet another definition here, this article indicates that the dominant outlook within lifelong learning policy is that of economic utility based on a perceived need to respond to the challenges of boosting national competitiveness within the context of globalisation (Coffield 1999).

Within this scenario, it will be argued that lifelong learning policy in England has been principally about labour power production: socially producing people with the skills, attitudes and personal qualities necessary for effective workplace performance. The focus is on England as there is not space enough to pinpoint differences between lifelong learning policy in constituent nations of the UK. After explaining some key concepts such as labour power and human capital, evidence is provided for the claim that lifelong learning policy is dominated by seeking to boost the quality of labour power. Finally, explanations of why this has occurred are explored.

Labour, labour power and human capital

In contemporary society, all the commodities that sustain us depend in various ways on our labour for their production. However, in turn the quality and quantity of our labour depends on our *capacity* to labour: our *labour power*. Karl Marx defined labour power as: 'the aggregate of those mental and physical capabilities existing in a human being, which he exercises whenever he produces a use-value of any description' (1867: 164). Thus when we labour in commodity production we organise our skills, knowledge and physical capabilities to produce the required result. As argued elsewhere (Rikowski 2002), the 'mental' characteristics include aspects of our personality and various social and work attitudes, and not just skills and knowledge. Therefore, labour power is an aspect of our personhood, our selves.

A use-value is a useful thing, something that has use for us. However, in capitalist society – the kind of society we live in today – our labour in the workplace also produces *value*, argues Marx (1867). Value is stored in commodities as we produce them. Some of this value is represented in the wage, but the rest becomes *surplus value*, which is unpaid labour. It is out of this surplus value that the owners and controllers of businesses receive their profits, after they have paid taxes and other deductions.

We can see from this that the working day, week, etc. is split into two parts: one part comprising value that goes to form wages, and another that yields surplus value and profits. As the quality of our labour power increases then we produce commodities more quickly, and this means we create the value represented in the wage sooner too; leaving more labour-time to produce surplus value and profits for the employer. This is why the *quality* of labour power is crucial for employers. Labour power is the fuel for what Marx called 'the living, form-giving fire' (Marx 1858: 361); that is *labour*, which transforms raw materials, designs and ideas into commodities.

In capitalist societies, through recruitment, contract and firing and redundancy processes, labour power is bought and sold as a commodity. Labour power in this sense can be seen as 'human capital', a term used by labour economists since the 1960s and increasingly by education researchers and writers. It is the accumulation of skills, knowledge and other capabilities that can be sold by individuals to employers for a wage. As the next section shows, lifelong learning policy in England is founded primarily on enhancing the quality of labour power (human capital).

The evidence

The foundations of contemporary lifelong learning policy in England can be traced to the first two *Competitiveness* reports of John Major's Conservative administration (DTI 1994, 1995). In these reports there was a concern with raising the quality of human capital. Furthermore, it was argued that education and training needed to be restructured to attain higher-quality human capital in the face of rising competition in a context of globalisation, where nation-states were engaged in economic struggles for shares of world trade. In the section on Education and Training in the first *Competitiveness* report (DTI 1994: ch. 4), it was argued that higher-quality human capital is crucial for the 'lifeblood of a modern, internationally competitive economy' (DTI 1994: 30).

The Conservative government's *Consultation Document* on lifelong learning (DfEE 1995) can be viewed as a deepening of the policy perspectives advanced in their first *Competitiveness* report. In the introduction, the Secretaries of State for Education and Employment, Scotland and Wales argued that: 'Creating a culture of lifetime learning is crucial to sustaining and maintaining our international competitiveness' (DfEE 1995: 3). The consultation document reiterated the links between lifelong learning, globalisation and national competitiveness. The 1996 policy framework document (DfEE 1996) made the same links.

Helena Kennedy's report to the English Further Education Funding Council (FEFC), *Learning Works* (Kennedy 1997), was the next significant official document to address the issue of lifelong learning policy; specifically, the role that the further education sector in England could play in promoting lifelong learning. The work for this report was mostly undertaken during John Major's Conservative government and appeared in June 1997, one month after New Labour's landslide election victory. *Learning Works* exhibited an altogether different outlook on lifelong learning, as did the Fryer Report which appeared later in 1997 (Fryer 1997). They had greater emphasis on personal and social development, citizenship and learning about the society we live in, although the usual references to learning for UK economic competitiveness were also present. However, for Kennedy, learning for 'life' and work were viewed as inseparable (1997: 16). The Kennedy Report also criticised the market-driven reforms in further education based on the incorporation of colleges in 1993, which placed colleges within a competitive environment to attract student customers whose recruitment brought in money.

Although both the Kennedy and Fryer reports received wide coverage in the educational press, the New Labour government largely ignored them. Instead, New Labour threw its efforts into the Green Paper, *The Learning Age* (DfEE 1998). As Kennedy and Fryer had widened the concept of lifelong learning, the Green Paper narrowed it down once more towards human capital development. In the 'Foreword' to the Green Paper, David Blunkett (then Minister for Education and Employment) noted that: 'Learning is the key to prosperity. . . . Investment in human capital will be the foundation of success in the knowledge-based global economy of the twenty-first century' (DfEE 1998: 7). Blunkett viewed the main aim of the consultation following *The Learning Age* as being about 'how learning throughout life will build human capital' (DfEE 1998: 7). While Blunkett also mentioned the importance of learning for making a civilised society, developing spirituality and promoting active citizenship, it was clear that enhancing human capital was lifelong learning's prime mission. The body of *The Learning Age* reiterated this message. The opening quotation from Tony Blair noted that 'Education is the best economic policy we have' (DfEE 1998: 9). For New Labour, lifelong learning's main goal was as a generator of human capital.

This theme was taken up once more in the White Paper, *Learning to Succeed* (DfEE 1999). The White Paper also proposed a new 'framework for post-16 learning' which was to result in the abolition of the Training and Enterprise Councils and the Further Education Funding Council and the emergence of the Learning and Skills Council in April 2001. The interesting thing about the White Paper was that lifelong learning seemed to have been downgraded as a policy issue. In so far as it was there, the White Paper indicated the triumph of lifelong learning as labour power development. New Labour aimed to build a new 'culture of learning' that would 'underpin national competitiveness and personal prosperity' (DfEE 1999: 6) in a situation where investment in human capital was replacing investment in 'plant, machinery and physical labour' (DfEE 1999: 12). People needed to learn throughout life to adapt to rapidly changing labour markets, for in these competitive times employers 'rightly put a premium on adaptability and the capacity to learn new skills' (DfEE 1999: 13). The rest of the White Paper outlined the New Labour's plans for delivering this form of lifelong learning. After the aberrant Kennedy and Fryer reports the same old show was back on track. But why did the Conservatives and New Labour hitch lifelong learning to labour power (human capital) enhancement?

Explanations

Explaining why lifelong learning policy in England is centred on labour power production and quality enhancement is a complex matter. Here, only some of the main strands of explanation are outlined.

First, analysts such as Perraton (1998) have argued that, as governments in developed capitalist countries have had problems controlling other forms of capital, human capital has seemed especially amenable to development by the state through supply-side education and training measures. Reforms and modernisation could yield higher-quality labour powers that would give nation-states a competitive edge in the international economic arena. Thus:

> Human capital policies are particularly attractive to contemporary governments.
> In an era when demand-led policies and traditional supply-side interventions

appear to lack potency, improving human capital seems to be a legitimate means by which governments can make a significant difference to their population's standards of living.

(Perraton 1998: 121)

Furthermore, compared to other forms of capital such as money, and increasingly means of production (e.g. factories), human capital is relatively stable, especially given immigration laws.

Second, Major's Conservative government and New Labour have emphasised the importance of labour power quality, and the significance of education and training in enhancing its quality, in relation to attracting foreign investment. High quality workers, it is held, will attract overseas operators to set up production, administrative and retail facilities in the UK.

Third, on reading the *Competitiveness* reports and the government publications on lifelong learning cited previously, it becomes clear that a particular set of relationships between lifelong learning, globalisation, economic competitiveness and the labour market is posited. Basically, because we live in an age of globalisation with capital moving around the world at increasing speeds, in order to be competitive as a nation we need to nurture human capital to attract and retain corporate and finance capital. In addition, as the pace of economic change is also increasing then people will need to learn new skills and knowledge throughout their lifetimes, requiring 'learning unto death' (Rikowski 1999) to keep up with rapid labour market changes.

Fourth, the previous point links in with New Labour's policy of creating a 'knowledge economy' (Finlayson 2003; Rikowski 2001). This is an economy where knowledge, rather than physical labour and manufacturing industries, becomes increasingly important. Intellectual property and Internet and educational services become particularly significant in this 'new' economy, argue its protagonists. Peter Mandelson heralded the knowledge economy in 1998 in New Labour's first *Competitiveness* report. To develop a knowledge economy and to stay ahead of rival knowledge economies, lifelong learning for the workforce is essential, especially in terms of updating and deepening information technology skills.

Conclusion

The problem with selling lifelong learning as an economic policy is that individuals have to be convinced that there is something in it for them. Hence the various advertising campaigns that try to convince us that 'learning pays'. Yet in sacrificing lifelong learning to upgrading labour power for economic competitiveness other notions of learning are implicitly downgraded. The idea of 'learning for its own sake', or learning for social and personal development, or for the critical appraisal of society, or for the sheer enjoyment of it appear to lose their magic in the shadow of New Labour's lifelong learning policy.

References

Coffield, F. (1999) 'Breaking the Consensus: Lifelong Learning as Social Control', *British Educational Research Journal* 25(4): 479–99.

DfEE (1995) *Lifetime Learning: A Consultation Document*, London: Department for Education and Employment, Crown Copyright.

DfEE (1996) 'Lifetime Learning: A Policy Framework', extracts in S. Ranson (ed.), *Inside the Learning Society*, London: Cassell.

DfEE (1998) *The Learning Age: A Renaissance for a New Britain*, Cm. 3790, Department for Education and Employment, London: The Stationery Office.

DfEE (1999) *Learning to Succeed: A New Framework for Post-16 Learning*. Cm 4392, Department of Education and Employment, London: The Stationery Office.

DTI (1994) *Competitiveness: Helping Business to Win*, Department for Trade and Industry, Cm. 2867, London: HMSO.

DTI (1995) *Competitiveness: Forging Ahead*, Department for Trade and Industry, Cm. 2867, London: HMSO.

Finlayson, A. (2003) 'Squaring the Circle: New Labour and the Ignorance Economy', *Mediactive: Ideas Knowledge Culture*, 1: 25–36.

Fryer, R. (1997) *Learning for the Twenty-first Century*, First Report of the National Advisory Group for Continuing Education and Lifelong Learning, London: NAGCELL1.

Kennedy, H. (1997) *Learning Works: Widening Participation in Further Education*, Coventry: Further Education Funding Council.

Marx, K. (1858) [1973] *Grundrisse: Foundations of the Critique of Political Economy (Rough Draft)*, Harmondsworth: Penguin.

Marx, K. (1867) [1977] *Capital: A Critique of Political Economy – Volume 1*, London: Lawrence & Wishart.

Perraton, J. (1998) 'Debate: Education and Growth (Introduction)', *New Political Economy* 3(1): 121–3.

Rikowski, G. (1999) 'Nietzsche, Marx and Mastery: The Learning Unto Death', in P. Ainley and H. Rainbird (eds), *Apprenticeship: Towards a New Paradigm of Learning*, London: Kogan Page.

Rikowski, G. (2001) *The Battle in Seattle: Its Significance for Education*, London: Tufnell Press.

Rikowski, G. (2002) 'Fuel for the Living Fire: Labour-Power!', in A. Dinerstein and M. Neary (eds), *The Labour Debate: An Investigation Into the Theory and Reality of Capitalist Work*, Aldershot: Ashgate.

Smith, J. and Spurling, A. (1999) *Lifelong Learning: Riding the Tiger*, London: Croom Helm.

Key readings

Hyland, T. (1999) *Vocational Studies, Lifelong Learning and Social Values: Investigating Education, Training and NVQs under the New Deal*, Aldershot: Ashgate/Arena (especially chs 1–2 and 4–6).

Merrill, B. and Hyland, T. (2003) *The Changing Face of Further Education: Lifelong Learning, Inclusion and the Community*, London: RoutledgeFalmer.

Peters, M. and Humes, W. (2003) 'Education in the Knowledge Economy', *Policy Futures in Education* 1(1), July, available at http://www.triangle.co.uk/pfie/.

Rikowski, G. (2002) 'Education, Capital and the Transhuman', in D. Hill, P. McLaren, M. Cole and G. Rikowski (eds), *Marxism Against Postmodernism in Educational Theory*, Lanham, MD: Lexington Books.

Focus question

Should learning throughout our lifetimes principally be about making us better, more productive workers?

CHAPTER 30

'GETTING YOUR LINES RIGHT'

Scripted communication in post-compulsory education

John Lea

Let's begin the exploration with the phrase 'Have a nice day!'. If you have pondered this much-used phrase when confronted with it as a farewell in a fast food restaurant you may also have come to the same conclusion as me. On the one hand it is simply another way of saying 'goodbye' and in this respect merits no more than a Garfinkel-like appraisal along the lines of 'shared meanings in a common-sense everyday world' (Garfinkel 1967a). On the other, it niggles as a form of irritation because of its false sincerity. But, what would be the point of getting angry? After all, it is only a script – as an employee, you learn your lines, you repeat them ad nauseam, largely because you want to keep your job, and, if it sounds insincere, it probably is, after all you're only working for the minimum wage.

It is easy to understand the employee's behaviour, but why has he or she been given it in the first place? Following Ritzer we might offer the following explanations: on the one hand, it offers customers the knowledge that they are in safe territory – a comfort zone where everything is predictable – and, on the other, it protects employers from inappropriate comments that might be uttered by employees, which might harm sales (Ritzer 2000). We might take this argument further by suggesting that 'learning a script' is an overlooked part of employee skills training. In this respect it might be further suggested that it is the retail sales equivalent of 'deskilling' – why trust employees to learn to communicate effectively when you can control them directly through a script? 'The managers assume the burden of gathering together all of the traditional knowledge which in the past has been possessed by the workmen and then of classifying, tabulating, and reducing this knowledge to rules, laws, and formulae' (Taylor 1911: 36).

In his seminal work, Braverman, utilising the notion of deskilling, looked at how routine non-manual work had fallen prey to this inexorable part of capitalist logic in his example of key-punch computer operators (Braverman 1974). But how far might the *professional middle classes* be deskilled? I do not intend to revisit his arguments here, merely to raise the question that scripted communication in middle-class professions might be viewed as an important part of the deskilling of the so-called soft skills.

The problem with pursuing this line of argument is that, by definition, middle-class professionals *are professional* and their need to make judgements, rather than follow rules, must preclude the possibility of scripted communication. However, in my role as a teacher trainer in a Higher Education Institution I find it easy to find examples of scripted communication. For example, each year I invite my trainee teachers to learn the language of 'inclusion, diversity and widening participation'. The story goes as follows: Teachers, sorry, *facilitators of other people's learning*, must recognise that some students, sorry, *learners*, might come from socially deprived, sorry, *culturally diverse*, backgrounds, and some may be disabled, sorry, have a *learning difficulty and/or disability*, sorry, are *differently able*. You get the point. I will lay my cards on the table here and admit to believing (almost wholeheartedly) in this agenda. However, I do not believe, as a matter of fact, that changing words changes the world, nor do I believe that learning this script is what I should be teaching. Enter 'political correctness'.

Although, as a teacher, I spent most of the 1980s supporting the progressive equal opportunities strategies of many London Boroughs and saw 'loony leftism' as a right-wing conspiracy, I have to admit that it was very often these very strategies that led to 'codes of conduct' (and in the United States 'speech codes') in many colleges and universities, resulting in many on the political left now seeing these as just as intrusive as 'political correctness' had always been portrayed by the most right-wing of libertarians. This is perhaps not that surprising – it has often been pointed out that the extreme left and the extreme right are not polar opposites but two adjoining parts of a circle. However, the first substantial point I wish to make in this chapter is that, as loud as the libertarian right have been in the United States, as an anti-pc brigade, it is the desire on the part of the State in Britain to call public sector professionals to account which is more pertinent in helping to understand some of the scripted communication we now see among these professionals. Furthermore, with respect to the left in Britain, these debates seem to have produced a significant split in thinking – an anti-pc group who believe that pc has simply replaced political action with debates about words and their meanings, and a pro-pc group who believe that equal opportunities strategies are not mere words and the dinosaurs of sexism and racism (etc.) must be policed by the enlightened vanguard.

With the benefit of hindsight it is now possible to suggest that throughout the 1980s in Britain the desire on the political Right to call to account public sector professionals coincided almost exactly with the desire on the Left to marshal the same professionals into an anti-discrimination crusade. This was complicated battleground: those public sector professionals who believed that a shake-up (and out) was long overdue became the new managers of their previous colleagues; those who saw this new form of accountability as nothing short of social control eagerly sought the means to subvert it. Alongside were those on the Left who saw the generation of 'codes of conduct' as the means to marshal the recalcitrant dinosaurs of sexist and racist behaviour, but who quickly became pitted against others with left-wing credentials who saw this as yet another attack (from their own side!) on professional autonomy.

If this scenario at least resonates with some truth it is clear why political correctness is a minefield. On the one hand, it could be used as a means to attack professional autonomy from the perspective of those who wanted a more accountable public sector. And, on the other hand, it could be used by the more libertarian left (if that is not a contradiction in terms) as a means to attack their more Stalinist comrades. In both cases political correctness became a derogatory term but for different reasons. However, what remained constant was the extent to which political correctness became associated with pandering to a political position. This interpretation is consistent with those who have tried to trace the origins of the term:

> The terms 'politically correct' and 'politically incorrect' can be traced to the counter cultural movements of the American new left in the late 1960s and

1970s. According to Ruth Perry's article 'A short history of the term *politically correct*', the source from which these groups adopted the phrase was probably the English translation of Mao's *Little Red Book*. Alternatively, Barbara Epstein has suggested a connection with 'correct lineism', a term used in the Communist Party.

(Cameron 1994: 19)

Of course, let's not forget that political correctness in ex-Soviet bloc countries was clearly the means to avoid an extended stay in Siberia, it thus having far more dire consequences for its miscreants, compared with those on the intellectual left in the West, where the phrase merely had a mocking irony attached to it. It is precisely in the Soviet contexts where we might talk about scripts not only as a way of life but also as an art form with its concomitant notions of 'reading between the lines' and disavowal. It is unlikely that such subversion could become that significant for McDonald's employees (although we should not dismiss this as a fruitful research area), but there might be much more significance when such 'scripting' takes hold in professional contexts – where 'reading between the lines' and forms of disavowal become a part of the everyday modus operandi of a professional organisation. Are we now seeing these subtle arts emerging in the very professions where we might least expect to see them? Where not only are the professionals reading from scripts, but also others are interpreting and interrogating what they might mean when they are being uttered?

This theme was recently explored by Morris when looking at the everyday decision-making we all undertake when faced with (often senior) colleagues we need to impress, i.e. it is simply too risky to depart from a corporate 'line' or 'script' if we want our ideas to be taken seriously (or even ourselves be employed in the first place!) (Morris 2001). But why has this type of behaviour become so entrenched in professional life? Ritzer is again instructive: 'fast-food restaurants tell employees what to say in various circumstances to make what they say, and what is said back to them, more predictable' (Ritzer 2000: 88).

The second substantial point I wish to make is that a coincidence of political agendas has occurred in professional life over the last 25 years. First, the right-wing political agenda in Britain has not only called public sector professionals to public account but has also engineered a corporate culture within the organisations in which these professionals work. These two strands of reform have been policed through forms of 'new managerialism'. The other political agenda, more clearly associated with the Left, has been concerned to create cultures of diversity, widening partici-pation and inclusion among the same professional organisations. This too is policed, although this time mainly by more enlightened professional colleagues. There is a 'predictability' required in both cases, not because the corporations wish to increase profits, as would be the case in private sector product-based organisations, but because professionals in public sector services are operating under forms of surveillance the like of which most have never seen before.

The result of this surveillance is that professional organisations have produced more and more scripts for professionals to learn. For example, corporate cultures do not sit easily with professionals who share a different professional ethic. In this context we need to ask ourselves the extent to which an ethic of public service has been replaced by an ethic of corporate enterprise and the extent to which this invites lip service by those who oppose the latter's imposition (see Hyland 1996). Furthermore, accountability is one thing, but government quangos with their own language of effectiveness is quite another. In this context we need to ask ourselves the extent to which the language of 'learning outcomes' is a lip service paid by many academics in order to be left alone to pursue their own more existential notions of the learning process. Finally, a language of diversity will not sit easily with professionals who believe that words can't change the world, or with those who believe that there is no substitute for straight talk. Each of these examples is likely to produce insincere 'scripted communication' and the accusation that we have filled educational establishments with trivial political correctness.

However, we need to ask to what extent is the discourse of 'corporations, customers, and mission statements' a script if it is believed in? To what extent is the discourse of 'inclusivity, learners, and diversity' also a script if it is believed in? The answers are surely obvious – the less they are believed in the more they are scripts, and the more 'politically correct' the script will be seen as being from the point of view of the disbeliever.

An important part of sociological work is to be seen to be documenting the nature of the interactions in which we all partake in everyday life. For better or worse, if professional organisations have become as I have described them we should be looking to see how professionals are coping with these changes in their everyday lives. I will, at this point, sketch three forms of behaviour likely to be observed where there is scripted communication: (1) '*keeping the front office appropriately misinformed*', (2) '*flying under the radar*', (3) the '*return of the repressed*'.

1   '*Keeping the front office appropriately misinformed*' is Garfinkel's phrase to help explain why there are 'good organisation reasons for bad clinical records' (Garfinkel 1967b). In this study of doctors in a hospital in the United States he documents how doctors will often produce deliberately poor patient records in order, on the one hand, to engineer more time to get on with what they see as their real job, i.e. patient care, but on the other, produce the documentation which will guarantee continued funding for the hospital. Written in 1967 this seems to describe precisely the process that many public sector professionals are involved in when time is short and inspection regimes are intrusive. It lends itself really well also to the notion of scripted communication. For example, write in one way for the 'bureaucracy', talk in another way, when actually engaged in 'client care'.

2   '*Flying under the radar*' refers to all those circumstances where you are protected from surveillance. I heard the phrase used to describe behaviour within the McCarthyite period in the United States, i.e. take a look around the room before you open your mouth! This is an inherently subversive activity and is extremely important to document. Lest it be thought in times of high surveillance that people either lie down and accept, or simply refuse to play, this phrase helps us to understand that human behaviour is far more subtle than that. Put simply, most professionals learn very quickly the rooms in which 'scripts' are not required; unfortunately there is rarely a public record of it for obvious reasons.

3   '*The return of the repressed*' is obviously borrowed from Freudian psychoanalysis. Clinical psychoanalysts might complain at this point about such promiscuous use of a clinical term in a cultural context but I will proceed to use it simply as a useful metaphor. The process is relatively straightforward. The more scripted a person's speech is the more they might be repressing what they really think and believe. This needs an outlet. How many politically incorrect jokes are actually told by the very professionals who were being politically correct not two minutes earlier? Does this mean that most public sector professionals don't share their currently conceived political agendas? Obviously not, but it might point to

the fact that in times when their behaviour is being policed there is a real desire to 'come off stage' whenever they can.

This brings me to my third and final substantial point – to what is, in essence, an impoverishment thesis. I am suggesting that public sector professionals are impoverished by the forms of the political correctness associated with their scripts. This might be said to have several dimensions. First, a culture of surveillance is unlikely to engender serious debate about the appropriateness of contemporary educational aims – it is much more likely to produce a dual culture where one's first thought is always 'who needs to know?' Second, the more that professional development is perceived as being the means by which corporate aims will be met, the less will be the space for the kinds of lateral thinking which is most likely to produce the more creative innovations. Finally, the more that professional training is perceived as 'learning one's lines' the less will be the chance to engage in serious debate about the appropriateness of any educational initiative.

Perhaps the most sinister development in this context is the extent to which the language of professional practice comes to be taken literally. *As if*, for example, appraisal could only be understood to mean one thing. *As if* offensive words have their meaning inherent within them. In the first case is it not possible to conceive of accountability operating outside of forms of managerialism? And, in the second case, is it not possible to conceive of words changing their meanings – of their meanings being subverted, or even inverted? 'Have a nice day!' is not a sentence *intended* to be delivered with irony. However, if we take phrases like 'Niggas With Attitude' or 'Queer as Folk' they clearly have (deliberately) multiple meanings. They are, at the same time, politically incorrect, and politically subversive. Surely the language of public sector professionalism is similarly constructed?

The current preoccupation in inspection regimes on 'measuring the measurable' and standardising the nature of provision in Post-Compulsory Education has as much to do with undermining professional autonomy as it does with improving quality and this is born from a right-wing agenda to make Public Service not only more business-like but more accountable to the State. My point, I hope, is obvious. There are other ways for professionals to be accountable, ways which are much more likely to diminish 'scripted communication'.

In many respects the Equality agenda is a more complicated matter. Although I would suggest that, on balance, we gained more than we lost with the progressive equal opportunities strategies of the last 25 years, it concerns me enormously that it has become possible with 'codes of conduct' and 'speech codes' to train people to become professionals rather than educate them, i.e. to tell people what they need to know rather than engage in critical debate. And this is precisely the context in which serious discussions concerning widening educational opportunities get lost in the more trivial discussions about appropriate language, which simply encourages the charge that it's all 'political correctness gone mad'.

References

Braverman, H. (1974) *Labor and Monopoly Capital*, New York: Monthly Review Press.

Cameron, D. (1994) ' "Words, Words, Words": The Power of Language', in S. Dunant (ed.), *The War of Words*, London: Virago.

Garfinkel, H. (1967a) *Studies in Ethnomethodology*, New York: Prentice-Hall.

Garfinkel, H. (1967b) ' "Good" Organisational Reasons for "Bad" Clinical Records', in H. Garfinkel, *Studies in Ethnomethodology*, New York: Prentice-Hall, pp. 186–207.

Hyland, T. (1996) 'Professionalism, Ethics and Work-based Learning', *British Journal of Educational Studies* 44(2): 168–80.

Morris, S. (2001) 'Political Correctness', *Journal of Political Economy* 109(2), April: 231–65.

Ritzer, G. (2000) *The McDonaldisation of Society*, New Century edition, London: Pine Forge.

Taylor, F.W. ([1911] 1947) 'The Principles of Scientific Management', in F.W. Taylor, *Scientific Management*, New York: Harper and Row.

Key readings

Dunant, S. (ed.) (1994) *The War of Words*, London: Virago.

Morris, S. (2001) 'Political Correctness', *Journal of Political Economy* 109(2), April: 231–65.

Focus question

Is it inevitable that professional accountability and professional autonomy will be inversely related?

PART VI

THE DIMINISHED ACADEMY

CHAPTER 31

A PROFESSION IN CRISIS?

Jon Nixon

Throughout the 1970s 'professionalism' was a dirty word: a means by which certain occupational groups sought to hang on to, or acquire, differential status over other occupational groups. During the 1980s, however, as the public and non-profit-making sectors had imposed upon them the values of the private sector, the term took on a different meaning: professionalism became the means by which the former resisted the ideological takeover of the latter through an insistence on the ethical, as opposed to status-oriented, values of the non-profit-making and public sectors. Workers within these increasingly beleaguered sectors found themselves having to mount a serious defence. They did so in the name of professionalism itself: its values, its traditions and its ethical orientation to the public sphere.

This was an odd and unpredictable turnaround. The sociology of the professions which had for decades been a backwater of sociological thought found itself central to a burgeoning literature on the significance of the need to protect the public sphere against the incursions of an increasingly privatised and market-driven society. Perkin's (1989) history of the rise of 'professional society' provided the groundwork for this new sociology of the professions, which has helped frame recent and current thinking on professional practice in terms of a radical reorientation towards the relation between professionals and their publics. From being a dirty word, 'professionalism' became one of the good words: part of the indispensable lexicon of those who would seek to consider, against the odds, the possibility of 'the good society' – or at least, as Margalit (1996) would have it, 'the decent society'.

The (mis)management of education

> ... the three horsemen of the new apocalypse – management, money and marketing.
>
> (Eyre 2003)

Professionalism so conceived is currently having to withstand two major trends which have already reconfigured the landscape of higher education. The first of these trends is the culture of performativity that remains the major legacy of new public management of higher education. Driven by the resurgence of neo-liberal market ideologies that dominated the last quarter of the last century, new public management was based on the assumption of a general breakdown of trust in the public and non-profit-making sectors and on the further assumption that public trust is best regained through systems of accountability that support competition across these sectors. If only the public and non-profit-making sectors could learn from, and behave as if they were a part of, the private sector, all would be well! From that forlorn hope unravelled the endless palaver of performativity – target setting, league tables, inspection regimes – that now characterises the university sector and dominates the working lives of those located within its institutions.

As O'Neill (2002) points out in her BBC Reith Lectures, this widely endorsed mode of institutional (mis)management is itself part of the problem, not part of the solution. Far from encouraging institutions within the public and non-profit-making sectors to engage with their publics, new public management has served to render them defensive and inward-looking: 'we are heading towards defensive medicine, defensive teaching and defensive policing' (O'Neill 2002: 50). The moral trajectory of professional practice towards public service through the exercise of professional judgement brought to bear on highly complex, indeterminate problems has thereby been deflected. Both the professionals and their publics are thereby the poorer. The accountability regimes which characterise the new public management of education have scored an embarrassing 'own goal'. In a bureaucratic effort to open up institutions, they have managed to close them in culturally.

The second major trend against which academic professionalism is having to define itself is the commercialisation of higher education. Bok (2003) analyses this process of commercialisation from the perspective of a seasoned senior academic, and respected legal scholar, within American higher education. Pointing to the 'rapid growth of money-making opportunities provided by a more technologically sophisticated, knowledge-based economy' (2003: 15), Bok cites as an example the fact that, in the United States, 'corporations doubled and redoubled their share of total academic research support, increasing it from 2.3 percent in the early 1970s to almost 8 percent by the year 2000' (2003: 12). 'Within a few short decades', he maintains, 'a brave new world had emerged filled with attractive possibilities for turning specialised knowledge into money' (2003: 13–14). Williams (1995: 177) points to a similar trend within the UK. 'The transformation has been dramatic', he argues: 'within ten years, students have been metamorphosed from apprentices to customers, and their teachers from master craftsmen to merchants'.

At issue are the underlying purposes of the professional practices traditionally associated with higher education. Those practices, argues Shumar (1997: 5) have 'come to be valued in terms of their ability to be translated into cash or merchandise and not in other ways, such as aesthetic or recreational pleasure. Eventually the idea that there are other kinds of value are lost.' That loss of all values other than the values of the marketplace further erodes public trust in higher education by restricting the notion of public concern to the narrow self-interests of the commercial sector. As Bok (2003: 208) concludes, 'universities will find it difficult to rebuild the public's trust. . . . In exchange for ephemeral gains in the continuing struggle for progress and prestige, they will have sacrificed essential values that are all but impossible to restore.'

A consequence of this Faustian exchange of 'ephemeral gains' for 'essential values' is, among other things, the low morale among academic workers: the sense of being under valued and of having no effective input into the way in which institutions of higher education are run or the direction in which they are heading. However, if loss of values is part of the problem, then the sense academics have of their own professional identity must be part of the solution. Any serious attempt at institutional change necessarily involves a commitment to professional reconstruction. Without that commitment, institutional change (and, indeed, broader policy change) lacks all substance. What academic workers clearly need to do is turn the change mechanisms on their head; or, to shift metaphor, achieve change from the inside out.

Change from the inside out

So, while it may be convenient, rhetorically, to see academic workers as constituting 'a profession in crisis', it is perhaps more appropriate to look to the changing conditions of academic work as an opportunity for realignment, reorientation and resistance. In particular, academic workers, in laying claim to professionalism within these new times, need to consider their changing relation to their publics, to knowledge and to the moral purposes of the university.

The changing relation of academic professionals to their publics

The presenting issues facing the university are very clear: an emphasis on access and participation leading to an increased diversification of the student body; the requirement that research should have demonstrable user-relevance and thereby be seen to impact upon policy and practice; the need for higher education to support economic regeneration at local and national levels; and the significance of global markets freed up by the new technologies and the technological apparatus of distance learning. These policy trends are having a profound influence on the ways in which institutions of higher education conceive of themselves and the ways in which learning operates within the context of higher education.

However, these policy trends also profoundly affect the ways in which academic workers construct their identity. The underlying issue that must be addressed concerns the moral foundations of the changing relation between academics and their publics. Unless that issue is addressed, then the policy changes are merely a cosmetic exercise: a kind of bureaucratic charade. Something very significant is happening in respect of the changing relation between higher education and the public sphere. The point is not only that academic workers must grasp the moral import of that changing relation, but that they must also track the shift that it occasions within their own professional identities. They must, that is, acknowledge the ontological dimensions of the challenge.

The changing relation of academic professionals to knowledge

They must also acknowledge its epistemological dimensions. The map of human knowledge has always been redrawn by those who seek to know. But now it seems as if whatever map might be available is of little use. The epistemological certainties attached to the notion of 'the disciplines' is still nostalgically recalled in the notion of 'inter-disciplinarity', but becomes increasingly redundant with the emergence of new fields of study that require their own methodological justifications and with the demise of traditional fields of study that call into question the old methodological justifications. Much that was solid is melting, or has already melted, into air.

Across the fluid and increasingly provisional boundaries, academic workers seek new ways of thinking and of talking thoughtfully. In spite of the epistemological meltdown, that process of intellectual engagement goes on. Therein, of course, lies the great line of continuity: the slender hope. Knowledge lies, at the cutting edge, not in what is already known, but in what is not known. That has always been the unexceptional case, in spite of the exceptional circumstances in which we now find ourselves. Knowledge has always been acquired by those who are intellectually courageous enough to admit that they do not know. That is the unique Socratic inheritance of those who seek to understand.

The changing relation of academic professionals to moral purposes

Ontological and epistemological uncertainties require a renewed sense of moral purposefulness. Higher education has always been hierarchical, but it is now deeply stratified as never before: witness the ratio of part-time to full-time academic staff, the erosion of 'tenure', the deep inequalities of funding for research across the sector and the lack of transparency regarding salaries for senior academic posts. (See, for example, Reid, 1996; Gamson 1998; Rhoades and Slaughter 1998.) Members of a highly differentiated workforce are having to hammer out their sense of purposefulness within an institutional context which is morally fractured: a context, that is, within which the development of a shared understanding regarding moral ends and purposes is rendered virtually impossible.

The leaders of our institutions have, with very few exceptions, deserted the field. They speak a language that would have been unthinkable not only in Plato's Academy and Aristotle's Lyceum, but even 50 years ago in the sector of which they are now the inglorious stewards. Of course, our Vice Chancellors and Principals, and their Deputies and Pro-Vice Chancellors, have to square up to a new enforced agenda of participation and cost effectiveness. They put up their little fights on the minor matters. But their abdication of moral responsibility is abject. It is to intellectual workers that we must look to reconstruct the moral agenda and refigure higher education for all our futures.

Conclusion

Academic workers, then, would seem to constitute 'a profession in crisis'. However, not all crises are catastrophic. Moreover, this particular 'crisis' is undoubtedly a chronic condition, which is undoubtedly wearing for those who have to endure it but does at least suggest that there may be ways through. One such way through, I am suggesting, is for academic workers to redefine their professional identity in terms of the values implicit in academic practice. That will not, of course, resolve the structural and systemic aspects of the 'crisis', but will ensure that those structures and systems have to square up to the scholastic traditions and practices of the academy.

References

Bok, D. (2003) *Universities in the Market Place: The Commercialisation of Higher Education*, Princeton, NJ, and Oxford: Princeton University Press.
Eyre, R. (2003) 'The BBC is One of the Few Things in Britain that Works', *The Guardian*, 27 September: 22.
Gamson, Z.F. (1998) 'The Stratification of the Academy', in R. Martin (ed.), *Chalk Lines: The Politics of Work in the Managed University*, Durham, NC, and London: Duke University Press, pp. 103–11.
Margalit, A. (1996) *The Decent Society*, trans. N. Goldblum, Cambridge, MA, and London: Harvard University Press.
O'Neill, O. (2002) *A Question of Trust* (The BBC Reith Lectures), Cambridge: Cambridge University Press.
Perkin, H. (1989) *The Rise of Professional Society: England Since 1880*, London: Routledge.
Reid, I. (1996) *Higher Education or Education for Hire? Language and Values in Australian Universities*, Rockhampton: Central Queensland University Press.
Rhoades, G. and Slaughter, S. (1998) 'Academic Capitalism, Managed Professionals, and Supply-side Higher Education', in R. Martin (ed.), *Chalk Lines: The Politics of Work in the Managed University*, Durham, NC, and London: Duke University Press, pp. 33–68.

Shumar, W. (1997) *College for Sale: A Critique of the Commodification of Higher Education*, Bristol, PA, and London: The Falmer Press, Taylor & Francis.

Williams, G.L. (1995) 'The "Marketization" of Higher Education: Reforms and Potentials in Higher Education Finance', in D.D. Dill and B. Sporn (eds), *Emerging Patterns of Social Demand and University Reform: Through a Glass Darkly*, Oxford, New York and Tokyo: Pergamon for The International Association of Universities Press.

Key readings

Perkin, H. (1989) *The Rise of Professional Society: England Since 1880*, London: Routledge.

Shumar, W. (1997) *College for Sale: A Critique of the Commodification of Higher Education*, Bristol, PA, and London: The Falmer Press, Taylor & Francis.

Walker, M. (ed.) (2001) *Reconstructing Professionalism in University Teaching: Teachers and Learners in Action*, Buckingham: The Society for Research into Higher Education and Open University Press.

Walker, M. and Nixon, J. (eds) (2004) *Reclaiming Universities from a Runaway World*, Philadelphia, PA, and Maidenhead: Open University Press/McGraw-Hill Education.

Focus question

What are the key values that shape academic practice within higher education?

CHAPTER 32

CORPORATE INVOLVEMENT IN INITIAL TEACHER TRAINING

Sonia Blandford

One of the potentially controversial policy developments over the last few years has been the active encouragement by government of closer links between education and business. Until recently these links have had little impact on teacher education. Now one innovative project, directly focusing on the values and methods of a successful international corporation, may be about to change teacher education forever. This initiative, branded 'Teach First', has gained support from a number of businesses and organisations who offer mentoring and training to participating recruits. These include:

McKinsey and Company	Citigroup
Corporation of London	Capital One
Canary Wharf Group	Deloitte and Touche
Freshfields	KPMG
Yahoo!	Deutsche Telekom
Mellon Bank	Sainsbury's
Morgan Stanley	Walkers
UBS Warburg	WHSmith

(www.teachfirst.org.uk)

In practice, Teach First combines the expertise of corporations, schools, education agencies and Higher Education Institutions (HEIs) to train and develop teachers for challenging London schools. After describing the origins of the Teach First programme, it will be argued here that corporate involvement in initial teacher training and continuing professional development in schools will provide new opportunities for those academics and practitioners engaged in school practice.

With every new initiative the British are inclined to take a questioning stance: staying with what we know and understand is what we do best. To introduce a scheme led by Americans, supported by a government lacking in popularity in a city that reflects the best and worst in educational practice would be considered foolish in the extreme. What would be the benefits to those involved? For the participants, graduating from Oxford, Cambridge and other institutions would almost guarantee them a head start in their chosen career. Teach First would have to offer similar or better prospects. For an HEI to consider involvement, Teach First would need to provide an opportunity for innovation that would enhance its standing in the educational community. Schools would also need to be convinced that young, untrained teachers would be an asset rather than a burden to their already over-stretched teaching resources.

These were the practical considerations; the ideological issues would prove to be far greater challenges to those involved:

- How could teachers become effective practitioners without the theoretical underpinning provided by full-time programmes?
- Can partnerships with global businesses and management consultants enhance initial teacher education?

From ideology to practice

Since Callaghan's 1976 'Ruskin College' speech, there has been pressure on those engaged in education to relate teaching and learning to the development of skills needed for business, industry and commerce (see Armitage *et al.* 2003: 261–2). While several schemes have been in place to engage non-educationalists in schools, colleges and HEIs, it has taken 25 years for the business world to link with government agencies, HEIs, London First – the agency tasked with bringing London's public sector, other institutions and London's businesses together – and a team of recruitment experts to recruit and train the best of UK's graduates to teach. This is set within a context of an ideological revolution, when universities across the globe are facing a time of unprecedented change. Challenges of scale, access, funding, demographics, internationalisation and new technologies create both competitive threats and new opportunities. The issues are complex and often contested, but they are unquestionably transforming the higher education market place. As identified in the recent White Paper (DfES 2003) new models and new suppliers are emerging, representing both competitive threats and possible new opportunities for existing institutions. Teach First represents the new, postmodern age of business that wishes to engage with the challenges found in city schools.

Teach for America

Teach First is based on a programme that was created by Wendy Kopp as described in her book, *One Day All Children: The Unlikely Triumph of Teach For America and What I Learnt Along the Way*. Kopp had felt that as a Princeton senior she was part of the 'me' generation. Most of the people she knew were heading for two-year programmes similar to internships in the business community. Kopp sensed that she was not alone and there were thousands of other seniors like her who were searching for jobs that would offer them significance and meaning. She suddenly hit on an idea: 'why didn't this country [United States] have a national teaching corps of recent college graduates who would commit two years to teaching urban and rural public schools'. She believed that the teacher corps would provide another option to the two-year corporate training programmes and graduate schools. The teaching corps would make teaching an attractive choice for top graduates by surrounding it with an aura of status and selectivity, streamlining the process of applying for teaching positions and assuring recent graduates a job and a steady income despite districts' inability to hire them until Labour Day.

On 12 April 1989 Kopp went to Princeton's library to look for the set of names and addresses of chief executive officers of major American corporations. She picked companies she recognised and those that surfaced in her thesis research as being committed to educational reform. Within a week, she had written to CEOs at 30 companies, such as Mobil Oil, Delta Airlines and Coca-Cola. Inevitably, Kopp did not get directly through to the CEOs, but the letter did make its way down various corporate ladders and she eventually met with executives of Xerox, IBM, AT&T, Metropolitan Life and New Jersey's Dodge Foundation. Kopp also met with an official in the Department of Education, the Dean of Harvard's undergraduate teacher education programme, the Head of Education of the States, which advises states in their efforts to improve education, and Stanley Caplin, the founder of the Test Preparation Company and a man deeply committed to education reform (Kopp 2001: 34).

Exactly one year and 10 days after Wendy Kopp had graduated from college she met with her 500 teaching corps members gathered in the University of Southern California's auditorium for the opening ceremony of Teach for America's first summer training institute. They were some of the country's most sought-after recent college graduates and they came from 100 colleges, including Ivy League schools, state schools and private universities. Teach for America alumni now have major roles in government and state departments. There are significant numbers (approximately 60 per cent each year) who remain in schools achieving high status in their communities.

The programme has not gone unchallenged by academics who find its relationship with businesses unpalatable. There is also the question of qualifications – many Teach for America graduates do not hold a teaching award. Those who do, gain the award when they become part of mainstream practice through university Masters programmes. There has also been a suggestion that the financial gain of Teach for America does not reflect its mission or 'not for profit status'.

Teach First

In 2000 a team of management consultants from McKinsey's relayed to the government, via London First, a report that identified the need to enhance teaching in London. The report focused on the usual indicators of success in schools: attendance, exclusions, examination grades and the recruitment and retention of teachers. The consultants were invited by the Prime Minister's office, teaching unions and major businesses to develop a scheme for recruiting young graduates from leading UK universities. Funded by the Department for Education and Skills (initially £500K) and guided by the TTA, the consultants registered a not for profit company, Teach First, with the aim of engaging a number of global companies and London schools to support the programme. Success with companies was linked to the consultants' access to executives through McKinseys and London First.

In parallel to the initial recruitment programme the Teacher Training Agency was directed to work in partnership with Teach First to appoint an HEI to develop, plan and deliver the initial training and ongoing school-based programme. In direct contrast with Teach for America, this initiative was to have award-bearing status.

In early November 2002 the TTA invited accredited Initial Teacher Training (ITT) providers working in partnership with London secondary schools to tender for the Provision of Employment-based ITT for Teach First. In February 2003, Canterbury Christ Church University College (CCCUC) was selected to deliver the Teach First training programme for able graduates who were to commit themselves to teaching for two years in London schools while undergoing an intensive programme of education and management training. A three-way partnership involving Teach First, CCCUC and London Schools provides the core of the training programme. It is preceded by an intensive six-week Summer Institute taught by the University College with additional activities provided by Teach for America alumni and the Teach First organisation.

Links with business

A central factor in this initiative is the role that businesses play in the scheme. By building a link with Teach First, leading figures within industry recognise the range of skills acquired by graduates through this prestigious scheme, potentially leading to careers outside teaching in the longer term.

The promise of an internship with leading UK and global companies, as experienced by the majority of the Teach First team, is also a huge incentive to Teach First participants. Major corporations are to provide additional training for the participants, thus allowing career choices that would extend beyond the two-year teaching commitment. It is anticipated that alumni will assume leadership roles, both inside and outside the field of education.

Teach First's business connections also help to demonstrate to potential applicants that the skills they gain while teaching provide them with rapid career progress within their chosen career once they have finished the two-year programme.

The involvement of businesses in education is not new; many schools were built through the patronage of the great industrialists of the Victorian era. The School Curriculum Project of the 1970s linked with corporations. Business in the Community has a 25-year history of working in partnership and training school leaders. More recently, school governors have been recruited to inner-city schools through the 'Governor One Stop Shop' initiative led by a retired United Biscuits executive. Earley and Weindling (1986) reported on the management exchange initiative, 'Management South'. The list goes on.

Conclusions

Those engaged in the Teach First initiative believe that highly motivated, focused individuals can make a significant impact on pupils' academic achievements. Teach First participants and business leaders aim to join with schools to raise the aspirations and levels of educational achievement for London's secondary school pupils, working with children from challenging backgrounds to ensure that they excel above and beyond their own expectations.

It has already been shown that London secondary schools benefit from the scheme through generating new energy in the classroom and creating a dynamic and creative approach to classroom management. Participating trainees will gain the opportunity to develop some of the classroom techniques, which are considered invaluable within business – specifically, communicating, planning, motivating, negotiating and presenting skills. Initially at least participants are engaging with theory through practice. However, they are provided with additional subject and professional studies sessions, enhancing their knowledge and experience.

The partnership with global businesses and management consultants has enhanced initial teacher education through the calibre and commitment of its recruits. The dedicated team of recruiters has impressed schools and HEI tutors; there is much to be learned from the expertise that exists in the market place.

Corporate involvement in initial teacher training and continuing professional development in schools will inevitably provide new opportunities for those academics and practitioners engaged in the initiative. Media interest has been intense, as has political involvement. Beyond the 'hype' pupils now have interested and engaged teachers who are highly qualified and are themselves receiving high-quality training. The evaluations are strong and the programme appears sustainable. As the late James Learmonth, who had a passion for improving inner-city schools commented, 'if the impact moves beyond the immediate and into the community it will have been a success' (2003).

Facts about the Teach First 'Class of 2003'

*   1,300 graduating students applied for the programme.
*   Teach First made number 63 in *The Times* Top 100 Graduate Recruitment list in 2003.
*   185 participants joined the Summer Institute in June 2003.
*   177 participants were appointed in 45 London schools in September 2003.
*   The majority of participants were from Oxford, Cambridge and Imperial College (University of London).
*   The majority of participants are qualifying to teach science, mathematics and modern foreign languages.
*   45 CCCUC tutors taught in the Inaugural Summer Institute; five Teach for America alumni also contributed to the programme; and Teach First provided additional support introducing aspects of management and self-development activities.
*   10 tutors provide ongoing support for participants with fortnightly visits to schools.

References

Armitage, A., Bryant, R., Dunnill, R., Hayes, D., Hudson, A., Kent, J., Lawes, S. and Renwick, A. (2003) *Teaching and Training in Post-compulsory Education*, 2nd edn, Milton Keynes: Open University Press.
DfES (2003) *The Future of Higher Education*, White Paper, London: HMSO.
Earley, P. and Weindling, D. (1986) *Secondary Headship: The First Years*, Windsor: FER-Nelson Publishing.
Kopp, W. (2001) *One Day All Children: The Unlikely Triumph of Teach For America and What I Learnt Along the Way*, New York: Perseus Books.
Learmonth, J. (2003) *ULF Meeting Notes*, Canterbury Christ Church University College: Centre for Education Leadership and School Improvement.

Key reading

Kopp, W. (2001) *One Day All Children: The Unlikely Triumph of Teach For America and What I Learnt Along the Way*, New York: Perseus Books.

To find out more visit the following sites:

Teach for America, http://www.teachforamerica.org/about.html.
Teach First, http://www.teachfirst.org.uk/.
McKinsey and Company, http://www.mckinsey.com/locations/london/index.asp.

Focus question

What are the advantages and disadvantages of corporate involvement in teacher training?

CHAPTER 33

THE McDONALDISATION OF LECTURER TRAINING

Laurie Lomas

It used to be the case that a Master's or Ph.D. was all that was required to lecture in a Higher Education Institution (HEI) and it was not necessary to have a teaching qualification as is the case in the compulsory education sector. However, in recent years the government, through organisations such as the Higher Education Funding Council for England and the Institute for Learning and Teaching in Higher Education (ILTHE), has encouraged the professionalisation of lecturing through the funding and accrediting of postgraduate certificate programmes. Since the Dearing Report (1997) and the formation of the ILTHE (see ILTHE 2002), many institutions have made it a requirement that lecturers new to higher education undertake a qualification such as a Postgraduate Certificate in Learning and Teaching or a Postgraduate Programme in Academic Practice. Occasionally, more experienced members of academic staff undertake these types of programmes as well.

I propose to demonstrate that there has been the gradual McDonaldisation of higher education in UK HEIs with the creation of the 'McUniversity'. As a consequence, there has also been the McDonaldisation of lecturer training, with lecturers now needing to be trained and prepared for a much more instrumental approach to higher education.

What is McDonaldisation?

At the outset, it is important to be clear what constitutes McDonaldisation in higher education. Ritzer's notion was developed initially in relation to worldwide corporate organisations such as Disney, Gap and McDonalds and is a depiction of global capitalism. Although McDonaldisation started out based on observations of corporations in the United States, there is transferability to a UK higher education context. Essentially there are four key elements of McDonaldisation:

1   efficiency – getting more students through the system by using 'appropriate' examinations;
2   calculability – with, for example, the introduction of league tables showing the comparative performance of HEIs on a wide range of performance indicators;
3   predictability – reducing ambiguity by standardising programmes, courses and learning outcomes;
4   control – ensuring lecturers teach in certain, usually 'student-centred', ways.
(Ritzer 1993, 1996)

McDonaldisation in HEIs

The drive for greater standardisation and efficiency has meant that large lectures and various forms of e-learning are becoming more widely used as teaching and learning strategies. There is now far closer congruity between what universities want to provide and the demands of students who are looking for a good deal, a low price (fee), the latest technology and efficient services. Students increasingly regard themselves as consumers, entitled to agreed standards of provision and full information about the quality of all academic and non-academic aspects of their higher education experience. They have the same expectations of standardisation, reliability and predictability when 'consuming' higher education as they do when purchasing a burger meal or dealing with their bank. Kneale's (1997) study of academic departments in 12 traditional and 10 modern universities found that 41 per cent of the departments that responded considered that they had problems with 'strategic' students who were predominantly instrumental in their attitude towards higher education. These students often had good A-level grades and were identified as those who had no particular interest in higher education per se, who refused to contribute in classes for which there was no mark, who preferred modules that did not have an examination and whose attendance was poor at modules where assessment was by means of an essay. Generally, they only attended sessions up to the point where their essay topic had been covered. One of the many quotes from students to undergraduate tutors sums up succinctly these attitudes: 'I can pass the year without doing the course work, so stop hassling me to give it in' (Kneale 1997: 121).

The emergence of this type of instrumental student is believed to be due, in large part, to a significant reduction in the use of tutorials; the increase in student numbers makes this teaching and learning strategy less practicable. For this reason, it is more difficult for tutors to get to know individual students and to ensure that course work is completed. However, it should be acknowledged that the 'strategic' student is at one end of a continuum of student attitudes that has the firmly committed student at the other end. Nevertheless, the 'strategic' student is an exemplar of an extreme form of consumerism, with the consumer having a very clear idea of what (s)he wants out of higher education.

The development of McDonaldisation in HEIs can be illustrated and illuminated through reference to Biggs' (2003) notion of constructive alignment. Constructive alignment is the term that describes a process based on the principle that a 'good' teaching system should align teaching methods and assessment to the learning outcomes stated in the objectives.

These aspects of learning, teaching and assessment are interlocked and interrelated so that they fully support the students' learning. This approach focuses lecturers' attention on the students' learning experiences by asking a series of questions (Jackson 2002), such as: 'What do I intend the students to learn (the outcomes required)?' 'What teaching and learning strategies are required in order that these outcomes are achieved by the students?' and 'What assessment tasks and criteria will inform the lecturer that the students have achieved the learning outcomes?' Great emphasis is placed on the structure and wording of the learning outcomes and the learner's performance increases in complexity through learning activities described by means of a hierarchy of verbs that move from identify and describe, through compare and contrast to theorise, generalise, hypothesise and reflect.

Constructive alignment helps to reduce ambiguity over what is expected of the student and the lecturer by ensuring calculability, predictability and control. These elements of McDonaldisation have also been secured by means of numerous Quality

Assurance Agency (QAA) codes of practice, including those relating to recruitment and admissions, programme approval, assessment and external examining as well as more centralised decision-making in HEIs (Macfarlane 2004).

Some academics have significant fundamental concerns about constructive alignment and its attendant predictability and control. For example, Cuthbert (2002) argues that constructive alignment is inappropriate for higher education curricula which, by their very nature, should be creative and consequently have unpredictable outcomes. He continues that there are limits to rationality when attempting to design a higher education curriculum that should be imaginative. In the context of the 'super-complexity' of HEIs, 'epistemological pandemonium' is a desirable feature when contemplating the place of knowledge and understanding in the curriculum (Barnett 2000). In summary, Barnett and Cuthbert are claiming that predictability and control are inappropriate in a higher education setting and constructive alignment is a simplistic rather than a simple concept.

Evans (2001) identifies some particular examples of this predictability and control associated with McDonaldisation. She claims that portion control in a McDonald's restaurant has its equivalent in the McUniversity in terms of course learning outcomes. Also, the QAA subject review handbook showed the atomisation of higher education knowledge and the assumption that knowledge is fixed, bounded, unambiguous and unproblematic.

Lecturer training

The greater prescription of both the content and delivery of the higher education curriculum through the McDonaldisation process has meant that lecturer training and development needs to be firmly linked to students' achievement of explicit, demonstrable learning outcomes.

There are plans to establish national professional standards for lecturers in higher education and, once these standards have been agreed by 2004, there will be the expectation that all new lecturing staff will obtain a standards-based teaching qualification from 2006 (DfES 2003). The proposals on lecturer training detailed in the government's recent White Paper, *The Future of Higher Education*, (DfES 2003) will consolidate and accelerate this approach to the training of lecturers as it makes clear in paragraph 4.14 that a competence-based framework is being advocated.

However, although such a framework is likely to bring greater predictability and control, it is also probable that lecturers' opportunities to develop students' creativity, innovation, criticality and in-depth analysis will be limited.

When arguing this point, Malcolm and Zukas' (2001) research is very helpful. They identify a pedagogical gap between the more cerebral, critical types of academic programmes and some of the more practical ones. The more cerebral programmes are concerned to develop a critical understanding of the social, political and institutional context of higher education, whereas some of the more practical programmes can be considered as reductionist because they distil pedagogic theory to a simple set of professional rules for practice. Indeed, there is a danger that these programmes reduce training to 'tips for new lecturers'. Often these programmes adopt a 'cafeteria' approach to educational theory that promotes a 'pick and mix' of theories. This is possible because higher education lecturing is often regarded as an undemanding profession that requires simple procedures rather than in-depth explanations (Entwistle 1998). Again, McDonaldisation provides simplicity and predictability, but by concentrating at a superficial level on what works in the lecture room there is the neglect of key underpinning philosophical, political and sociological questions.

These types of training programme that are technicist, practical and skills-based do not fully engage the participants in detailed debate and discussion based on relevant underpinning literature on philosophical, sociological, psychological and political issues. Ritzer claims that a consequence of the McDonaldisation in UK HEIs, as in commercial and public sector organisations throughout the world, is products, services and experiences that are devoid of meaningful, substantive content.

Malcolm and Zukas' pedagogical gap between the more practical and the more research-based lecturer training programmes can be looked at another way by using Macfarlane's work. He makes the distinction between study *for* higher education and study *about* higher education. Study *for* higher education is more concerned with a technicist approach that stresses practical aspects of content and skills, whereas study *about* higher education looks in detail at underpinning philosophical, political, managerial and social issues related to teaching. It would seem that the White Paper, with the move to a competence framework, is promoting study *for* higher education with an emphasis on the content and skills required in the lecture hall or seminar room. Charles Clarke, the Education Secretary, illustrated the prevailing view that higher education should be utilitarian when, in 2003, he told his audience at University College Worcester that higher education should have 'clear usefulness'. He went on to say that taxes should not be used to fund learning for learning's sake and he concluded with an attack on 'ornamental' subjects such as medieval history.

Conclusion

It has been argued that the gradual McDonaldisation of higher education during recent years is having an impact on the type of lecturer training that is now provided. McDonaldisation, with its emphasis on efficiency, predictability and control, has led to a much more structured and rigid approach to the curriculum and assessment. Through QAA codes of practice and subject reviews HEIs have been steered by government to constructively align teaching methods and assessment with learning outcomes. As well as HEIs providing students with a more structured unambiguous curriculum, students as consumers are now tending to demand the same standardisation, reliability and predictability that they expect of any other product or service.

Lecturer training is becoming more skills-based in order to prepare new academic staff for the more prescriptive nature of both content and delivery. The research-based training programmes are felt to be inappropriate and now the more utilitarian programmes are in the ascendancy with the growing assumption that knowledge is fixed, bounded and unambiguous. Study *about* higher education is giving way to study *for* higher education.

It is acknowledged that McDonaldisation has merit in that it encourages greater clarity and certainty, but the concern is that this is at the expense of creativity, innovation and criticality; all key attributes that should be central to higher education.

References

Barnett, R. (2000) *Realizing the University in An Age of Supercomplexity*, Buckingham: SRHE/Open University Press.

Biggs, J. (2003) *Teaching for Quality Learning at University*, 2nd edn, Buckingham: SRHE/Open University Press.

Cuthbert, R. (2002) 'Constructive Alignment in the Worlds of Institutional Management', paper presented at LTSN Generic Centre Conference, 4 November, London.

Dearing, R. (National Committee of Inquiry into Higher Education) (1997) *Higher Education in the Learning Society: Report of the National Committee*, London: HMSO.

Department for Education and Skills (DfES) (2003) *The Future of Higher Education*, Cmd. 5735, Norwich: HMSO.

Entwistle, N. (1998) 'Conceptions of Teaching for Academic Staff Development: The Role of Research', paper presented at Development Training Conference for Academic Staff, Goldsmith's College.

Evans, M. (2001) 'Did I Come Here For This?', paper presented at The McDonaldization of Higher Education Conference, Institute of Ideas/Canterbury Christ Church University College.

Jackson, N. (2002) 'Growing Knowledge about QAA Benchmarking', *Quality Assurance in Education* 10(3): 139–54.

ILTHE (2002) 'National Teaching Fellowship Scheme', *Institute for Learning and Teaching in Higher Education Website*, available at http://www.ntfs.ac.uk (accessed 28 August 2002).

Kneale, P. (1997) 'The Rise of the "Strategic" Student: How Can We Adapt to Cope?', in S. Armstrong, G. Thompson and S. Brown (eds), *Facing Up to Radical Changes in Universities and Colleges*, London: Kogan Page.

Macfarlane, B. (2004) *Teaching with Integrity: The Ethics of Higher Education Practice*, London: Kogan Page.

Malcolm, J. and Zukas, M. (2001) 'Bridging Pedagogic Gaps: Conceptual Discontinuities in Higher Education', *Teaching in Higher Education* 6(1): 33–42.

Ritzer, G. (1993) *The McDonaldization of Society*, Thousand Oaks, CA: Pine Forge Press.

Ritzer, G. (1996) 'McUniversity in the Post-modern Consumer Society', *Quality in Higher Education* 2(3): 185–99.

Key readings

Hayes, D. and Wynyard R. (eds) (2002) *The McDonaldization of Higher Education*, Westport, CT: Bergin & Garvey.

Ritzer, G. (ed.) (2002) *The McDonaldization Reader*, Thousand Oaks, CA, and London: Pine Forge Press.

Focus question

How far is the 'McDonaldisation' of Higher Education stifling creativity and innovation?

CHAPTER 34

THE THERAPEUTIC TURN IN EDUCATION

Dennis Hayes

'Educationalists' is a loose categorisation of actors that includes teachers, teacher trainers, academics and policy makers, among others. If we were to hazard a guess as to what they could have in common it would no longer be the vision of education that Matthew Arnold called 'a disinterested endeavour to learn and propagate the best that has been known and thought in the world' (Arnold 1864/1964: 33). If this conjecture is correct, and the traditional idea of education as being fundamentally about the acquisition of knowledge is disappearing, what is replacing it?

The answer to this question depends on the values dominant in wider society. These values are increasingly what sociologists call 'therapeutic' values. One pointer to the truth of these broad sociological claims is that educationalists have clearly adopted or succumbed to a therapeutic ethos. They are promoting, and are engaging future teachers in promoting, forms of therapeutic education. If this bold assertion is true, we are at the beginning of an era of educational decline that is unique in its rejection of any notion of the transmission of what is worthwhile to new generations, with an uninspiring vision of all children and young people as being hapless and hopeless and in need of therapy.

The knower and the known

The abandonment of the search for knowledge is expressed in four ways, which are fairly familiar: the idea that knowledge is now problematic or challenged; the idea that there are many 'knowledges' or many 'truths'; the idea that much knowledge is useless to society or the economy; and, most often, the claim that knowledge is changing so much that it is soon out of date.

These ideas focus on what is known. They have been subject to some very strong rebuttals and criticisms, particularly in so far as they tolerate relativistic viewpoints. But in any proposition about any subject there is also the knower – the subject or person who makes the knowledge claim. It is towards this human subject that the therapeutic turn is addressed.

The abandonment of the search for knowledge is an entirely spurious idea. Knowledge is just as essential to society as ever. What is really being rejected is the subject of knowledge – the knower. It is the knower not the known that is ultimately the target of the problematisation of knowledge. The fourfold attack on 'knowledge' is paralleled by an attack on the knower. We are told that our identities are now problematic; that we have multiple identities or selves; that the traditional individualistic competitive 'masculine' self is no longer effective or appropriate in 'postmodern' or 'risk' society; and that we need to constantly change and create new identities.

At the core of this reconstruction of the identity of the knower is the idea that we are all vulnerable. This is often termed the 'victim culture'. Even the term 'knower' seems odd. We are much more at ease with the term 'learner' and the notion that 'we are all learners'. But these terms place everyone in a position of uncertainty and vulnerability. A 'knower' has the authority of knowledge, a clear sense in which 'knowledge is power'. A 'learner', on the other hand, needs support and help.

A victim culture does not result from political policy-making and is certainly not an outcome of any conspiratorial activity. It has little to do with the impact of the science of therapy that aims to treat real mental illnesses. Even the growth in counselling activities is an expression of victim culture and not its cause. Victim culture arises spontaneously as a consequence of broad social and political changes that, over a period of time, are reflected in policy (see Hayes 2003). James Woudhuysen (2002: 2) has a simple abbreviation that encapsulates what he sees as the essence of New Labour's public policies:

$$\boxed{\textbf{T2V}}$$

or, *Therapy to Victims*. Of course, except in the case of the responses to major disasters and traumatic incidents, T2V will never be explicitly stated as the guiding principle of policy. The therapeutic ethic is adopted because it reflects the prevailing understanding of human nature rather than issuing in a deductive way from a clearly articulated philosophy of education. Teacher training, in all its various forms, is perhaps the key area of government policy were this therapeutic approach is becoming clearest, because the role government prescribes for teachers embodies its vision of future generations. However, bringing this therapeutic tendency out still requires a particular methodology.

The great German philosopher, Immanuel Kant, discussing the paucity of examples in his own work, concluded with the memorable phrase 'examples are ... the go-cart of judgment' (Kant 1781/1978: 178). In what follows, many examples will be given to show that T2V is now the dominant trend in teacher training. Teachers and students of education will be able to supply many more from their reading, from training courses and from their teaching experience.

Therapeutic talk

The first set of examples comes from the increased use of 'therapeutic language', much of which we can extract from a recent pamphlet produced by an internationally recognised centre for school leadership that argues for the importance of the 'emotionally competent' school. Here are some of them: 'self-esteem', 'self-worth', 'being our self', 'accepting', 'respectful', 'resilience', 'empathetic', 'responsive', 'playful', 'soothing' and 'feel(ing) secure and confident in (our) own identity' (Gerlach and Bird 2002). To this therapeutic language we can add 'schooling the emotions', 'emotional literacy' and 'emotional learning', terms made popular as a result of Daniel Goleman's books on 'emotional intelligence' (1996, 1998). The equivalents of this therapeutic talk in policy documents will be terms like 'empowering', 'enabling' and 'inclusive'. These terms, particularly 'empowerment', often had radical origins but have been usurped into therapeutic talk. The message of therapeutic talk is: we are all emotionally vulnerable.

The therapeutic 3Rs

What might be called the basics of education are even being challenged, and the traditional 3Rs (Reading, (W)riting and (A)rithmetic), now have competition from therapeutic alternatives, such as the 3Rs of goodcharacter.com (Responsible, Right and Respect). Throughout America there is emphasis on new 3Rs relating to pupils who are 'different' (Rights, Responsibilities and Respect). The message of all the new 3Rs is that we need to move away from the Gradgrind philosophy of education as being about knowledge and facts. We need to put the emotional basics first because we, and those who are 'different', have one thing in common – our *vulnerability*.

The therapeutic primary school

The huge popularity and increased use across the primary curriculum of 'circle time' in order to build up children's self-esteem and allow the 'safe' discussion of any subject does not need elaboration. The DfES have singled this technique out as an aspect of school pedagogy that children are positive about. The sheer popularity of the books by Jenny Mosley is illustrative of the dominance of this therapeutic idea (sample them on www.circle-time.com). Her best seller is *Quality Circle Time in the Primary Classroom* (1996/2002). Another of her best sellers is *Quality Circle Time in the Secondary School*. How long before we have *Quality Circle Time in Further Education* and *Quality Circle Time in Higher Education*?

But the use of 'circle time' in the primary school is not the only therapeutic initiative. An edition of the *TES* published in early 2003 contained a picture of a smiling 'Emotional Literacy Worker' from a Primary School in Southampton holding up a smiley badge. Her headteacher declared that: 'Until children are emotionally literate, they can't learn'. And the local educational psychologist argued that 'We are trying to redress the balance so schools are not just about academic attainment' (Kirkman 2003).

More recently schools have been encouraged to undertake emotional literacy audits (ELAs) of pupils. As 'emotional literacy' is something of a movable feast, making it a priority means that children are seen as psychologically flawed and they will never start up the ladder of learning. As we will see, this does not matter, as they will be preoccupied with their emotional states throughout what used to be called 'education'.

The therapeutic secondary school

In secondary education it is the 'cross-curriculum' issues that are most likely to provide examples of the therapeutic turn in the secondary school. The vehicle for this is often the more socially concerned and even 'radical' or 'socialist' teacher trainer. All issues such as 'racism', 'bullying' and 'personal relationships' now have a 'safe' circle time approach to them. One discussion of the future of citizenship education after the Iraq war eulogised the opportunity it presented: 'Citizenship education was made for just these situations. It creates a space in which views can be expressed, debated and analysed in an emotionally safe environment' (Klein 2003).

It is left-wing teachers and teacher trainers who are most at ease with what is an invasion of the curriculum by a political project. One 'radical' view, of what we can only call the 'therapeutic school', argued that 'real progress for education' meant longer-term investment in 'building the self-esteem of *all* our children' through putting 'Pastoral care policies and the building of a positive whole-school culture ... at the *heart* of our education system' because they 'are the way we enable our children to become more human' (Parker 1999: 83). Schools are 'doomed to failure' unless they build up pupil self-esteem. This is a sentimental and impoverished conception of humanity dressed up in the form of a progressive innovation in schooling.

The therapeutic transition: Connexions

Connexions is the policy initiative that provides the strongest evidence of therapeutic policy-making. There are approximately 1,231,000 therapeutic workers in Britain today, a grand total that includes guidance workers, mediators, counsellors (632,000) and therapists (Heartfield 2002: 236). The pathologising of ordinary life has become so extensive that people are believed not to be able to cope with any of life's vicissitudes without guidance from therapeutic 'experts'. The original aim of the Connexions strategy was to make sure that this number of therapeutic workers increases dramatically by ensuring that every young person has a 'personal adviser' (PA) to guide them into education, work and adult life. The therapeutic turn is now explicit and the 'C' word (careers) is rarely used; an advertisement for the service has a youngster proclaim: 'There's plenty of people who know about careers. I need someone who knows about me' (Loga 2003). Young people in what used to be the exciting transition to adulthood are now seen as 'at risk' and in need of therapeutic support.

The therapeutic further education college

In a survey of 2,729 further education practitioners reported in 2002, 92.5 per cent agreed that students 'experience improved self-esteem'. Self-esteem was clearly at the top of a list of perceived wider benefits of further education (Preston and Hammond 2002: 9). The therapeutic turn is also there in the curriculum. A popular book on further education argues that we need a 'high trust' and 'democratic' education system; a system that 'respects learners and their experiences, listens closely to their expressions of interest and need, builds partnerships between teachers, learners, parents, the community, and employers so that young adults learn what they wish to learn, and how they wish to learn' (Harkin *et al.* 2001: 140). The language here, 'trust' 'partnership' and 'respect' for 'learners and their experiences', is that of the therapist. Education is about taking young people out of the narrowness of their local and personal interests. This respectful approach merely traps them there.

The therapeutic university

Teacher training is now becoming accepted as a requirement for lecturers in higher education. However, as higher education is an adult world, it cannot focus on the usual subject matter of the social and psychological development of children and young people. Out of the search for a new professional focus have come influential advocates of a therapeutic approach. Sometimes they are quite explicit and one professor of higher education argues that: 'university teaching in general, and educational enquiry on the part of university teachers in particular, can usefully draw on therapeutic insights' (Rowland 2000: 107). These insights will result in 'a closer harmony with ourselves' and build 'more authentic relationships with our students' (Rowland 2000: 114).

But the therapeutic approach is often indirectly expressed. Another professor of higher education argues that, in the university, 'Knowledge and control are not, thankfully, available. (That belief partly led to Auschwitz.) What is both necessary and possible – just – is an enlightened societal self-monitoring' (Barnett 2000: 68). To facilitate this, the university must reorganise itself around the 'uncertainty principle'. This will transform it into an institution that 'contributes to our uncertainty in the world' through research; 'helps us monitor and evaluate that uncertainty' through criticism; and 'enables us to live with that uncertainty' through its teaching (Barnett 2000: 69). This is a vision of the 'therapeutic university' – an institution that makes students feel safe and secure, and does not challenge them at all.

Lifetime therapy

As a final example we can show that the concept of lifelong learning is not the liberating one of the middle of the last century. It would be better called 'lifelong dependence'. There is no escape from the therapeutic classroom. 'Reminiscence therapy' is being used by Norwich's Adult Education service as part of a living memory project described by NIACE as 'exemplary'. It was originally designed to treat people with dementia but 'is now increasingly used to revitalise other vulnerable pensioners'. And the teacher/therapist is enthusiastic – she says: 'It makes them smile. The work is fantastic for rebuilding their confidence' (Levis 2003). The report does not say whether smiley badges are used. But from the cradle to the grave teaching is now therapy.

Opposing the therapeutic turn

Educationalists, and teacher trainers in particular, now encourage people, who came into teaching because they love their subject, to fashion their teaching around a range of therapeutic and counselling techniques and an overriding concern with their own and their pupils' or students' feelings. They are transforming education into therapy, and the liberating project of education has been abandoned in favour of helping people to live with their flawed selves.

Examples are indeed the go-cart of judgement and they show that seemingly progressive educational rhetoric disguises a view of future generations as made up of hapless and hopeless people who need lifetime therapy. Being alert to these and other examples will help in recognising and rejecting therapeutic initiatives in education. Only with this rejection will come the possibility of teachers being able to inspire pupils and students once more with the best that has been known and thought.

References

Arnold, M. (1864/1964) 'The Function of Criticism at the Present Time', in *Essays in Criticism*, London and New York: Dent, pp. 9–34.

Barnett, R. (2000) *Realizing The University in an Age of Supercomplexity*, Buckingham: SRHE/Open University Press.

Gerlach, L. and Bird, J. (2002) *Feel the Difference: Learning in an Emotionally Competent School*, Occasional Paper No. 6, Canterbury: Centre for Education Leadership and School Improvement, Canterbury Christ Church University College.

Goleman, D. (1996) *Emotional Intelligence*, London: Bloomsbury.

Goleman, D. (1998) *Working with Emotional Intelligence*, London: Bloomsbury.

Harkin, J., Turner, G. and Dawn, T. (2001) *Teaching Young Adults: A Handbook for Teachers in Post-compulsory Education*, London: Routledge/Falmer.

Hayes, D. (2003) 'New Labour New Professionalism', in J. Satterthwaite, E. Atkinson and K. Gale (eds), *Discourse, Power, Resistance: Challenging the Rhetoric of Contemporary Education*, Sterling, VA, and Stoke-on-Trent: Trentham Books, pp. 27–42.

Heartfield, J. (2002) *The 'Death of the Subject' Explained*, Sheffield: Sheffield Hallam University Press.

Kant, I. (1781/1978) *Critique of Pure Reason*, translated by Norman Kemp Smith, London and Basingstoke: Macmillan.

Kirkman, S. (2003) 'An ABC of Emotions', *TES*, 4 April.

Klein, R. (2003) 'Rallying Round', *Education Guardian*, 1 April.

Levis, N. (2003) 'Profits at the Bank of Shared Memory', *TES*, 4 April.

Loga, C. (2003) 'Making the Connection', *Education Guardian*, 11 March.

Mosley, J. (1996/2002) *Quality Circle Time in the Primary Classroom*, Wisbech: LDA. Also available at http://www.circle-time.co.uk/.

Parker, J. (1999) 'School Policies and Practices: The Teacher's Role', in M. Cole (ed.), *Professional Issues for Teachers and Student Teachers*, London: David Fulton Publishers, pp. 69–84.

Preston, J. and Hammond, C. (2002) *The Wider Benefits of Further Education: Practitioner Views*, London: Centre for Research on the Wider Befits of Learning.

Rowland, S. (2000) *The Enquiring University Teacher*, Buckingham: SRHE/Open University Press.

Woudhuysen, J. (2002) 'Organisational Innovation in Public Services: A Kind of Devolution', *BT Public Policy Forum*, Insight paper, available at http://www.egovernment.bt.com/ppf_open/insight_reports.html.

Key readings

Furedi, F. (2003) 'Making People Feel Good About Themselves: British Social Policy and the Construction of the Problem of Self-esteem', inaugural lecture, University of Kent at Canterbury, 24 January, available at http://www.timesonline.co.uk/article/0,,2–552622, 00.html.

Hayes, D. (2003) 'New Labour, New Professionalism', in J. Satterthwaite, E. Atkinson and K. Gale (eds), *Discourse, Power, Resistance: Challenging the Rhetoric of Contemporary Education*, Sterling, VA, and Stoke-on-Trent: Trentham Books, pp. 27–42.

Two websites promoting therapeutic education are the Self Esteem Advisory Service and Jenny Mosley Consultancies:

http://www.emotionalintelligence.co.uk/seas.htm.
http://www.circle-time.com.

Focus question

What would be the alternative to therapeutic talk and practice in education?

CHAPTER 35

'ACADEMICUS SUPERCILIOSUS'
The beast revisited

Mary Evans

The term *Academicus Superciliosus* was first used by E.P. Thompson in *Warwick University Ltd*, a critique he edited in 1970, about what he saw as the invasion of Warwick University by the values of the market place and the subordination of academic standards and decisions to those of private industry. Thompson was scathing in this volume about the willingness of dons to be bought by concerns about money and economic prestige. In a passage in *Warwick University Ltd* he wrote:

> I have never ceased to be astounded when observing the preening and mating habits of fully-grown specimens of the species *Academicus Superciliosus*. The behaviour patterns of one of the true members of the species are unmistakable. He is inflated with self-esteem and perpetually self-congratulatory as to the high vocation of the university teacher; but he knows almost nothing about any other vocation, and he will lie down and let himself be walked over if anyone enters from the outer world who has money or power or even a tough line in realist talk. ... *Superciliosus* is the most divisible and rulable creature in this country, being so intent upon crafty calculations of short-term advantages – this favour for his department, that chance of promotion – or upon rolling the log of a colleague who, next week, at the next committee, has promised to roll a log for him, that he has never even tried to imagine the wood out of which all this timber rolls. He can scurry furiously and self-importantly around in his committees, like a white mouse running in a wheel, while his master is carrying him, cage and all, to be sold at the local pet-shop.
>
> (1970: 154)

Thompson, writing over 30 years ago, probably had every reason to suppose that his account of universities, and their inhabitants, would not change very much in that time. It would be wrong, therefore, to suggest that Thompson would be surprised by what has happened in British universities or that he would raise his hands in horror and mourn the passing of an idyllic era when universities were governed by little else than a concern for scholarship and a mutual interest in the pursuit of truth. Thompson, like others writing at the same time as him, and indeed throughout the twentieth century, recognised that just as much as universities did contain individuals with a passionate commitment to scholarship, so they contained others who were much concerned to articulate little other than those ideas which would be most likely to maintain their privilege and the privilege of those like them. Universities, Thompson knew full well (and to his own professional cost) were nothing if not places of ideological and material struggle.

The question here, however, is not whether or not Thompson was correct in his assessment of the horrible *Academicus Superciliosus*, but exactly how, and why, this beast has changed since Thompson first named the species. First, we need to note that the species has not become extinct and so we do not have to embark upon an expedition to the furthest reaches of the academy in order to find the last remaining member of the species and bring it back to live in carefully monitored and controlled captivity. *Academicus* is alive and well, and has not only avoided extinction but has actually begun to mutate, in that while the beast discovered by Thompson was exclusively male, there is considerable evidence that *Academicus*, unlike Frankenstein's Creature, has found himself a mate. There were always brief sightings of female academics in the early part of the twentieth century, but those sightings were brief and it was apparent that the conditions of the academy were not such as to encourage the existence of the female.

By the beginning of the twenty-first century, however, all British universities have had to commit themselves to policies that encourage the appointment of both male and female academics. The extent to which this policy has changed the gender divisions within the academy is relatively limited; despite the pious statements of all advertisements for jobs in universities, equal opportunities policies are more easily voiced than implemented. Thus, although the gender intake of students to British universities is now virtually equal, the proportion of women academics (and particularly senior women managers and professors) remains significantly lower than that of men.[1] Since being an academic does not involve physical strength (except to move around boxes of books – an activity which university restructuring exercises frequently involve) we need to note that although *Academicus* now comes in both sexes, the academic habitat is more welcoming to the male than the female. Women and men have always had a different relationship to the academy; from the days of Virginia Woolf's *Three Guineas*, there has been a well-documented sense in which the culture of the universities does not 'belong' to women.

We might, from this, suppose that women academics would have had a more radical and critical view of the universities than men. In the early days of second-wave feminism this was certainly the case and numerous well-known women academics voiced their criticism of a world that seemed to marginalise both the work of women and women themselves. Women, in the words of the famous account of women and history by Sheila Rowbotham (1993), were 'hidden from history'. Yet just as women became more visible in the academy – and as the curriculum of the universities was changed to include a greater discussion of women – so the academy, academics and all, was picked up and carried off, to become a full part of the British state. This was not an exercise in which academics were carried off one by one as Thompson predicted; on the contrary, this was a post-Jarrett Report (1985) exercise in which all the cages were carried off together. *Academicus*, although modernised by now being visible in two sexes (and a variety of ethnic and racial hues), was now very firmly relocated within the pet shop.

The *Academicus*, which now lives and is being bred within the new post-Jarrett pet shop, is a beast which retains many of the characteristics he had when Thompson first identified him. *Academicus* still retains that ability to be impressed by the most facile of promises from the world outside the ivory tower; successive governments have promised academics that they will acquire more independence and retain their autonomy, while all the time the cages become smaller and the freedoms that were once enjoyed disappear. *Academicus* was, as Thompson suggested, a species that did not find it easy to be loyal to its own, and in that lies the saddest part of the history of *Academicus* in the past 30 years. A truly loyal member of any species or tribe might be expected to protect all others of the same kind; not so *Academicus*, which has shown himself only too willing to be divided and ruled. Old universities have pitted themselves against new; more elitist old universities have tried to distance themselves from less elitist old universities. Within universities, departments have been set against one another in battles about spending provoked by the hideous ideology of the internal market. An *Academicus* in any institution finds himself (or even occasionally herself) evaluating his standing in the light of the credit rating of his department: to be in a 'deficit' department defines *Academicus* as scarcely better than an inmate of Dickens' Marshalsea. Should *Academicus* be in a 'successful' university then his best policy is to ensure that his cage is rigidly defended against others of his kind from less 'successful' institutions. In *Three Guineas* Virginia Woolf wrote, with some sadness, of the effects of education on some people; her remarks have an uncanny resonance with the behaviour of many academics:

> education, far from teaching the educated generosity and magnanimity, makes them on the contrary so anxious to keep their possessions, that 'grandeur' and 'power' of which the poet speaks, in their own hands, that they will use not force but much subtler methods than force when they are asked to share them?
>
> (1992: 193)

The *Academicus* of Thompson's version of university life could console himself that many people would take it for granted that he had a right (even a responsibility) to teach and research in his subject as he thought most appropriate. The beast may have characteristics that the zoologist could only regard with a certain amount of distaste, but as zoologists know, no animal species is absolutely pleasant and well behaved to its own and its neighbours. Nevertheless, left alone, most animals live in reasonable harmony. So it was with *Academicus*: not wholly lovable, but not entirely savage. Then the habitat underwent a transformation: the feeding ground changed and resources became scarcer at the same time as the barriers to obtaining them became more difficult. Poor old *Academicus* became a beast that is more easily an object of pity rather than an object of dislike and satire. The pet shop in which *Academicus* now lives is neither well guarded nor well appointed: circling all around it are truly hostile species who would like to see the end of *Academicus* altogether and his replacement by a 'knowledge provider' (in the deadly phrase of the Quality Assurance Agency). The 'knowledge provider' (who would definitely be committed to the provision of skills rather than education or understanding) would not only not know much about other vocations, there is a reasonable chance that he or she would not know much about his or her own, given that the marginalisation of the curriculum in favour of an emphasis on the process of learning does little to encourage subject specialisation.

The government which took a job lot of *Academicus* was that of Mrs Thatcher; petrified Vice Chancellors, fearing that every *Academicus* (and its masters) would be sold off into something approaching chattel slavery, engineered an agreement with the government which ensured a crucial turning towards not just the interests of the state but a particular version of the interests of the state. The version endorsed by Mrs Thatcher, and the version which sealed the fate of *Academicus* as E.P. Thompson knew him, was one that could not understand the value of any form of knowledge or inquiry other than the utilitarian. So the form of the academic remains, but arguably the substance is different: *Academicus* is alive and well, but alive and well in the sense that an animal bred in captivity is very different from the animal bred in the wild. The more elderly of the species retain folk memories of the days of universities as communities, and indeed of exchanges between scholars, but the younger members of the species know that they have a very well-defined function to fulfil and any deviation from it is likely to produce hostile reactions from the keepers of the pet shop. Indeed, the keepers of the pet shop have become considerably more vigilant in their policing of the behaviour of *Academicus*: each and every specimen is now expected, for example, to be awarded a Ph.D. degree and membership of the bizarre organisation, named the 'Institute of Learning and Teaching'. Job advertisements for vacancies in the pet shop request clearly defined characteristics and skills: *Academicus* is unlikely any longer to be superciliosus, since he or she will be far too busy submitting a response to the most recent assessment exercise. Pet shops for *Academicus* are, in the twenty-first century, kept ruthlessly free of difference and diversity, except of course that form of difference and diversity which is an attribute of the general population. Thus the pet shop is expected to contain certain numbers of women and members of 'ethnic minorities', who, it is assumed, in an entirely essentialist way, will maintain differences of ideas.

It is difficult, given the previous behaviour of *Academicus*, to express much sympathy for the new conditions of his life. *Academicus* did not have the courage of his convictions when faced with the blurring and erosion of boundaries between the state and the university. The species has survived, and with that survival some vestiges of the world which he represented. But more than the changes that have occurred to the species (domestication, feminisation, incorporation and marginalisation being foremost) have been the crucial changes to the habitat; if once *Academicus* lived and worked in a cage of his own making, that cage has now become the wider world all around him. In this world there is increasingly no need for cages, since there is little that *Academicus* can do that might involve the need for constraint or captivity. If we have to mourn, then our mourning might be grieving, not for the extinction of a species, but for the extinction of the idea that the academics had something important enough to merit a cage, or at least a degree of surveillance and constraint. There is no longer, we might conclude, any need for cages for *Academicus*; we have become free-range animals in a managed and controlled environment.

Note

1   The Higher Education Statistical Agency figures for 2001/2 show that female professors constitute 12 per cent of the total, although women constitute 56.2 per cent of the total number of undergraduate students.

References

Jarrett Report (1985) *Report of the Steering Committee for Efficiency Studies in Universities*, London: CVCP.
Rowbotham, S. (1993) *Hidden from History*, London: Pluto Press.
Thompson, E.P. (ed.) (1970) *Warwick University Ltd.*, Harmondsworth: Penguin.
Woolf, V. (1992) *Three Guineas*, Oxford: Oxford University Press.

Key readings

Graham, G. (2002) *Universities: The Recovery of an Idea*, Exeter: Imprint Academic.
Thompson, E.P. (ed.) (1970) *Warwick University Ltd.*, Harmondsworth: Penguin.

Focus question

Are today's university lecturers more concerned with student learning and 'knowledge provision' than the development of independent thought and new ideas?

CHAPTER 36

CHALLENGING STUDENTS

James Panton

From exams, tutorials and essays, many of the traditional institutions and pedagogic techniques of higher education have been the subject of criticism and debate in recent years. Few would argue explicitly with the idea that universities should serve to challenge and stretch students intellectually and to push them beyond the world of their immediate experience. So we ought to welcome a debate about standards in the university sector and encourage an educational climate that is open to critical assessment, revision and improvement in its institutions and methods. In this chapter I want to consider some of the criticisms and debates around examinations, tutorials and essay writing. A survey of some of the debates as they have appeared in the academic press reveals that, problematically, much of the discussion is motivated less by a concern for higher standards than by a sense of diminishing horizons in terms of the capabilities of students and our capacity to inspire and stretch them intellectually.

One of the clearest examples of traditional approaches to teaching and examining is the Oxbridge tutorial and exam system, which has been the subject of some debate and controversy within those universities and within the academic and educational press over the past few years. The tutorial system asks students to produce essays or written work for weekly tutorial meetings with tutors, either individually or in pairs, while the examination system grades students entirely on the basis of examinations sat at the end of three years (in Oxford) or each year (in Cambridge). These are systems that place a high emphasis upon students' self-motivation and autonomy. The tutorial system allows tutors to keep a close eye upon students' progress, to tailor their teaching and expectations to the needs and interests of individual students and, perhaps most importantly, to put students under serious academic and intellectual pressure to develop and defend their ideas and argument (Palfryman 2001). Complementing this, a system of assessment based on written examinations sat at the end of each year, or even at the end of three years, in contrast to the increasingly popular systems of continuous assessment based on coursework or tests at the end of each module, gives students the time to develop a more sophisticated and mediated understanding of their discipline. Many of the ideas and concepts studied in academic disciplines that may seem obvious on first consideration reveal themselves to be more complex and contradictory with further thought. To understand them with any sophistication requires reflection over an extended period, and a reflection on the mediation between those concepts and others – a process which is impossible if students study, complete and are tested on a subject within the space of one module or semester.

Of course, there are equally important arguments for considering methods other than Oxbridge-style tutorials and examinations. For example, while tutorials work well for many students, and in many disciplines, they are an inefficient means of imparting general information or data. And, while the low tutor–student ratio makes teaching students in a rigorous and challenging way easier, in a more rigorous educational climate that expected students to engage actively in their own learning the level of intellectual pressure that can be achieved in tutorial could also be achieved with larger groups. Similarly, it may well be the case that, in certain disciplines, testing students through a combination of examinations and termly or occasional papers may be a better way of testing their ability than exams alone. However, the arguments currently presented against tutorials and examinations seem less concerned with these issues of rigour, standards and challenging students, and more concerned with presenting an image of vulnerable students who must be protected from the stresses of the academic environment.

A recent consultation document into learning and teaching in collegiate universities published by the Educational Policy and Standards Committee at Oxford suggested that the traditional tutorial system often places such high demands on students that it can lead to a lower quality of learning for students who, faced with the rigours of weekly and often twice-weekly tutorial meetings and essays, are left with too little time for reflection (Sanders 2003). However, while it is true that high demands in terms of workload are placed on students at Oxford University during term times, it is worth remembering that term-time accounts for only 24 weeks, or less than half a year. One of the original principles behind this system was that students take tutorials, classes and lectures during term-time and use vacations to expand their reading and assimilate the work performed during term. Yet the idea that students might be able to cope with such pressures during term, and that they might draw upon such self-discipline during vacation, seems unpopular in an educational climate in which pressure and stress is understood in entirely negative ways. One critic argues against the essay as a means of assessment on the grounds that expecting students to produce essays in only a few weeks at the end of a course gives them too little time to do too much work and inevitably leads them to 'panic' (Winter 2003); while other research warns that work- and exam-related stress may lead students towards depression, self-harm and even suicide (Currie 2000).

If it is true that students experience more stress than might once have been the case, we ought not conclude from this that the demands placed upon them are too great. Rather, the framework of meaning through which difficult and stressful experiences are interpreted has been transformed.

If we accept the idea of higher education as a process in which we should push and challenge students to excel, then we must also accept that this will be experienced as a difficult and often stressful process. Most of us are aware that a reasonable degree of 'stress' is a precondition for working efficiently. Working to tight deadlines and preparing for examinations are difficult challenges, but they are also challenges that teach students to manage their time and to channel their stress in positive ways. In a climate in which the subjective experience of stress is understood in entirely negative ways, however, rather than seeing examinations or essays as challenges to be faced and overcome – a process that involves students challenging themselves and their own limitations – they are transformed, in the students' subjective experience, into almost insurmountable problems.

The problematisation of what were once standard aspects of university education is encouraged by a broader cultural climate in which students are seen to be vulnerable, their sense of self in constant doubt and their capacity to face difficult challenges much diminished. Examples of this diminished image of students are striking. The Committee of Vice-Chancellors and Principals, for example, in their guidelines on student mental health, call on universities and academics to 'help students capitalise on the positive mental health benefits of higher education', which positive benefits include a 'sense of personal achievement', 'creativity' and 'increased self-esteem' (Currie 2000). The chancellor of the University of Derby, Sir Christopher Ball, argues that rather than understanding students who do not enter higher educa-tion, or who perform badly once there, as lacking ability, we should be aware that they suffer from 'low self-belief'. He proposes that our role as academics should not be to focus on students' ability but rather to enhance their sense of self-esteem (Ball 2003). A critic of traditional modes of assessment argues for the idea that students should be allowed to decide for themselves how they should be assessed on the grounds that this will give students a sense of ownership of their education and raise their self-esteem (Baldwin 2003); while professor of education at Anglia Polytechnic University, Richard Winter, challenges the essay as a form of working which is 'alien' to many and thus disenfranchises individuals who would be capable of embodying their understanding of ideas in other, less formal, styles and genres. In place of the essay Winter proposes a 'patchwork text' composed of such assignments as lecture notes, accounts of personal experiences, a poster representation of relationships between ideas, a project proposal or even a poem or short story. The results of experiments with this approach, he reports, have been an increase in students' morale and an increased sense of ownership of their own learning (Winter 2003).

Ironically, although motivated by an attempt to enfranchise students and encourage their intellectual growth and development, the emphasis placed upon students 'sense of self', the avoidance of 'alienating' experiences and the importance of a sense of 'ownership' over their education are more likely to result in a much-diminished educational experience which sells students short.

An educational process that seeks to challenge and develop young people and to encourage them to move beyond their immediate experience necessarily involves posing a challenge to students' sense of themselves, a challenge that is both foreign and alienating to young people with no previous experience of academic life. Such a process assumes that in order that students can develop intellectually they must engage with concepts, ideas and frameworks of meaning that are beyond the commonplace, and it demands of students that they question their assumptions about the world around them, their place in it and their limitations. To organise such a process around protecting students' sense of themselves at their current stage of development rules out of court the kinds of challenges and tests that might allow development in the future.

There is good reason to question and challenge some of the traditional methods of teaching and assessing students in higher education. Unfortunately, these reasons are rarely considered in current challenges to essays, tutorials and examinations, which depend rather upon an image of students as vulnerable and easily damaged.

The demands placed upon students by traditional pedagogic and assessment tech-niques, such as essay writing, tutorial teaching and written examinations, are great. They depend upon an assumption that students are young adults engaging in a process of initiation into academic life, an environment in which they are asked to engage as intellectual equals with academics in tutorials, and in which they are taken seriously enough that their ideas presented in essays and written examinations might be worthy of challenge and critique. By contrast, the image of students presented in many of the contemporary challenges to traditional methods and institutions is an image that makes challenging young people, pushing them intellectually and providing them with the kind of transformative experience that is at the heart of higher learning difficult, if not impossible. The result is that rather than providing a rigorous and challenging educational experience to young people, we will present them rather with little to aspire to, and encourage in them a diminished sense of themselves.

References

Baldwin, J. (2003) 'Students get Personal', *The Times Higher Education Supplement*, 23 May.
Ball, C. (2003) 'Inspire Your Students to Blow Their Own Trumpet', *The Times Higher Education Supplement*, 27 June.
Currie, J. (2000) 'Not All in the Mind', *The Times Higher Education Supplement*, 28 April.
Palfryman, D. (2001) *The Oxford Tutorial*, Oxford: Oxford Centre for Higher Education Policy Studies.
Sanders, C. (2003) 'Overworked Students Suffer Lower Quality of Learning', *The Times Higher Education Supplement*, 20 June.
Winter, R. (2003) 'Alternative to the Essay', *The Guardian*, 10 June.

Key texts

Fox, C. (2002) 'The Massification of Higher Education', in D. Hayes and R. Wynyard (eds), *The McDonaldization of Higher Education*, Westport, CT: Bergin & Garvey.
Palfryman, D. (2001) *The Oxford Tutorial*, Oxford: Oxford Centre for Higher Education Policy Studies.

Focus question

To what extent does our image of students impact upon our capacity to inspire and teach them?

PART VII

THE STUDY OF EDUCATION

CHAPTER 37

PRACTICE MAKES IMPERFECT

Shirley Lawes

Sound theoretical knowledge is essential to teachers and the development of this knowledge must begin at the start of the initial training period. However, preparation for teaching is no longer a question of *education* involving an academic as well as practical initiation into the profession, but a question of *training*. Initial teacher training today is prescribed by a framework of mandatory competence-based standards, largely of a practical orientation, which places theoretical knowledge on the margins of beginning teachers' professional knowledge. Student teachers express high expectations of their courses in terms of developing their practical expertise, but relatively low aspirations of becoming autonomous professionals. The PGCE offers an intensive, highly structured and regulated period of initial professional training which student teachers see as coherent and generally meeting their needs as they perceive them, but which appears to 'limit the development of broader perspectives on education' (Whitty 2002: 76).

It is only through a sound knowledge of theory that real professionalism is possible. Theoretical understanding may not offer much in the way of 'tips for teachers', but there is a more important outcome: sound theoretical knowledge implies 'generalisability', gives a framework of understanding that ultimately improves the quality of practice and leads to the transformation of subjective experience. But to make the case for teachers to have greater theoretical knowledge right from the start of their preparation for teaching does not necessarily mean a return to the separation of theory and practice, but the development of a balanced approach to the two that requires a re-examination of the unity of theory and practice. To work towards this, it is necessary to emphasise theory above all else. Developing even a minimal level of independent critical thought implies a philosophical understanding of education (Tibble 1966; Dearden 1984) as a first step, together with a historical knowledge of the development of educational thinking and education systems along with psychology and some sociology of education.

However, there is a body of opinion within education, at the level of both policy and practice, which maintains that teaching is essentially a practical activity. This is confirmed by the emphasis in initial training on both classroom skills and pedagogical issues. The view held by many is that once practical skills, which are implicitly based on theory, are mastered, the teacher is more able to benefit from a more explicit knowledge of the theoretical underpinnings of their work when they are established in their career. Hence the range of higher degree and professional diploma opportunities offered by Higher Education Institutions and the array of government initiatives in their Continuing Professional Development (CPD) strategy. This is all well and good, but unless future teachers, right from the beginning of their training, see their chosen profession as having a substantial body of academic knowledge with which it is essential that they be acquainted, as well as a corpus of practical skills, they will be mere technicians and feel themselves to be such. Teachers may *say* they are not interested in theory, but only because policy makers consistently attack the value of theory and teacher trainers are sometimes guilty of undermining it by going along with the prevailing idea that classroom competence is all that matters. In so doing, we undermine our own profession. It is at the initial teacher training stage that expectations should be set and aspirations raised.

The desirability of educational theory and subject theory both in Initial Teacher Training (ITT) and in CPD is supported by a number of educationists working in the field at the present time (Furlong and Smith 1996; Wilkin 1999; Pring 2000). There is, however, some diversity of opinion as to what 'theory' means and what sort of theory is 'useful' and 'relevant' to teachers. Smith (1996) is critical of the loss of theory in initial training inasmuch that it is a transformative experience which encourages us to re-evaluate and develop our practice and gives a broader understanding of a variety of perspectives, not just a personal one. Theory does not necessarily apply in any direct form to practice. What is often seen as 'theory' on PGCE courses at the present time is really no more than *guidance for practice*, which, while based on theoretical principles, has no transformational capacity – it does not change the way we see things or provide conceptual understanding. Moreover, questions of theory are easily ignored because the notion of 'reflection' is seen as key to effective professional development.

Reflective practice is *the* guiding principle in teacher professional development and this signals a shift in the way 'theory' is understood. It is reflective practice rather than theory that underpins both policy and practice in teacher training and education. At a policy level, the 'reflective practitioner' is the exemplification of individuation of thought and an individualistic response to problems that stress the capacity of reflective practice to enable teachers to develop their 'personal theories' of practice. This redefines and reduces 'theory' to the particular, and might be seen as a contradiction in terms. Are 'personal theories' any more than opinion based on experience? Twenty years ago it seemed obvious to ask: why should every teacher have to 'reinvent the wheel' for themselves? (Dearden 1984); today that reinvention is the orthodoxy and is celebrated and required.

The process of reflection as a psychological phenomenon is necessarily subjective, and necessarily inward-looking. Far from encouraging a critical perspective, reflective practice is more likely to encourage conformity and compliance, particularly within a competence-based training setting, which is guided entirely by the notion of spreading good practice in a functional sense. As such, it is an inadequate basis for the profession of teaching. Michael Grenfell, in his 1998 book, *Training Teachers in Practice*, expresses just such a view:

> Reflection and the reflective practitioner are powerful metaphors; certainly ones which ring true to many involved in professional training. But do they exist in reality? Is reflection anything more than a romantic notion? We all reflect in a manner. We do not walk down the street without setting in place a whole set of explicit and implicit know-how and knowledge bases. We learn from experience, we anticipate, we act with intent and adjust accordingly as we go along. In other words, human beings are by nature reflective creatures. Is the 'reflective practitioner' therefore anything more than a truism, the product of previously simplistic models to link instruction and practice? Does it have sufficient weight to base an entire system of teacher training on it, as appears to be the case in England?

(1998: 177–8)

While it is sometimes argued that reflective practice does not preclude knowledge of theoretical perspectives, nevertheless the underpinning ethos of reflective practice points to a redefinition of 'theory' in education – that *practice* has become theory (Lawes 2003).

A further problem is that the growth in influence of relativist and, to a lesser extent, postmodern ideas has contributed to the undermining of educational theory. While most teacher educators would not see themselves as postmodernists or are even aware of their espousal of relativist ideas, elements of this body of thought have either been unconsciously absorbed into teacher education or have been consciously adopted. The influence of relativism and postmodernism, through their rejection of objective truth, and any attempt to understand society in its totality, has had a corrosive effect on educational thought in general and has led to an undermining of academic confidence in the project of education. These points are familiar, but what is less familiar now that they have become commonplace is that they mask a fundamental shift in the role and significance of theory in teaching and the professional development of teachers that is embodied in the national curriculum for teacher training and the standards required for the award of Newly Qualified Teacher status (DfES/TTA 2002). How do we account for this?

At the level of government and policy-making, lack of confidence is often expressed by their fear of things being out of their control, particularly in the traditionally independent spheres of knowledge-creation in universities, colleges and schools. They are therefore keen to regulate and control whatever is left to them. Education is an easy target. The imposition of draconian inspections and a national curriculum for teacher training are examples of the lack of trust on the part of policy makers in teachers to educate future generations and in teacher educators to train good teachers. However, such initiatives are more indicative of their uncertainty about their own policies than of the quality or lack of it in education. Today's society is characterised by compliance, caution, conservatism and conformity. We live in a time where a strongly anti-theoretical climate abounds and where a sceptical view of ideas and progress is prevalent. Educational thinking has become much more orientated towards attitudes rather than knowledge. The demand for theoretical explanation and understanding at a social and political level has been marginalised and this has impacted on educational theory. Hayes (2000) identifies a loss of confidence in the academy by academics themselves, which he attributes to wider uncertainties and anxieties in society. Hayes argues that lack of confidence in the academy is an important aspect of a loss of confidence in wider society.

Some educationists in Higher Education now lay the blame for the wholesale adoption of competence-based initial teacher training in the early 1990s and the subsequent demise of theory on the then Prime Minister, Margaret Thatcher, and New Right ideology. There is undoubtedly some truth in this, but many teacher educators themselves were highly critical of teacher education courses at the time, although for different reasons. Pring (1996) points to the rejection of educational theory as not just being a feature of government policy, but as being supported from within the ranks of the academic establishment (O'Hear 1988; Lawlor 1990). However, criticisms came not only from the 'academic establishment', but from a younger generation of academics in education departments who, influenced by intellectuals of the Left, were promoting the importance of 'practice' over theory. In 1993, John Elliott talked of the deliberate government policy of denigrating and deriding educational 'theorists' by associating them with the 'loony left'. He pointed to the 1988 Education Reform Act as key to the removal of any theoretical underpinning of educational policy (Elliott 1993a). But Elliott had, for a number of years, been prominent in 'endorsing a move towards experientially-based professional learning'. He supported the involvement of Higher Education in ITT but noted: 'On the one hand we have a theory-based and impractical form of training emanating from higher education and on the other hand we want a more realistic, practically based form of training based in the schools' (1993b: 1).

Thus, on the one hand, New Right influences, refusing to recognise the value or even existence of education studies as an academic discipline, rejected the importance of theoretical knowledge in teacher education in favour of a purely practical initiation into teaching. On the other hand, academics in teacher education from a purportedly more left-wing perspective sought not to *develop* the epistemology of education, but to abandon it in favour of a more pragmatic solution to problems. What was created in the 1980s and early 1990s was a theoretical vacuum, which has been replaced by practice represented as theory through reflective practice. In the intervening decade, reflective practice has become the sanctuary of teacher trainers who have lost confidence in, or even their belief in, the value of theoretical knowledge for teachers. Reflective practice is entirely compatible with the current technical approach to developing teacher expertise and the restricted view of teacher professionalism of policy makers.

However, it is theory, not reflection, that should be at the heart of practice. Theoretical knowledge, of both a subject-specific and general nature, should be what student teachers expect of their initiation into teaching and what they are exposed to. By elevating their expectations of what it means to be a teacher beyond classroom competence it is possible to engender a set of aspirations and an elevated sense of professional identity that provide a more firm foundation for future development. The consistent failure to introduce theory and its absence from ITT programmes is the primary underpinning feature of the de-professionalisation of teachers.

It is time to mount a new defence of teacher *education* and to reintroduce a more liberal programme including all aspects of educational and applied theory, alongside the teaching of practical skills. This latter has now been, more-or-less, refined. Teachers who have studied theory and who have risen to this theoretical challenge throughout their initiation into teaching will have confidence in knowledge, a vision of education, more commitment to the profession and certainty about the value of their professional knowledge *as well as* their practical skills. Without such teachers, 'education' will just mean social training.

References

Dearden, R.F. (1984) *Theory and Practice in Education*, London: Routledge & Kegan Paul.
Department for Education and Skills/Teacher Training Agency (DfES/TTA) (2002) *Qualifying to Teach: Professional Standards for Qualified Teacher Status and Requirements for Initial Teacher Training*, London: Teacher Training Agency.
Elliott, J. (1993a) 'Professional Development in a Land of Choice and Diversity: The Future of Action Research', in D. Bridges and T. Kerry (eds), *Developing Teachers Professionally: Reflections for Teacher Education*, London: Routledge.
Elliott, J. (1993b), 'Introduction', in J. Elliott (ed.), *Reconstructing Teacher Education*, London: The Falmer Press.
Furlong, J. and Smith, R. (1996) *The Role of Higher Education in Initial Teacher Education*, London: Kogan Page.
Grenfell, M. (1998) *Training Teachers in Practice*, Clevedon: Multilingual Matters.
Hayes, D. (2000) 'Confidence and the Academy', conference paper, BERA 2000, University of Cardiff, 7–9 September.

Lawes, S. (2003) 'Trends in Modern Foreign Languages Teacher Education: The Role of Higher Education', *Language Learning Journal* 25: 22–8.

Lawlor, S. (1990) *Teachers Mistaught: Training in Theories or Education in Subjects?*, London: Centre for Policy Studies.

O'Hear, A. (1988) *Who Teaches the Teachers? A Contribution to the Public Debate of the Green Paper*, London: Social Affairs Unit.

Pring, R. (1996) 'Just Desert', in J. Furlong and R. Smith (eds), *The Role of Higher Education in Initial Teacher Training*, London: Kogan Page.

Pring, R. (2000) *Philosophy of Educational Research*, London: Continuum.

Smith, R. (1996) 'Something for the Grown-ups', in J. Furlong and R. Smith (eds,) *The Role of Higher Education in Initial Teacher Training*, London: Kogan Page.

Tibble, J.W. (1966) *The Study of Education*, London: Routledge & Kegan Paul.

Whitty, G. (2002) *Making Sense of Education Policy*, London: Sage.

Wilkin, M. (1999) 'The Role of Higher Education in Initial Teacher Education', UCET Occasional Paper No. 12, London: UCET.

Key readings

Bartlett, S., Burton, D. and Peim, N. (2001) *Introduction to Education Studies*, London: Paul Chapman Publishing.

Carr, D. (2003) *Making Sense of Education: An Introduction to the Philosophy and Theory of Education and Teaching*, London: RoutledgeFalmer.

Halsey, A.H., Lauder, H., Brown, P. and Stuart Wells, A. (1997) *Education Culture Economy and Society*, Oxford and New York: Oxford University Press.

Focus question

What theory features in the Initial Teacher Training programme that you are involved in, or have some knowledge of, and what do you think is the ideal proportion of theory to practice?

CHAPTER 38

WHY DOES TRUTH MATTER?

Richard Bailey

> There are no universal truths to which our construction is a more or less good approximation.
>
> (Guba and Lincoln 1989: 16)

> There is no realm of 'objective' truths to which science has exclusive access, no privileged position that enables philosophers to transcend the particulars of their culture and traditions.
>
> (Carr 1995: 80)

These quotations provide examples of a growing condition affecting educational research: veriphobia (Bailey 2001), or a general aversion to talk of truth or its associates, such as fact, knowledge and evidence. Technically, veriphobia is a 'virus of the mind' (Dawkins 2003), passed from mind to mind via journal articles, conferences and seminars. These viruses can travel both longitudinally (from master to pupil) and horizontally (from peer to peer), and, as such, they have great virulence and potency. Potentially fatal to research and enquiry, veriphobia can be extremely virulent and resistant to treatment.

This chapter reports on the symptoms and aetiology of veriphobia, especially as it affects the practice of educational enquiry.

The aetiology of veriphobia

Veriphobia has been defined as 'a denial of the merit, or even the possibility, of truth' (Bailey 2001: 161). It is a common condition, mainly affecting academics, and is associated with a wide range of symptoms, including the rejection of traditional research concepts and values, and excessive use of plurals, speech marks, parentheses and word-processing effects – realities, 'truth', (re)search, facts.

Veriphobic thinkers come from across the academy, but predominate among the social sciences. They go by many names, such as postmodernists, social constructivists, pragmatists and eco-afro-feminists, but they are characterised by a shared denial of the traditional goals of research and enquiry, including the pursuit of truth, objectivity and the growth of knowledge. In the words of one group of concerned onlookers, 'a fluid scepticism now covers the intellectual landscape, encroaching upon one body of thought after another (Appleby *et al.* 1994: 243). We are told, for example, that 'there is no universal truth' (Guba and Lincoln, 1989: 16), that 'instead of only one truth, there are many' (Scott and Usher 1999: 3), and that, if it makes any sense at all to talk of truth, we ought to recognise that it is 'multiple, historical, contextual, contingent, political and bound up in power relations' (St Pierre 2000: 23). We are also warned of the dangers of tolerating those who resist the lure of veriphobia, although the severity with which they should be judged is a matter for debate. So, some writers feel pity for these poor souls, describing them affectionately as 'prigs' (Rorty 1982: 8), or dismissing them as living under an 'illusion' of an objective reality (Elliot, cited in Hayes 2003: 154). Others are more harsh, denouncing truth-seekers as 'conceited, ignorant, superficial, incomplete and dishonest' (Feyerabend 1988: 25).

In case the reader assumes that these are merely embittered rejections of the mainstream from those at its edges, it ought to be noted that each of the cited authors is a well-established figure within the academic world. Veriphobia is no longer an alternative to the mainstream; it *is* the mainstream.

Expressions of veriphobia

Veriphobia can express itself in many ways. For the sake of illustration, we will consider two of the more common forms.

Consensus veriphobia

The American philosopher, Richard Rorty, has equated objective truth with solidarity or consensus. He supports those who would 'replace the desire for objectivity – the desire to be in touch with a reality which is more than some community with which we identify ourselves – with the desire for solidarity with that community' (Rorty 1991: 39). According to this stance, what we rather grandly call 'truth' is really little more than an assertion of which we have been persuaded.

A consequence of the consensus view of truth is that it is impossible to compare one group's assertion with that of another; in the language of Thomas Kuhn (1962), the beliefs are 'incommensurable'. Different groups are likely to have different practices and standards, and, as such, say the consensus veriphobes, it makes no sense to seek support for your own viewpoint with reference to truth, since there can be no truth that is based on anything outside of those practices and standards (Rorty 1979).

Domination veriphobia

The French philosopher, Michel Foucault, took another tack in his denial of truth. He suggested that truth can only be understood in the context of power relations. He wrote that:

> Each society has its regime of truth, its 'general politics' of truth; that is, the mechanisms and instances which enable one to distinguish true and false statements, the means by which each is sanctioned: the techniques and procedures accorded value in the acquisition of truth; the status of those who are charged with saying what counts as true.
>
> (Foucault 1972: 131)

The particular appeal of Foucault's version of veriphobia is its reliance on strong emotive language and appeal to a moral subtext. His talk of 'regime of truth' identifies truth as a tool of domination, power and control. Others have developed this line of argument, by suggesting that the notion of truth (and its accomplices, rationality and objectivity) have a masculine and Western origin and character, and have been used to sustain inequalities of power between men and women, between the West and the rest, between those with influence and those without it. It is no surprise that science, with its unapologetic pursuit of truth, stands as the focus of condemnation by veriphobes, captured nicely by Sandra Harding (1986: 250), when she writes that science is 'not only sexist but also racist, classist, and culturally coercive'.

Veriphobia only affects other people

An interesting feature of veriphobic writing is a failure to recognise that the logic (for want of a better word) of its critique undermines its own position. That is to say, if veriphobia's claims were accepted, they would also have to be rejected.

Consider an example from the philosopher of education, Wilfred Carr (1995). Following an extended critique of the 'Enlightenment' distinction between the 'knowing subject' and the 'objective world', Carr goes on to suggest (he is actually talking on behalf of postmodernism, but it seems clear that he is supportive of such views) that, 'the subject's knowledge of the world is always preinterpreted: *it is always situated in a conceptual scheme* ... knowledge is never "disinterested" or "objective"' (Carr 1995: 80, emphasis added). But surely there is some difficulty with this line of argument. On the one hand, Carr is making a claim about how things really are, and on the other hand, he is explicitly denying that it is ever possible to make such claims.

Thomas Nagel (1997) refers to this situation as the 'impossibility of thinking from the outside'. Sociological insights into the practice of research serve a valuable role in raising our awareness of the context of our work, and may even lead us to change our practice. But such insights lose their force if stretched too far. It is useful to be reminded that our education, our background and our cultural origins all influence the way we approach the world, but it is erroneous to assume that just because our knowledge of the world is 'situated in a conceptual scheme' these things do not exist (Siegal 1998). The difficulty that veriphobes face time and again is that truth is difficult to banish from our discussions of the world as it is presupposed in such discussions (Carr 1998).

So, when writers such as Foucault assert that claims of truth merely represent regimes of power and domination, they are making, whether they like it or not, claims of truth. In the same way, Rorty's reduction of truth to agreement does not only derive from his upbringing or position, but from his belief that he is stating something that is the case, something that is true. And, this problem is not solved when they claim that they are not offering us a 'theory', but only an 'interpretation' of events. Why should we listen to them and their claims of inequality and unfairness at all, unless they are supposed to represent the way things really are?

There is nothing new in this response to veriphobia. Indeed, its origins can be traced back to Plato, who was the first to show the difficulty of throwing truth out with the sociological bathwater. Truth keeps coming back.

In practice, both consensus and domination veriphobia lead to a bind. The medicine, science and technology that each of us takes for granted as we make our ways around the world are premised on a conception of truth that it is not merely a matter of time, place or personality, but that is objective and universal. Richard Dawkins captured the flavour of this difficulty for the veriphobes when he wrote: 'Show me a cultural relativist at 30,000 feet and I will show you a hypocrite!' (Dawkins 1994: 17).

Veriphobia is fatal

There is a difference between an open mind and a hole in the head.

(Anon)

It is a peculiar irony of the current popularity of veriphobia among educational researchers that the condition is so harmful for research. Research is inherently related to truth, and a denial of that connection leads to the sorts of contradictions that litter the work of veriphobes like Carr, Rorty and Foucault.

The consequences of veriphobia for researchers can be profound. Truth offers a sense of direction and purpose to enquiry and, without these, research becomes a decorative activity, filling the time of academics, but making no contribution to society or its understanding of the world. In the words of philosopher, C.S. Peirce (1931–58: 57–9), 'man loses his conception of truth and reason ... (and comes) to look about reasoning as mainly decorative. The result ... is, of course, a rapid deterioration of intellectual vigour'. Although he was writing before the emergence of contemporary styles of veriphobia, Peirce has spotted a pattern in much such writing. Indeed, one of the founding fathers and heroes of postmodernism, Jean-François Lyotard (cited in Bailey 2001: 171) held his hands up and admitted: 'I made up stories, I referred to a quantity of books I'd never read, apparently it impressed people, it's a bit of a parody'.

So, veriphobia too easily descends into trivia. But, there can also be sinister consequences of the abandonment of the pursuit of truth. Veriphobic theorists present their ideas as radical or progressive, but their denial of truth leads them to consequences that are fundamentally reactionary. The casual manner in which some writers denounce traditional forms of enquiry, like science, as inescapably sexist, racist and classist (such as Sandra Harding), if accepted, immediately creates a barrier for the participation among marginalised groups, warning them that they are destined to fail. Aside from the dishonesty of this approach, it is also deeply offensive to those groups. By denying the vital distinction between truth and falsity, fact and fiction, veriphobia disempowers the very people it claims to represent.

Truth is the only salvation for the minority view. Without it as a clear and unapologetic goal of enquiry, the lies and deception of the tyrants, the liars and sometimes the majority will remain forever unexposed. Researchers can and should be troublemakers in the realm of ideas (Hayes 2003), and their most potent weapon in this context is the ability to stand up with authority, and say: 'That is not true!'

References

Appleby, J., Hunt, L. and Jacob, M. (1994) *Telling the Truth About History*, New York: Norton.
Bailey, R.P. (2001) 'Overcoming Veriphobia: Learning to Love Truth Again', *British Journal of Educational Studies* 49(2): 159–72.
Carr, D. (1998) 'Introduction: The Post-war Rise and Fall of Educational Epistemology', in D. Carr (ed.), *Education, Knowledge and Truth*, London: Routledge.
Carr, W. (1995) 'Education and Democracy: Confronting the Postmodern Challenge', *Journal of Philosophy of Education* 29(1): 221–38.
Dawkins, R. (1994) 'The Moon is a Calabash', *THES*, 30 September.
Dawkins, R. (2003) *A Devil's Chaplain: Selected Essays*, London: Weidenfeld and Nicolson.
Feyerabend, P. (1988) *Against Method: Outline of an Anarchistic Theory of Knowledge*, 2nd edn, London: New Left Books.
Foucault, M. (1972) *The Archaeology of Knowledge*, A. Sheridan trans., New York: Random House.

Guba, E.G. and Lincoln, Y. (1989) *Fourth Generation Evaluation*, Newbury Park, CA: Sage.

Harding, S. (1986) *The Science Question in Feminism*, Ithaca, NY: Cornell University Press.

Hayes, D. (2003) 'The Truths About Educational Research', in J. Lea, D. Hayes, A. Armitage, L. Lomas and S. Markless, *Working in Post-Compulsory Education*, Maidenhead: Open University Press, pp. 153–67.

Kuhn, T. (1962) *The Structure of Scientific Revolutions*, Chicago, IL: University of Chicago Press.

Nagel, T. (1997) *The Last Word*, New York: Oxford University Press.

Peirce, C.S. (1931–58) *Collected Papers*, C. Hartshorne, P. Weiss and A. Burks (eds), Cambridge, MA: Harvard University Press.

Rorty, R. (1979) *Philosophy and the Mirror of Nature*, Princeton, NJ: Princeton University Press.

Rorty, R. (1982) *Consequences of Pragmatism*, Hassocks: Harvester Press.

Rorty, R. (1991) *Objectivity, Relativism and Truth*, Cambridge: Cambridge University Press.

Scott, D. and Usher, R. (1999) *Researching Education: Data, Methods and Theory in Educational Enquiry*, London: Continuum.

Siegal, H. (1998) 'Knowledge, Truth and Education', in D. Carr (ed.), *Education, Knowledge and Truth*, London: Routledge, pp. 19–36.

St Pierre, E.A. (2000) 'The Call for Intelligibility in Postmodern Educational Research', *Educational Researcher*, June/July 29(5): 25–8.

Key readings

Bailey, R.P. (2001) 'Overcoming Veriphobia: Learning to Love Truth Again', *British Journal of Educational Studies* 49(2): 159–72.

Carr, D. (ed.) (1998) *Education, Knowledge and Truth*, London: Routledge.

Haack, S. (1994) *Evidence and Inquiry: Towards Reconstruction in Epistemology*, Oxford: Blackwell.

Nagel, T. (1997) *The Last Word*, New York: Oxford University Press.

Focus question

Why is veriphobia so virulent in educational research?

CHAPTER 39

CAN EVERYBODY BE A RESEARCHER?

Ray Godfrey

Like all interesting words 'research' means different things to different people. At a recent international conference on educational research, there was a discussion of the difficulties of encouraging students in professional preparation courses to engage with the research training elements. Part of the problem was that students do not seem to understand 'research' in the same way as their tutors.

One Australian participant thought that students saw research as what you did in the library before you wrote an essay at school. This involves simply gathering other people's knowledge to reproduce it, with or without giving it your own structure or contributing your own ideas. If that is what research is, then obviously everybody could be a researcher, though given the quality of many undergraduate essays it would be of doubtful value.

The Europeans, including me, were concerned that students saw research in terms of the sort of thing that appears in the media – drugs trials, large-scale social surveys – difficult and expensive things done by academic or other research institutions. If this is what research is, obviously there could never be enough funding in the world for everybody to be a researcher. It is quite easy to see why students might think that training for that sort of activity is irrelevant to someone who wants simply to be a teacher, a nurse or a social worker.

Another unhelpful notion of research is found in activities described as 'action research', which very often is all action and no research. Some possibly very useful innovations are made in the practice of some teacher, school, nurse or hospital ward, but little or no evidence is gathered or reported to justify the claims made. Such things may spark off ideas in other practitioners. In just the same way, when I was a mathematics teacher I used to read descriptions of lessons people had enjoyed in *Mathematics Teaching*. These short articles or letters were sometimes inspirational, but no one would describe them as research.

For the rest of this chapter I shall use the word 'research' to apply to activities in which investigators not only try things out or try to find things out but also try to gather evidence that might justifiably convince other people of the validity of what they have to say at the end of the process. This can be much more demanding than gathering evidence that is enough to justify changes in practice to yourself. Many years ago when lecture groups in teacher training began to grow larger, I had to rethink how to arrange the furniture in my lecture room. I tried a few things and noted how they affected students' attention to me and to each other, and how they affected the quality of discussion and other things of that type. Eventually I was satisfied that I could choose an arrangement that worked best for me and my classes. This was sensible professional development, but it was not research. I did not even consider the possibility of making detailed records that could be analysed and presented to other people as evidence that my arrangement was superior to others. Perhaps I should have written a letter to *Mathematics Teaching* about it.

Research is enquiry conducted in such a way that the results are of value to those who have not been party to the research. You usually get slightly more out of your own research than anyone else does, but this is not a characteristic of research. It is a characteristic of human activity. You probably get more out of running in an Olympic final than others do out of watching you. This extra bit that you get is not what makes an enquiry count as research. The important characteristic of research is that it is carried out in a way that almost gives you a right to be heard by other people. The evidence collection, organisation and presentation is done with such care that if anyone is interested in your research topic then, in a sense, they ought to read what you have to say – not because of your human right of free speech but because of the stature and quality of what you have done.

This is the fundamental idea behind the notion of a systematic review of literature on a topic. The reviewers accept that they have a duty to consider all the research evidence that meets a certain standard. It would be wrong of them to overlook any published research on the topic. But they do not feel bound to search through every single lesson description in *Mathematics Teaching*.

There is something awkward about the idea of a piece of research which is not suitable for publication. That is not to deny that publishers may decide not to publish it and that the people who funded the research may decide to suppress it. There is also a possibility that someone who has carried out a high quality investigation may not be able to write about it clearly.

It is almost a logical requirement of research that the researcher should be trying to contribute to the knowledge of some sort of community. The community decides whether the research counts as research and judges the quality and importance of the results. Of course opinions may be divided within the community. It may take a long time for the community to come to a consensus. The community may get it wrong. It has frequently happened in the history of science and mathematics that the academic community has completely rejected the work of a particular researcher, calling it worthless or even nonsense, only for the research to be rediscovered years or centuries later and to become the basis for major progress. It is hardly surprising if in educational research the same thing can happen.

If everybody was doing research there would be a need for vastly more publication outlets. Alternatively, if the quality was generally poor, it would only be necessary to have vastly more editors working for existing outlets in order to handle the job of rejecting the great majority of submitted articles. Although some might think the internet makes it possible for everybody to publish virtually as much as they wish, it is not the physical business of printing and distributing journals that is the main problem. The chief obstacle to vastly increased publication is the business of quality control – of making sure that research that deserves to be read does get to be seen and research which does not make the grade is not put before an over-burdened public.

If you have an interest such as teaching mathematics to pupils with learning difficulties or teaching primary school history or reducing school exclusions, it is difficult enough now to keep up with all that is written on the subject. There is hardly room for more research literature on the subject, especially if the quality is not high.

Why is it that all sorts of professions now require students to undertake research training as part of their preparation? It cannot be because the world needs every single professional to be a researcher. The world could not cope if they were. Presumably the benefits of this training are meant to come from the effect it has on the practice of the individual practitioner in a world where research is very important.

We want teachers, nurses and occupational therapists to be intelligent users of research. Even in this respect, though, we do not necessarily want them to be using research independently of colleagues. What we really need is professionals who have a sufficiently intelligent and critical appreciation of research evidence to enable them to make a useful contribution to discussions of policy and practice.

We also want professionals who will be prepared to test out their own ideas about how to conduct their practice, rather than simply pressing on through prejudice or inertia. Only if this is done very formally does it need to look like research.

It is not necessary during initial training for anything to be done with a view to teaching all students to be researchers. Those who wish to do their own research need to take a masters course and those who are really serious should take a doctorate. During initial training teachers and other such professionals need only to be taught to appreciate critique and use research. It seems of little value for them to spend a term producing questionnaires (often of very poor quality), administering them (often without a pilot and to a completely inadequate sample), analysing the results (often using inappropriate techniques or no techniques at all) and coming to conclusions (seldom justified by the evidence and usually believed before the 'research' even began), thus learning (if anything) to do really bad research and gaining a totally wrong impression of what research is. It would be more useful if trainers could identify the skills required to appreciate, critique and use research, devise tasks which would enhance those skills and let students spend a term carrying out something that will teach them something useful.

For example, we could tell a group of students to imagine that they were the staff of a school which had decided to do something about creativity across the curriculum; that they were not satisfied with national and local guidelines and they have a few weeks to find out what research (as well as other forms of literature) has to say on the subject and then come up with a policy, strategy and plan of action. Writing this up and justifying the decisions made would probably be more useful than writing about a piece of 'research' done so badly that it is really best ignored by the rest of the world.

For the past two years the National Foundation for Educational Research (NFER) has been engaging a small group of teachers in an exercise quite similar to this. They have conducted a systematic review of research on environmental education. Their claims to have benefited from this have in my opinion been more convincing than the claims of teachers who have actually engaged in and presented their own research. Most of those I have spoken with agreed with me that this sort of exercise would be more useful for students than doing a poor research project. Some thought that the experience of doing a research project may have helped them and helped motivate them in carrying out this systematic review.

There is really no way of saying which of these two possible views is correct, though I definitely know which one I favour. What we need is a research project.

Key readings

Blunkett, D. (2000) 'Influence or Irrelevance: Can Social Science Improve Government?', speech to the ESRC on 2 February, reprinted in *Research Intelligence* 71, BERA Newsletter.

Elliot, J. (1998) 'Living with Ambiguity and Contradiction: The Challenges for Educational Research in Positioning Itself for the Twenty First Century', keynote address, European Conference for Educational Research (ECER), Ljubljana, September.

Hammersley, M. (1997) 'Educational Research and Teaching: A Response to David Hargreaves' TTA Lecture', *British Educational Research Journal* 23(2): 141–61.

Hargreaves, D.H. (1996) 'Teaching as a Research-based Profession: Possibilities and Prospects', Teacher Training Agency Annual Lecture 1996, London: Teacher Training Agency.

Hargreaves, D.H. (1997) 'In Defence of Research for Evidence-based Teaching: A Rejoinder to Martyn Hammersley', *British Educational Research Journal* 23(4): 405–19.

Hayes, D. (2003) 'The Truths about Educational Research', in J. Lea, D. Hayes, A. Armitage, L. Lomas and S. Markless, *Working in Post-compulsory Education*, Maidenhead: Open University Press, pp. 153–67.

Swann, J. and Pratt, J. (1999) *Improving Education: Realist Approaches to Method and Research*, London and New York: Cassell.

Focus question

Do all teacher educators need to be researchers, or do they only need to be engaged in far more rigorous criticism of research than their students, something that can be achieved by attending research conferences?

CHAPTER 40

SCHOLARSHIP REINSTATED

Gill Nicholls

A few years ago 'scholarship' seemed almost an archaic term. Nowadays it appears everywhere in academic papers, policy documents and mission statements, but its meaning is ill-defined. One thing that is clear is that the term is no longer linked almost exclusively to *research* but is used most often in relation to *teaching*. Does this matter?

Scholarship and status

Part of the remit of the Institute for Learning and Teaching (ILT) was to accredit programmes in teaching and learning for lecturers in higher education, and to encourage them to become members of the institute. The ILT requires members and associates to exhibit 'Professional Values' and within this category it states that they will be expected to show 'a commitment to scholarship in teaching both generally and within their own discipline'. But what does this mean? Increasingly the ILT, Educational Development Units (EDUs) and Staff Development and Training Units (SDTUs) have linked the word scholarship to teaching as a means of raising the status and credibility of the programmes that are run or accredited. This move is ill-advised and, it will be argued, entirely detrimental to the project of enhancing learning and teaching in higher education. Examining some contemporary definitions will reveal what is at stake.

Defining scholarship

'Scholarship' now means different things depending on the purpose of the individual or organisation. Sometimes a very traditional notion of 'scholarship' is retained. For example, a major grant-awarding body in the United States declares that 'scholarship' can be defined as any activity of 'critical, systematic investigation in one or more fields and the submission of one's findings for criticism by professional peers and the public through published writings, lectures, or other modes of presentation'.

Scholarship in this sense has three key characteristics: it must be public, open for critical review and accessible and available for use by other members of a scholarly community (Shulman 1998). But the meaning is becoming ever more promiscuous as a result of direct attacks on this 'ivory tower' concept of scholarship. One of the first writers to draw attention to what was becoming seen as the academic profession's 'narrow' conception of scholarship was Ernest Boyer in his book *Scholarship Reconsidered* (1990). His work is seminal and some familiarity with it is necessary if the threat to learning and teaching is to be understood.

Scholarship Reconsidered revisited

According to Boyer, 'Scholarship is not an esoteric appendage; it is at the heart of what the profession is all about'. This is a useful corrective to current arguments for 'teaching only' universities, or universities with staff divided up into 'teachers' and 'researchers'. He passionately believed that, 'All faculty, throughout their careers, should themselves remain students. As scholars they must continue to learn and be seriously and continuously engaged in the expanding intellectual world. This is essential to the vitality and vigour of the undergraduate college' (Boyer 1990: 36).

It is interesting that here we get an early version of the popular idea that we are all learners (students) – an idea that undermines the authority of lecturers. This is not Boyer's intention, but as we shall see there are many unintended consequences to his work. One of his main concerns was that academics traditionally saw three components to their work: scholarship, teaching and service. He suggested that, although these three components are related, for many purposes the academic community treats them as separate. For example, when an academic is considered for promotion each of the three components is evaluated separately. Boyer suggested that dividing the academic's professional life in this way is misleading. Instead, he argued that academics are first, foremost and, perhaps exclusively, *scholars*. Boyer however, does not associate scholarship solely with research and creative activity. He saw scholarship subsuming all traditional roles of an academic. This unified role is of the utmost importance.

Boyer's analysis of scholarship identified four key roles: discovery, integration, application and teaching. Boyer considered teaching not simply as a matter of dissemination and the transmission of knowledge, but as a form of scholarship. By this he meant the transformation and extension of knowledge through the process of classroom debate and a continual examination and challenge of both content and pedagogy.

The four forms of scholarship

Boyer's first form of scholarship was that of the 'scholarship of discovery', which relates to the discovery of new empirical data or creating novel artistic forms. The scholarship of discovery equates closely to the traditional mission of research activity. Boyer emphasised that the scholarship of discovery, or research, is a 'pervasive process of intellectual excitement' rather than just a concern with outcomes in the form of new knowledge. Boyer also realised that the extension of the frontiers of knowledge was not enough, and that academics need to be constantly involved in the interpretation of knowledge. The 'scholarship of integration' relates to the interpretation given to the new emergent data or artistic forms as they are integrated with other results and compared to other creations. This allows academics to make connections between knowledge and models gained from different disciplines. It requires a divergent approach to knowing. The 'scholarship of application' was defined as professional activity in practice and service, which had to be subject to the rigour of evaluation and accountability.

Finally, and he suggests that this is the important of all the scholarships, is the 'scholarship of teaching'. Boyer suggests that the scholarship of teaching has integrity of its own, but is deeply embedded in the other three forms. The particular characteristics are, first, its *synoptic capacity* – the ability to draw the strands of a field together in a way that provides both coherence and meaning; second, *pedagogical content knowledge* – the capacity to represent a subject in ways that transcend the split between intellectual substance and teaching process; and, third, *what we know about learning* – scholarly inquiry into how students 'make meaning' out of what teachers say and do.

Boyer's view and interpretation of the scholarship of teaching was that of an inclusive activity. This perspective suggests that academics should take a scholarly approach to teaching by reflecting on the knowledge gained from educational research in relation to particular contexts in which they teach. It emphasises the important reciprocal relationship that exists between theory and practice, and the value of the practitioners' experienced-based knowledge.

Before considering the implications of Boyer's four forms of scholarship, it is important to note that Boyer was very conscious of the dangers of his analysis. He was worried, with justification as it turned out, that he was creating divisions that would seem as separate as the traditional tripartite conception of academic work:

> We acknowledge that these four forms – the scholarship of discovery, of integration, of application and of teaching – divide intellectual functions that are tied inseparably to each other. Still there is value, we believe, in analysing the various kinds of academic work, while also acknowledging that they dynamically interact, formatting an independent whole.
>
> (Boyer 1990: 25)

Boyer was quite explicit in his defence of the integrated nature of the 'scholarship of teaching'; however, his untimely death left the concept open to examination and reinterpretation. A consequence of this has been that the last decade has seen an increased interest in the notion, and some very different interpretations of 'the scholarship of teaching' (Prosser *et al.* 1994; Kember 1997; Kreber 1999, 2000, 2002a, 2002b; Kreber and Cranton 2000; Trigwell *et al.* 2000).

The scholarship of teaching

Trigwell and his colleagues work will serve as an example here. They suggest that there are *five* qualitatively different, hierarchical interpretations of the scholarship of teaching which move from what the teacher does to a focus on student learning. According to Trigwell they differ in four dimensions: information, reflection, communication and conceptions of teaching. The four key dimensions can be summarised as follows: the source of information teachers draw upon, the focus of their reflection, the nature and extent of their communication of insights and their conceptions of teaching and learning. The model put forward suggests that to engage in higher order activities within the scholarship of teaching requires academics to: consult discipline-specific literature on teaching and learning, focus reflection on specific areas of one's practice, focus teaching on students and learning, and publish results of teaching initiatives through peer-review mechanisms. As a consequence academic staff can engage in the scholarship of teaching to varying degrees.

It is clear from this analysis, the elements of which parallel the usual definition of academic scholarship, that the scholarship of teaching has now been separated out as a distinct field of study in its own right. The isolating of the scholarship of teaching as a field of study is a confused enterprise. It is not surprising that many writers see this as a problem, but only one of definition. Kreber, for example, argues that 'the scholarship of teaching, despite its long intuitive appeal to many, to date has been a concept lacking a unified definition' (2000: 8).

Polemic and academic scholarship

Another useful approach to 'scholarship' may help us see what lies behind the widespread and confused use of the notion of 'scholarship of teaching'. We can distinguish between polemic *scholarship*, which is a form of scholarship that promotes a particular position, specifically designed to advance a cause, and *academic scholarship*, which is neutral and has no particular aim other than finding out the truth (Shulman 1987). The idea of the scholarship of teaching is an example of polemic scholarship. It is an example of concept-building to enhance the power base of individuals and agencies that are promoting a particular agenda. That agenda is most clearly stated in the title of one influential paper on HE, 'Changing the culture of scholarship to the culture of teaching' (Brookfield 1995). This goal is simply to make the role of the academic focus on teaching rather than the advancement of their subject knowledge. The social and political context of this agenda is the creation of a mass higher education system that has to process more students. There is simply less time for *real* scholarship. The ILT was the most important and powerful institution to introduce scholarship of teaching as a professional value, thus trying to raise the social and economic value of teaching within a society that still prizes highly the notion of scholarship as represented by Boyer's scholarship of discovery. Their absorption into the new Higher Education Academy will not stop but only enhance this process. Adopting and changing the meaning of 'scholarship' so it applies to 'teaching' is one weapon used to undermine both learning and teaching in HE.

References

Boyer, E. (1990) *Scholarship Reconsidered: Priorities of the Professoriate*, Princeton, NJ: Carnegie Foundation for the Advancement of Teaching.
Brookfield, S.D. (1995) 'Changing the Culture of Scholarship to the Culture of Teaching', in T. Schuller (ed.), *The Changing University*, Buckingham: SRHE and Open University Press, pp. 128–38.
Kember, D. (1997) 'A Reconceptualization of the Research into University Academics' Conceptions of Teaching', *Learning and Instruction* 7: 325–51.
Kreber, C. (1999) 'A Course-based Approach to the Development of Teaching-scholarship: A Case Study', *Teaching in Higher Education* 4: 309–25.
Kreber, C. (2000) 'How Teaching Award Winners Conceptualise Academic Work: Further Thoughts on the Meaning of Scholarship', *Teaching in Higher Education* 5: 61–78.
Kreber, C. (2002a) 'Controversy and Consensus on the Scholarship of Teaching', *Studies in Higher Education* 27(2): 151–67.
Kreber, C. (2002b) *The Scholarship of Teaching: A Comparison of Conceptions Held by Experts and Regular Academic Staff*, Edmonton: University of Alberta Press.
Kreber, C. and Cranton, P.A. (2000) 'Exploring the Scholarship of Teaching', *Journal of Higher Education* 71: 476–95.
Prosser, M., Trigwell, K. and Taylor, P. (1994) 'A Phenomenographic Study of Academics' Conceptions of Science Learning and Teaching', *Learning and Instruction* 4: 217–31.
Trigwell, L.K., Martin, E., Benjamin, J. and Prosser, M. (2000) 'Scholarship of Teaching: A Model', *Higher Education Research and Development* 19(2): 155–68.
Shulman, L.S. (1987) 'Knowledge and Teaching', *Harvard Educational Review* 57: 1–22.
Shulman, L.S. (1998) 'Course Anatomy: The Dissection and Analysis of Knowledge Through Teaching', in P. Hutchings (ed.), *The Course Portfolio*, Washington, DC: American Association for Higher Education.

Key readings

Boyer, E. (1990) *Scholarship Reconsidered: Priorities of the Professoriate*, Princeton, NJ: Carnegie Foundation for the Advancement of Teaching.

Brookfield, S.D. (1995) 'Changing the Culture of Scholarship to the Culture of Teaching', in T. Schuller (ed.), *The Changing University*, Buckingham: SRHE and Open University Press, pp. 128–38.

Focus question

What barriers stand in the way of re-establishing a traditional conception of scholarship in HE?

WHAT ARE THE KEY DEBATES IN EDUCATION?

Tyrrell Burgess

Perhaps the first question to be asked is, 'Why debate at all?' The spirit of the age in education is against it. There are many, not least in government, who think that they know 'what works' and that all that is needful is that this be 'implemented' forthwith and universally. There are, however, two answers – one general and the other personal. In general human knowledge, understanding and practice are improved not by doing the same things over and over again and everywhere but by trial and error. In brute beasts this trial and error is immediate, practical and frequently lethal. Humans, by contrast, have language and so can discuss, criticise and argue. By these means we can discover error before the trial has damaging consequences. In Karl Popper's memorable phrase, our theories can die in our stead. To eschew debate is to inhibit progress.

Personally, debate is equally fruitful. One seldom knows anything unless one can explain it to others and defend it against criticism. It is a powerful aid to understanding and improvement. Without it people are unlikely fully to know what they are doing, still less to be able to do better.

Education today offers a paradox. It is the object of unprecedented dissatisfaction and complaint. The government leads the way in claiming that what goes on in it is not good enough. This might be expected to call for sustained thought, argument and experiment, in other words for informed debate such as has been offered in the preceding pages of this book. Yet readers will be aware that in the country at large educational debate is simply not taking place. What we have instead is educational 'news', which consists largely of the latest central 'initiative', ministerial speeches, pages of league tables, pictures of nice young women getting A-level results, the occasional 'dispute' and incidents of abused children or victimised teachers. It is as if people want a grievance more than they want an argument.

This state of affairs is at least a quarter of a century old. It was in 1976 that the then Prime Minister, James Callaghan, called for a 'great debate' on education. It did not take place. The present Prime Minister has been having 'conversations' with people about many things, including education, but asking people nicely to say the first thing that comes into their heads is not the same as having a debate. The very habit of debate seems to have been lost. There are no doubt many reasons why this is so. Some may be rooted in profound social changes, but there are three which are specific to education and are remediable. The first is the busy activity of the Education Department. When imposed change is frequent and sudden, debate is stifled. If what is compulsory today becomes optional or even prohibited next year, there seems little point in arguing. If decisions are all taken centrally and in a hurry, there is no enticement to discuss. Callaghan's call led to no debate because Secretaries of State, with a noble exception or two, did it all without asking.

The second reason is that the institutional basis for debate was destroyed. The Education Act 1944, which founded the modern system, provided that the Secretary of State should have a Central Advisory Council which was to report to him periodically on a subject of his or its own choosing. Successive Councils reported on 15–18-year-olds, on 13–16-year-olds of average or below average ability and on children in primary schools. There was a separate but similar report on higher education. The point about these Councils was the way they worked. Once established they invited 'evidence' from anyone who might wish to submit it, and many individuals and institutions did so. Most of this was published. There was, during the time that the Council sat, continuous reporting of the arguments on the topic of the moment. In other words there was a great debate. By the time that Callaghan called for one, his Secretaries of State had been breaking the law by failing to appoint the Council, and the framework for national argument had gone.

The third reason is that, since local government has been turned into little more than an agency of the centre, there has been no local argument either. When selection at the age of 11 was ended in the late 1960s, the Secretary of State requested local authorities to prepare plans for their own 'comprehensive' system. The matter was argued in every local newspaper in the land. The present establishment of specialist schools, which many think will undermine the comprehensive principle, is taking place with little or no local and thus no national debate. The point is not whether one is for or against selection in any form, but the way in which any change might be introduced.

In the absence of an institutional basis for debate, parents, teachers and the public at large must do what they can. One recourse is to write books, articles and letters, but for this to be effective it must grow from a renewed habit of debate, in schools, higher and further education and particularly in places where teachers are trained and educated. This book is one attempt to effect the renewal, presenting many of the topics on which more knowledge, understanding and above all debate are required. It may help to summarise here what these might be.

First is the knowledge of the way in which children grow and develop. Here it is not the knowledge that is problematical. Much is known and has been for some time. It includes the speed of growth, fast at birth and adolescence, slower in between; differences in rates of development both between the sexes and among children of the same sex; and earlier maturation. Some principles of development are also familiar, including the notion of a developmental age, that is the point an individual has reached in the sequence of growth that all go through; sensitive periods in development when outside influences may be critical; and above all the interaction of heredity and environment in individual growth. These facts and ideas are familiar to teachers, to any parent with more than one child and indeed to any moderately observant person.

The last of the Central Advisory Council's reports, on primary education, opened with a statement of what was known about children's growth and development and even based some of its recommendations on this. This had not happened before and has not happened since. This knowledge raises severe problems for formal education. If children grow at different rates, it may not be wise to teach them in narrow age-groups. Given the disparities between two 14-year-old boys, one still a child the other virtually a man, the age of 14 can have no educational significance. It raises the question of why every child of the same age should be required to sit and pass the same test. If there are other reasons for insisting on it, unrelated to the interests of individual children, then those doing so should at least say how they propose to avoid individual harm. They never do this because there is no debate. What every parent knows is excluded from the making of education policy. It is time to make it central.

A second topic for debate concerns the nature of learning: what is it that happens when learning takes place? The case here is worse than with child development. Facts are scarcer, and many of those that there are, in neuroscience for instance, do not readily suggest any particular practice. Theories there are in plenty, some of them over 2,000 years old, some a few hundred years and some quite recent, but they are inconsistent and often incompatible with each other. Some, which have been discredited, are still held by teachers and policy makers. None of them is explicitly taken as a basis for practice in schools. The public discussion of education, increasingly dominated by government, scarcely ever mentions learning; instead it concerns what should be taught, methods of teaching, standards of performance, forms of assessment and, mostly and worse, how the fashionable view of these should be enforced. It is not surprising that after prodigious efforts along these lines government and people remain disappointed. Lacking any firm base in fact or theory, any success the measures may have had will have been random.

When one considers what has been officially done in education in the last quarter of a century, one is forced to the conclusion that it is based on an implicit and on the whole unacknowledged theory, that is that learning takes place by transmission. Somebody teaches, and somebody else receives and learns what is taught. There is a subsidiary theory that if what has been taught can be reproduced it has been learned. The whole apparatus of National Curriculum and standard tests, prescribed literacy and numeracy hours and the worship of public examinations is inexplicable without an assumption of learning by transmission. This assumption has never been made explicit, except once to be denied by a government adviser, reminding one that one should never believe anything until it has been officially denied. The assumption is suspect. It is commonly recognised that children do learn in school, but seldom quite what they have been taught. Many who pass examinations have forgotten what got them through before the results come out. It is incumbent on those who make the assumption, or do things that seem to depend upon it, to say how they think transmission works. Or, if the transmission theory is not what underpins their actions and proposals, what does?

There is a challenge here for teachers and those who train them. Have they themselves a useful theory of what happens when learning takes place? My own is based on the one idea common to many traditional theories: that learning takes place through the initiative and activity of the learner. The idea that it takes place through the activities of the teacher, the Secretary of State, his department or a committee set up by him strikes me as fanciful. Learning seems to me to take place when we find we do not know or cannot do something and set out to discover how to know or do it. Children do this spontaneously long before they go to school. Most of the things they learn then, especially critical things like walking and talking, they do without being taught or tested. School could be a marvellous place for learning like this, and some schools have been. The range of books, equipment, space and expertise available is greater than all but a few homes. There are more other children from whom they might learn. The question is whether schools can fulfil their potential for helping children to learn or whether as now they will go on stultifying them. I do not ask teachers to accept my view of learning or even my strictures on the official one, but a debate on learning is long overdue.

Knowledge, understanding and debate about child development and learning, with their implications for educational practice and policy, should underpin all other educational discussion, if only because if they are wrong little else will be right. Other topics include the purposes of education, the means by which its outcomes are to be judged, the nature of teaching, the standing of teachers and education's relationship with society and the state.

There is a consensus about what education is for. It is to mitigate or even banish the evils of ignorance, incapability and dependence. However, this immediately raises other questions, like 'Who is this for?' and 'Does the present structure of formal education help or hinder this?' There has been an age-old debate about whether education is a good 'for its own sake' or whether it should respond to external demand. I have elsewhere characterised as 'autonomous' and 'service' the two traditions operating here. The establishment of polytechnics in the late 1960s followed a White Paper in which the question was argued seriously. The polytechnics became universities in the early 1990s without any argument at all. But the question remains, and not only in higher education. If the answer is 'both', what is to be the balance between them and how is this to be expressed in schools and colleges? There is an even further question. Within the service tradition is the service to be to the individual or to society, the economy or the state? Again, if, as seems plausible, the answer is 'both' how is this to be achieved, and how does one contrive that service to the one does not make impossible service to the other?

As to the present educational structure, it might be argued that it is apt for filling children, as did Dickens' Mr Gradgrind, with facts by the imperial pint, but what it does not do is encourage capability and independence. To be capable one has to be responsible. Formal education has seldom offered children responsibility for initiating or managing their own learning, and recent measures have largely removed responsibility from teachers as well. It is no use talking of democracy or citizenship to those working in institutions where the conditions for their exercise do not exist.

A similar difficulty attends the question of judging education's outcomes. There seems to be no alternative to tests and examinations, even though most people know where they inexorably lead. The test is meant to show how far the curriculum has been mastered, but what happens is that the curriculum becomes a preparation for the test. Children can be trained to pass the tests, but it is doubtful in those lessons at least whether they learn much else. The debate that is needed here is about what form of judgement would show that something had been learned and how this might gain public acceptability. One solution was officially proposed in the early 1980s in the form of records of achievement for 16-year-olds, but it was soon reduced to mere form-filling.

The big debate that teachers are not having is on what they themselves are for. Their earlier lack of clarity on this helped in the destruction of their professional autonomy. It is a long time since government ministers looked to teachers to know what and how to teach. If teachers are ever again to be other than purveyors of official prescriptions, they will have to know what it is that they uniquely bring to their pupils. My own belief is that this consists of knowing something thoroughly, knowing how to get at other things and knowing when and how to offer this to pupils. They can give their pupils the self-confidence needed to motivate their efforts and be critical of the outcomes. Little improvement is possible here, however, without a developed sense of professionalism, which recognises each child as a client to whom teachers' training, experience and judgement are made available.

Professionally teachers are not yet fully organised. They have unions to look after their individual and collective interests; they have an element of self-regulation in the General Teaching Council; and they have an embryonic professional body in the College of Teachers. They need to support such a body, because until they understand, as doctors and engineers do, the necessity of a professional body, until they themselves determine the nature of their profession, they will be ill-placed to help either their pupils or themselves.

Education is embedded in society and must relate to it. At present it is heavily controlled. Teachers are inspected, appraised, paid by performance and threatened into compliance by publicity. Nobody has ever explained why this is necessary, or how it is expected to work for the better. There is justified fear that it is doing harm. The last great debate centres round accountability. Is this to mean simply doing what you are told and showing that you have done it, or are there better ways of securing the national interest in education? There is a lot to talk about, so that we can be sure that whatever is done may be apt, fruitful and free from harm.

INDEX